Cindy

ChamPage Wishes
a great cooking

R_ de!
TVFN

Robin Leach's
HEALTHY LIFESTYLES
COOKBOOK

Robin Leach's
HEALTHY LIFESTYLES COOKBOOK

MENUS AND RECIPES FROM
THE RICH, FAMOUS, AND FASCINATING

produced and written by
Mardee Haidin Regan

PENGUIN
STUDIO

PENGUIN STUDIO
Published by the Penguin Group
Penguin Books USA Inc., 375 Hudson Street,
New York, New York 10014, U.S.A.
Penguin Books Ltd, 27 Wrights Lane,
London W8 5TZ, England
Penguin Books Australia Ltd, Ringwood,
Victoria, Australia
Penguin Books Canada Ltd, 10 Alcorn Avenue,
Toronto, Ontario, Canada M4V 3B2
Penguin Books (N.Z.) Ltd, 182–190 Wairau Road,
Auckland 10, New Zealand

Penguin Books Ltd, Registered Offices:
Harmondsworth, Middlesex, England

First published in 1995 by Viking Penguin,
a division of Penguin Books USA Inc.

1 3 5 7 9 10 8 6 4 2

Photography credits appear on page 251.

Note: Susan Povich, of The Cake Bar & Cafe, and Daisy Fuentes, of ¡Dish!, operated their
restaurants until the summer of 1995.

CIP Data Available

ISBN 0-670-85730-0

Printed in the United States of America
Set in Bembo
Designed by Joseph Rutt

This book is dedicated to the memory of my parents, Phil and Dougie Leach, who lived the best lifestyle of all but who passed away within eight weeks of each other in late 1994, still sharing the love they could never be separated from.

It is also dedicated to Al Masini, the first-run syndication television pioneer who took "Lifestyles" and turned it into a television phenomenon, and to Reese Schoenfeld, who gave me my first real on-camera TV assignments at a fledgling CNN, and who went on to launch cable's other major success story, the Television Food Network—where you'll find me every night with my own talk show, "Talking Food."

And most important, it is dedicated to an incredibly loyal family of viewers who have tuned in to my merry adventures these past twenty years. I send you all Champagne Wishes and Caviar Dreams. THIS BOOK IS FOR YOU! Read, learn, play, and taste its delicious contents so you can all revel in HEALTHY LIFESTYLES. As they say in Italy (and as I named my house in the island paradise of Jumby Bay, Antigua), SOGNI D'ORO! . . . Golden Dreams!

CONTENTS

INTRODUCTION

◆ ◆ ◆ ◆ ◆ ◆ ◆ ◆ ◆ ◆ ◆ ◆

Just what is a "healthy lifestyle"? We've asked everyone and, honestly, we've come to this conclusion: It's indefinable—no one particular thing or practice can encompass all that a healthy lifestyle is or can be. A healthy lifestyle is personal to each of us—in many ways, a state of mind in which the end goal is contentment with how we live our lives. Indeed, what works for one won't do for others; what works for many won't work for some. But often, within what works for one person, there's a nugget of "healthful truth" that we can incorporate into our very own healthy lifestyle.

One thing is for sure: A healthy lifestyle is not merely eating healthfully, working out regularly, or avoiding stress altogether. It's a much larger goal, which may or may not include dieting for weight loss. Who among us has not at some point pledged: "From now on, I'm going to change my ways. I'm going to eat better, get more sleep, reduce the stress in my life, exercise more, get a checkup, break my bad habits, cut down on alcohol and/or tobacco." Whoa, there. Is anyone up to such a task, or are they doomed to failure by the sheer scope of the assignment? Let's break it up into smaller bits—one day at a time, step by step, or nugget by nugget.

For Cheryl Tiegs, a healthy lifestyle includes a view of the Pacific, a hike in the mountains, a stroll on the beach, and a simple, tasty, relaxing picnic on the bluffs. For the New York Giants football team, a healthy lifestyle is one that leads to optimal performance on the field. Harvard-trained lawyer Susan Povich gave up her work as a Wall Street attorney, went to cooking school, found a business partner, and opened a restaurant in New York's Greenwich Village. Was the stress any less? No, not really. Was she happier? Yes—really. Was her father, talk-show host Maury Povich, proud of her? You bet. And was she not "healthier" for doing it? Just ask her.

Susan Powter (we like to call her "The Enabler") is passionate about sharing the life and style lessons she learned the hard way. With enthusiasm to burn, this powerful lady is more than vocal on what works for her in the hope that it will be helpful to others. Equally frenetic are Wolfgang Puck and Barbara Lazaroff, emperor and empress of a wide-ranging restaurant and food empire. At home, they glean a good measure of their healthfulness and contentment in the company of their children and pets, over—what else?—a delicious, healthful family meal.

What we offer in *Robin Leach's Healthy Lifestyles Cookbook* is a peek into the lives and styles of some well-known, accomplished people. We've asked them how they live, what they eat, and how they go about seeking and finding contentment. We hope that we can learn by following their example. Indeed, if imitation truly is the sincerest form of flattery, we salute them.

AN IMPORTANT NOTE TO ALL READERS:

THIS IS NOT A DIET COOKBOOK. This book focuses on how some very successful, very smart people combine the needs of their lives with the needs of their bodies. If there was any single theme that nearly everyone we spoke with mentioned, it was this: It's all about balance and moderation. And whether it's the time you devote to work, what time you give yourself to play, what you eat, when you eat, who you eat with, where you eat, or what you wear when you eat, balance and moderation are the keys.

Not every recipe or menu in this book is low in fat, low-to-moderate in protein, and high in grains, fruits, and vegetables. But all can be part of a healthy lifestyle. What we most definitely offer are some special-occasions-only dishes, lots of everyday mainstays, and the occasional I-can't-believe-this-has-no-fat treat. The balancing part is up to you—with just a bit of advice from us. Don't try to balance your food intake within every single day, consider it over a whole week at a time. Inevitably, there will be one day that you are faced with Le Cirque's crème brûlée or crave a gooey slice of chocolate birthday cake. You needn't forgo it; go ahead, have it, but take care to offset that treat by cutting back on fat or sugar on another day.

Balancing and moderation don't require abstinence and they don't apply just to food; they're about fitting what you want into a broader, more expansive scheme of things. As it turns out, you *can* have your Champagne Wishes and Caviar Dreams—right along with a healthy lifestyle. Go live life to the fullest and for as long as you can—healthfully!

On the set of the Television Food Network (clockwise from top left): movie director and vineyard owner Francis Ford Coppola; former first daughter Patti Reagan Davis; co-host Kate Connelly; and New York City's first lady Donna Hanover Giuliani, who hosts "Food News and Views" for TVFN.

ROBIN LEACH

◆ ◆ ◆ ◆ ◆ ◆ ◆ ◆ ◆ ◆ ◆

*"WORK HARD, BELIEVE IN YOURSELF, AND YOU WILL WIN.
BE DEDICATED, BE DILIGENT, AND NEVER GIVE UP ON YOUR DREAMS.
DON'T MAKE MONEY THE ULTIMATE GOAL. MAKE SUCCESS THE TARGET, AND
ALWAYS HELP THOSE LESS FORTUNATE THAN YOURSELF."*

MY WORK LIFE

It's hard for me to believe that "Lifestyles" is now into its thirteenth incredible season and that it airs on some 150 American television stations and in more than 25 countries around the world. Ever since my good friend Al Masini and I launched the show in 1983, I have ceaselessly searched the world for the best it has to offer: the finest homes; the most wonderful hotels, resorts, and vacation destinations; extraordinary people from the worlds of show business and big business; plus fabulous food and marvelous restaurants. Nice work if you can get it? Yes, it is fun and I truly do enjoy it, but it's also a great deal of work.

Be it a sunrise breakfast with Brooke Shields while on safari in Kenya, a lazy lunch with Roger Moore overlooking the Mediterranean in the south of France, or an incomparable dinner with Joan Collins at Le Cirque in New York, it all has been a fabulous journey, gastronomic and otherwise. I log nearly 300,000 miles a year, flying virtually everywhere that airplanes go, and have visited every country in the world except New Guinea and Myanmar (formerly Burma). You must be able to imagine how my "workstyle" has taken its toll on my lifestyle. With 18-hour workdays and a grueling 300 days a year away from home, does it come as a surprise that, well, I've sometimes overeaten? Indeed, sometimes I think that "spanning the girth of the world" is a more apt description of my waistline than my line of work.

CLOCKWISE FROM TOP LEFT: *From the worldwide travels of "Lifestyles,"
Robin with entertainer Wayne Newton, singer Barbara Mandrell, actor
Donald Sutherland, and actress Morgan Fairchild.*

But it's all been an incredible adventure—meeting extraordinary people in unbelievable locations and conducting 250 interviews and video segments each year since '83. Yep, that's 3,000 "Lifestyles" stories since day one! Now you know why my hairline has receded and I don't look as young as I did back then!

But being older and wiser didn't stop me two years ago, when I had the opportunity to take on yet another project. The subject, you see, was right up my alley; it involved talking—which I like to think I'm good at—with all sorts of celebrities about one of my very favorite topics: food. Thus, "Talking Food," my one-hour talk show that airs nightly on cable's Television Food Network (TVFN), was born.

We've had some great conversations with all sorts of people—everybody from Kenny Rogers to Geraldo Rivera, Debbie Reynolds to Ismail Merchant. You'd be surprised at just how many of our favorite stars and headline personalities are cooking enthusiasts; in fact, our lively conversations can get downright hilarious. Many of our guests have been eager to go into our "Talking Food" kitchen with my sidekick-chef, Kate Connelly, and share their favorite foods with our viewers. But on some nights, when our visiting celebrity is too busy or doesn't feel like cooking, Kate invites a famous restaurateur or chef to prepare the star's favorite dish. Superstar chefs—Wolfgang Puck, Jeremiah Tower, Larry Forgione, Bobby Flay, and Michael Lomonaco, among them—have revealed some of their secrets to us, and many of them you'll find in this book.

And so, I keep going, but I'm learning too—every day. About two years ago, it struck me that rather than burning out from work overload, I had to take a firm stand. I vowed to take time off and reorganize my work life. The goal was to cut back on work time in order to have a total of two months each year to myself. Mind you, I wasn't thinking of two full months, just the equivalent—60 days or so—spread out over several very long weekends. I wanted to find a special place where there'd be no phones, no fax, no discos, no neon lights, just plain, old-fashioned, simple peace and quiet. And therein lies a tale. . . .

Casa di Sogni D'Oro—House of Golden Dreams—Jumby Bay, Antigua.

MY REAL LIFE—JUMBY BAY ISLAND

We all have our own idea of paradise on earth, but mine is and always has been glorious sunshine, gentle, warming breezes, blindingly white sandy beaches, and swaying palm trees. As a teenager, living on the outskirts of London through miserably damp and chilling winters, I had a dream of one day living in paradise. Visions of relaxing in a hammock overlooking a sparkling blue sea and being able to pluck a mango or papaya from a nearby tree were a constantly recurring theme.

It wasn't long after moving to New York in late 1963 and battling the harsh East Coast winter storms that I had the great good fortune to find myself wandering the different islands of the Caribbean. I guess that being English I was naturally attracted to the British islands, and whenever I visited, I would pick up real estate brochures and occasionally look at homes for sale. In time—all the while saving my money—I narrowed my choice to the sunshine island of Antigua. Located more or less at the crossroads of the Caribbean, Antigua was perfect: populated with wonderful, happy, kind, caring people; dotted with 365 sandy beaches (one for every day of the year), and already possessing an international airport that offered direct service to both America and Europe.

Then, in 1986, while producing a "Lifestyles" segment about luxury resort developments in the Caribbean, I discovered Jumby Bay Island—a tiny, 300-acre paradise just two miles north or six minutes by motorized catamaran from the Antigua airport. The very moment I stepped ashore, I knew I had found my future home and the place where I eventually would retire. I returned annually for vacations to the growing hotel property, and when the owners unveiled plans for constructing a limited number of elegant private villas, I was among the first to put down a membership deposit.

By 1990, I had purchased a nearly three-acre beachfront site at the end of quiet, beautiful Pasture Bay. It took almost two years to transform architect Andrew Goodenough's plans for the Italian-style home I wanted into a reality. (Building on a small Caribbean island is no small undertaking, and despite a six-week delay on decorative tiles being shipped from Italy, everything was completed perfectly.) It was on July 4, 1992, that the Dutch construction company of Balast Nedham turned over Casa di Sogni D'Oro (House of Golden Dreams) to me right on schedule. My dream had come true.

It may sound strange, but my house has only one bedroom! Around the grounds are two fully equipped guest houses for visiting friends and two other potential guest quarters that double as recreation areas near the swimming pool and tennis court. I couldn't give up my pool table or collection of antique fairground games and jukebox just because I was going to the tropics!

Casa di Sogni D'Oro has a warm, comfortable feel to it. To take advantage of the year-round perfect weather, it's very open; the warm trade winds blow through the two working offices (so much for no phones, no fax), living room, and media room. The dining room, with its built-in table for ten, is completely open on one side.

ABOVE: *The pool, guest house, and alfresco dining area at Sogni D'Oro.*

LEFT: *The Jacuzzi is the perfect spot to hang out with a glass of juice squeezed from the garden's plentiful fresh fruit.*

OPPOSITE: *The swimming pool at Sogni D'Oro, designed so that the water in the swimming pool and the sea look like one to the swimmer.*

Robin's built-in tiled dining room table seats twelve. The ceramic candle holders and napkin rings were made by Cecilia Nord in the Sogni D'Oro pottery studio.

The view from the dining room reveals the croquet lawn and beach. Orchids picked fresh from the gardens grace a ceramic vase made by Cecilia Nord at the villa.

LEFT: *Robin's just pottering about in his ceramic studio—it's fully outfitted with a kiln and potter's wheel.*

BELOW: *The main living room features the metal art of Pal Kepeynes, a Hungarian sculptor who lives and works in Acapulco, Mexico. Robin has been collecting his powerful artwork for the past twelve years.*

OPPOSITE: *An Italian hideaway in the gardens, perfect for enjoying Pavarotti and a glass of red wine at sunset. What started as almost barren land has become a tropical jungle in just three years.*

After sunset, with the house alight with masses of candles and the illuminated palm trees beyond, the effect is almost magical. I simply love it.

My kitchen—remember, I love to cook—was designed to be the busiest room in the entire house. A work island in the center lets me go full steam ahead whether I'm prepping vegetables at the sink, grilling them on the range, grabbing ingredients from the fridge, or baking and roasting in the double ovens. There's a separate large pantry for dry goods and staples, and the wood counters are deep enough to keep all of my cooking machines close at hand. Whether it's bread, pizza, pasta, juice, or ice cream, all of my hardware for making it is always ready to go.

My dream of paradise has always included an element of self-sufficiency. And though I've always enjoyed shopping for food, when Mother Nature is so generous in your own backyard, you have to revel in her bounty. Just outside the kitchen is a large herb garden and beyond that six small vegetable plots. All of the lettuce is grown by the fishpond, since koi love fresh-grown too! And I have abundant crops of tomatoes, eggplants, sweet corn, onions, squash, cucumbers, zucchini, and beets, plus a never-ending supply of my favorite herbs—basil, parsley, ginger, rosemary, and cilantro, among others. I order all of my seeds from Shepherd's Garden Seeds,

an incredible mail-order supplier in Connecticut, and the combination of my Antiguan gardener, Uncle Will, and his partner, Ken, with Nature watching over, produces year-round perfect harvests.

It's a constant marvel for me to watch how quickly plants grow in perfect weather. So, we take advantage of it with our orchard of fruit trees—guavas, papayas, mangos, limes, lemons, oranges, bananas, and grapefruits. Lemongrass stalks, aloe plants, and even the famous black Antiguan pineapples ring the property. This has to be heaven on earth!

Horticulturist Paul Richnow, who is based in Antigua and Fort Lauderdale, gets the credit for making the designs of this garden gem come to life. He has faithfully supervised every palm, ficus, bougainvillea, hibiscus, sea grape, orchid, and bird-of-paradise and has turned what was a barren building site into a veritable Garden of Eden. Apart from going to the main island to buy fresh dairy products, I can live off my land. Why, even the local fishermen will drop off fresh-caught red snapper or lobster at the Jumby Bay Island dock!

As I write this, I can barely believe that it's been just three years since move-in day. What was a scenic but empty lot now sustains a beautiful home, and the soil has been coaxed into extraordinary gardens filled with flowers, fragrances, and food! When I started work earning just $10 a week at my first newspaper job, I never guessed that I could wind up where I am now. But years of hard work, diligence, and dedication can pay off when you stick to one goal with unwavering determination. That's really been the underlying message on "Lifestyles": Never quit, work hard, and you can make your dreams come true. My paradise is now reality; may yours be too. As I've always said, you have my Champagne Wishes—and may all of your Caviar Dreams come true.

RIGHT: *Picking tomatoes in the garden.*

BOTTOM LEFT: *One of the six vegetable gardens at Sogni D'Oro.*

BOTTOM RIGHT: *A corner of the croquet lawn. This oriental figure was discovered in Thailand while Robin was filming "Lifestyles" there and then imported to his garden on Jumby Bay.*

SOGNI D'ORO MEALS

A typical healthy dinner for guests at the House of Golden Dreams uses as many freshly picked fruits, vegetables, and herbs from the garden as possible:

APPETIZER: Butternut Squash Soup
Whole Wheat Bread

MAIN COURSES: Rich and Famous Chicken (see my first cookbook,
The Lifestyles of the Rich and Famous Cookbook)
Turkey Burgers and Fresh-Made Pasta
"Poached" Red Snapper Supreme

VEGETABLES: Papaya Salad
Eggplant and Tomato Pie
Beet Salad

DESSERTS: Black Antiguan Pineapple Sorbet with Fresh Mangos

I love fresh homemade whole wheat breads served with meals. Using the programmable timer on my automatic breadmaker, I can preset the machine for the exact moment I want a loaf of still-hot, fresh-made bread to serve right away with the first course. With the pasta machine, it's easy, economical, and efficient to make batches of pasta just hours—or minutes—in advance of a meal. And with an abundance of fresh basil and tomatoes from the garden, we make large batches of tomato and pesto sauces and freeze some of each for later use. Mixing the pesto and tomato sauces is my idea of the ultimate topping for the pastas.

I try to keep preparation time to under one hour and cooking time to less than another hour so I'm not exhausted or agitated when guests arrive. With sufficient planning I can cook most of the dinner in advance—that way there's time to shower, cool down, and change for the evening's enjoyment. Fifteen minutes of last-minute fussing and heating is all that should be needed as guests arrive. They can

even join you in the kitchen with a glass of good Champagne for that quarter of an hour to make them feel part of the overall dinner experience. Always remember to fill the coffeepot with water and ground beans before guests arrive so you can flick the switch as you serve the main course!

It's said that many pianists play by ear. I think I cook in a similar way: by feel and by smell. Sometimes the guesswork goes awry, but I remember the next time to add fewer sliced onions or cut back on the hot mustard so the meal isn't overpowered. My recipes all tend to be in unlimited quantities rather than specified for a particular number of people.

If you don't want to make soup, butternut squash is perfect for baking in a casserole dish. After peeling, rinse, and remove the seeds; cut into cubes. Layer the squash in a baking dish. Top with a touch of butter, sugar, salt, and pepper. Add 2 tablespoons white wine to 2 tablespoons of cold water; pour over the squash. Bake for about an hour at 375°F. until tender. You can stir the mixture once or twice during the cooking. Serve with lemon juice and chopped basil leaves sprinkled atop.

BUTTERNUT SQUASH SOUP

All varieties of squash grow rapidly in the gardens of Antigua, and I've selected butternut for this recipe because you can get it, inexpensively, almost anywhere and anytime. If you prefer, you can substitute pumpkin.

Peeled butternut squash, sliced and cubed
Apples, peeled, sliced, and cubed
Chicken broth, depending on how many people you plan to serve and over how many meals, anywhere from 4 to 6 cans
Oil
Onions, as many as you want for taste—chopped tiny
Flour, no less than 1 tablespoon
Ginger, finely grated
Sugar, or you can use orange juice
Salt and pepper to taste
Grated nutmeg, no less than 1 teaspoon, but keep adding as much as you wish

Put the cubes of squash and apple into the broth and bring to a boil. Then they should be allowed to simmer until they are fork-tender but don't break apart. Put to one side and let the mixture cool.

In a second deep pan, heat the oil, add the onions, and cook till clear but not browned. Add the flour and keep stirring.

Meanwhile, puree the squash and apples with some of the broth in a food processor. Stir the puree into the onion and flour mixture. Immediately add the ginger. Add some of the remaining broth until the soup is as thick or liquid as desired. Finally, add the sugar, salt, pepper, and nutmeg to your own taste requirements.

It's very safe to make up a large batch and store it in plastic containers in the fridge for up to 5 days or in the freezer for a month or more.

"POACHED" RED SNAPPER SUPREME

Why do I call it Supreme? To be honest, if I'm feeling grand, I substitute Champagne for the wine or beer and then the bubbles really work their way inside the fish. On Jumby Bay, we wrap it in banana leaves, but simply tightening aluminum foil over an open baking dish works just as well. I have a collection of French restaurant cookware, so I use both methods at the same time. I use wine or beer and all manner of herbs so that as the fish cooks, all of the magical, mystical flavors add to its taste. And if you don't serve all of the marinade with the meal, keep it in the kitchen and make a fish stock out of it later. Fish frightens some at-home cooks, but this recipe is foolproof and worry-free.

Onions
Lemongrass
Basil
Lemon juice
Wine or beer
Ginger
Soy sauce
White Worcestershire sauce
4 to 6 fillets of red snapper

Make a marinade of all of the ingredients (except the fish). Add the fish fillets and let marinate in the fridge for 1 hour. Cook in a preheated 375°F. oven for 25 to 30 minutes, or until the aroma is delicious and the fish is soft and tender.

I like to create unexpected vegetable dishes to accompany the main dish. For this menu I created a cold papaya salad—almost Thai-style—to complement the snapper, and an eggplant and tomato pie without a pastry crust. Instead, I just let the layer of basil leaves atop provide the finishing touch.

PAPAYA SALAD

My eldest son, Steven, is a whiz with this Leach-created dish. It can be made as a serve-alone brunch salad by adding half a cabbage or an amount of cabbage equal to the amount of papaya. However, when it is served as an accompaniment to the red snapper, the cabbage is omitted.

Green or fully ripened papaya, depending on your taste, skin
removed, the fruit either grated or diced
Tomatoes
Green, red, and yellow bell peppers
Finely chopped lemongrass stalks
2 large garlic cloves
Small scallions
Diced peanuts

Diced dried shrimp
Fresh lime juice
1 teaspoon sugar or palm sugar or Hawaiian sugar
Sprigs of parsley or cilantro or basil

In a salad bowl, combine the papaya, tomatoes, bell peppers, lemongrass, garlic, and scallions; grate or chop together.

Add all of the remaining ingredients and sprinkle sprigs of parsley or cilantro and chopped basil on top for eye appeal when serving.

It's unusual and exotic and always wins raves, with everybody asking for the recipe. Now you've got it!

EGGPLANT AND TOMATO PIE

This dish grew out of the need to find ways to use up the overabundant supplies of tomatoes and eggplants that grow like wildfire in my garden. A generous layer of fresh basil leaves atop the layers of tomatoes and eggplants adds to the taste and the appearance—and does away with the need for a pastry top or bottom. And it's much healthier!

Some people complain that eggplant has a slightly bitter taste (easily solved by salting it before cooking). Some people fry eggplant, some bake it inside bread crumbs, some whip it up with tahini for dips, but I love it in its natural state. Eggplants come purple-black or with pink and white streaks. They come long or round and can be sautéed or pickled—every person to his own choice. My recipe is remarkably simple, very healthful, totally tasty, and, again, a unique side course of vegetables to go with the red snapper.

6 eggplants, halved
4 large beefsteak tomatoes, each cut into 6 slices
Parmesan cheese, grated
Oil
Fresh lemon or lime juice
Pepper
Basil leaves

In a preheated 375°F. oven, bake the halved eggplants in a baking dish for 20 to 30 minutes. Remove and let stand for 5 to 10 minutes. Slice the eggplants about the same thickness as the tomatoes. Layer into the baking dish the eggplant, tomatoes, grated cheese, and drizzle with oil and lemon juice. Sprinkle on pepper, and completely cover with basil leaves, as if it were pastry topping.

Bake for 1 hour, timing its completion to just after you've served the appetizer course.

Turn the oven off and let the pie sit until ready to serve as the accompaniment to the red snapper main course.

This recipe is very simple, very tasty, and very healthful. You can use the same procedure and add lamb or other minced meats to make meat casseroles. If you like garlic, slice up a clove and add to the eggplant.

If you really like the papaya salad and just want to have a cold eggplant salad to go with it, here's another quick Leach family eggplant recipe.

Broil or grill eggplants until burned and charred. Set aside.

Then dice the following: cucumber, garlic, pepper, lemongrass, onion. Peel, seed, and dice tomatoes. Add pepper and the juice of two lemons; mix with very little oil. Scoop the flesh from inside the eggplant; do not use the charred skin. Combine the mixture and the eggplant. Garnish with lots of basil and parsley.

This can be presented as a stand-alone dish by heaping it in the center of a plate and using garden herbs and fresh ground pepper around the rest of the plate. If you want to turn this into a one-course meal in its own right, take 6 ounces of boneless, skinless cooked chicken breasts and finely chop them. Add some fish sauce. Combine the mixture with the eggplant.

NOTE: You probably will not want to use more than 2 teaspoons of fish sauce—obtained easily from Asian and Indian food shops or specialty markets.

I've talked about many quick, simple variations for eggplants, but you can achieve the same with tomatoes. Stir-fry some 3 dozen cherry tomatoes with chopped garlic, chopped scallions, basil, oregano, and pepper in a pan containing olive oil and a little heated butter. Don't exceed 2½ minutes of frying time! Or, make a tomato tart using the same directions and ingredients in the eggplant dish. Obviously, omit the eggplant and instead add eggs, milk, and grated Monterey Jack cheese. Tomatoes made this way have to cook for only 30 minutes or so, and it's advisable to use a pie shell. Always stem and core your tomatoes.

Making tomato sauce at home is easy. Once you've got the basic sauce recipe down pat, feel free to experiment and heat it up with chiles, garlic, red wine vinegar, salt, and pepper. We often add mint leaves to kick up the natural flavors. Here's the easiest tomato sauce in the world:

Peel as many pounds of tomatoes as you wish and cut each tomato into 4 sections. Cook over medium heat for 2 to 3 hours, or until the tomatoes are quite soft and the liquid has almost evaporated. Strain. Add chopped basil and mix into a pesto sauce when serving over pasta. Again, this sauce can be frozen for later use.

Use basil leaves atop pasta dishes, add them to curries, fry them in a crispy batter as a garnish for roasts, or cut them into chiffonade. Chiffonade is thin long strips or shreds of a vegetable or herb; here's the easy way to do it: Stack several basil leaves (the bigger, the better) atop one another. Starting on a long side, roll up the leaves into a long, tightly packed tube. Thinly slice crosswise with a sharp knife and *voilà*—long, thin, frill basil chiffonade. If we have an oversupply of basil leaves, we let them sun-dry, hanging upside down, and then crumble the leaves into a mason jar for whenever we need them or to take back to friends in Connecticut.

You know from reading these recipes that I'm also in love with lemongrass and use it whenever I can. Fortunately, it grows like a weed in Antigua. It can be used in drinks and teas but I use it as an addition to soups and whenever I'm making vegetables and salads. Chop or mince it, or you can leave it as whole stalks when roasting chicken. A zesty flavor comes when lemongrass is used with fish sauce, sake, ginger, garlic, coriander, and rice wine as a paste for marinating shrimp. And then you can barbecue the shrimp with stalks of lemongrass—much as you would roast using branches of rosemary.

Mix lemongrass with sugar, water, and lemon slices and then boil to dissolve the sugar. Let cook and store in the refrigerator. You can brush this lemongrass syrup over pears and other fruits—even my old friends the mango and papaya—which gives you another perfect dessert.

However, I've selected a different dessert to complete your healthful Caribbean menu:

· ·

BLACK ANTIGUAN PINEAPPLE SORBET WITH FRESH MANGO

This favorite Caribbean recipe applies to all pineapples, be they Hawaiian or otherwise. We're blessed with black pineapples in Antigua. They're not black, but food experts will swear they're the best-tasting, sweetest-tasting pineapples on the face of the earth. They grow in abundance on Antigua and Jumby Bay Island, and they've begun to be exported in fair quantities to the East Coast. When we've chopped off the top of one, we let the top sit in a glass of water for 4 days and then we plant it right back in the soil again. A year later it will have grown itself back to full size, sprouting six other pineapples!

SORBET:

1 large pineapple, trimmed, cored, and cut into chunks
Sugar: I don't use any because Antiguan pineapples are so sweet, but you might want to use up to 2 cups for sweetness
2 cups water
2 tablespoons white Antiguan rum

MANGOS:

Mangos
Fresh lime juice
Dark rum
Angostura bitters
Sugar
Ground cinnamon

Puree the pineapple chunks in a food processor until smooth; strain, reserving the juice, and compost the remaining pulp.

Combine the sugar and water in a saucepan and bring to a boil. Cook until the sugar dissolves. Let cool. Add sufficient syrup to the pineapple juice and mix in the rum—stirred not shaken! Refrigerate until it's cold. Freeze in an ice-cream maker.

Peel and pit the mangos. Smother with the fresh lime juice, dark rum, Angostura bitters, sugar, and cinnamon. Scoop the pineapple sorbet on top.

Since this is a healthy lifestyle cookbook I won't dare tell you how delicious it would be to add whipped and chilled heavy cream on top. It's too sinful! But if you're going to splurge, then this is the dessert to do it with!

I hope your meal and its variations are as delicious as the ones we enjoy in our House of Golden Dreams on Jumby Bay. Cold Nicolas Feuillatte Champagne is perfect to serve with the appetizers, and South African, Australian, New Zealand, Chilean, or California Chardonnays are perfect to serve with the main course. Cheers!

· ·

JUMBY BAY ISLAND

Jumby Bay Island is consistently ranked among the world's top three resorts, lauded in publications such as *Departures, Travel & Leisure, Gourmet, Condé Nast Traveler, Town & Country, Forbes, Caribbean Week,* and *Caribbean Travel and Life.* Check the top-secret guest-registration book and you'll find a stellar lineup: George Harrison, David Copperfield, Roseanne, Oprah Winfrey, LeVar Burton, Meryl Streep, Liam Neeson, Glenn Close, John Cleese—but not Princess Diana, because the hotel turned her down, fearing an invasion of paparazzi in helicopters disturbing the peace. My friends Alan Thicke and his bride, Gina, honeymooned on Jumby Bay Island, and one of my former British newspaper colleagues, famed novelist Barbara Taylor Bradford, and her husband, Robert, renewed their wedding vows in a ceremony that marked their thirtieth wedding anniversary. Best-selling author Ken Follett is moving into a new home built just 100 yards from mine, and Terry Anderson, the Beirut hostage, took his "R&R" here while writing his life story and experiences. Stylistically worlds apart, both Howard Stern and Kathie Lee Gifford agree on one thing: Jumby is the best place in the world to vacation.

Although the Jumby Bay Island resort has only thirty-eight hotel rooms and eighteen privately owned villas that can be rented, it is not just for the rich & famous! Yes, the $1,000-a-night rate for two people sounds pricey, but it includes *everything*—all meals, all drinks, all sports, everything! In fact, on Jumby nobody ever carries money, because once the reservation rate has been paid, absolutely everything is included. And prices drop dramatically once the Christmas-to-Easter high season ends and the quieter summer months come along.

OPPOSITE: *Sailboats at rest on Jumby Bay Island's main beach.*

The Jumby community also includes ten estate homes, and some of the owners even rent their guest cottages as part of the Jumby experience. It is very exclusive, very private, and very, very special, but just what makes it that way for visitors and Jumby Club members?

Everybody has a different answer: For some, it's the serenity, the friendly, warm, efficient staff, the absolute feeling of security (guests don't even bother with room keys), the sunny days and starry nights, the soft, white-sand beaches and inviting waters, or the incredible service (a staff of 300 caters to every whim and request).

Many visitors are happy to stretch out under palm trees or lemongrass-thatched umbrellas on one of the two white beaches. The more active swim and play tennis or croquet. Walking or biking the three-mile meandering roadway that circumscribes the island is easy, and it's impossible to get lost: There are no cars and therefore no traffic jams or noise. Pick up a bike in one spot and leave it in another—there's plenty for everybody.

Jumby Bay Island is also home to the endangered hawksbill sea turtle. Since 1985, a team of students from the University of Georgia works for eight months of each year on Jumby, protecting the turtles, monitoring the nesting, and helping newborn baby turtles survive. It is truly one of the most wondrous experiences of life to watch a mother sea turtle laying up to 100 Ping-Pong-ball-size eggs, and then ninety days later, to see the eggs hatch under the sea grapes, the baby turtles scampering through the sand, and swimming off into the sea.

Whatever the natural attractions a world-class resort island may offer, on Jumby Bay Island food ranks as the most important of all. The executive chef is Rex Hale, a James Beard Award winner, who is brilliantly assisted by his number-two, big, friendly, Antigua-born Nigel Gore. Their teamwork assures artistry—and nonstop raves from food critics, food and travel magazines, and even rival chefs and restaurateurs who vacation here.

OPPOSITE: *The three-hundred-year-old stone steps that lead up to the resort's Estate House, where cocktails and evening meals are served.*

Rex's menus strongly emphasize native dishes enhanced with classic French or contemporary American touches. Any ingredient that can be grown on Jumby is, but nonnative goods are flown in from impeccably monitored sources. One day a week, usually on Saturdays, Rex and his staff invite hotel guests to join them on an 8:00 A.M. launch over to the main island. The goal is to tour the local farmers' market and fishermen's wharf for close scrutiny of everything from red snapper and crabs to passion fruits and avocados. As Rex observes, "Anything that grows in the Caribbean has a brighter flavor."

Take a look at just a few choices from his menus. Clearly this is a man who can marshal his resources into interesting and flavorful combinations of fresh ingredients. And much of what he chooses from is close at hand; Rex oversees two acres of Jumby Island land dedicated to a hundred varieties of herbs and vegetables.

Formerly with world-famous Commander's Palace and Brennan's restaurants in New Orleans, and more recently at the amazing Lost Palace resort in Sun City, South Africa, Rex believes that Caribbean-influenced food will be the next "hot craze in the food world." Why? "Our cooking is a blend that results in the best— it's more nuanced and layered through the continued infusion of the bright Caribbean flavors."

JUMBY BAY RECIPES
BY CHEF REX HALE

....

CHILLED TUNA ESCABECHE

Every individual part of this recipe can be used for its great, fresh flavor, but when you combine all the parts—that's artistry!

Serves 6

MARINADE:
1 red onion, coarsely chopped
1 bunch cilantro, stems removed
5 serrano or other chile peppers, trimmed and seeded
¼ cup chili powder
3 tablespoons ground cumin, toasted
2 garlic cloves
3 cups chicken or fish stock or broth
½ cup white wine vinegar
Salt and freshly milled black pepper

SEASONINGS AND TUNA:
1 tablespoon chili powder
3 tablespoons coarse (kosher) salt
1½ tablespoons freshly milled black pepper
2 tablespoons olive oil
1 pound center-cut, top-quality yellowfin tuna fillet, cut into 3-x-2-inch pieces

FOR SERVING:
West Indian Fruit Relish (recipe follows)
Curry Sauce (recipe follows)
Fresh herbs, for garnish (optional)
Plantain or cassava chips

1. Combine all of the marinade ingredients in a food processor or blender and process to a puree. Pour the mixture into a nonreactive saucepan and bring to a boil over high heat. Reduce the heat to low and simmer for 10 minutes.

2. Pour the marinade into a deep bowl or container. Cover and refrigerate until chilled. (The marinade can be made a day or two ahead; refrigerate until needed.)

3. When the marinade is cold, combine the seasonings to make a wet paste. Generously rub the seasoning mixture all over the tuna, coating well.

4. Place a nonstick skillet over moderately high heat until a drop of water sizzles and evaporates on contact. Add the chunks of tuna to the pan and sear quickly—just until opaque—on all sides, 1 to 2 minutes total. Transfer the tuna to the marinade and submerge it. Cover and refrigerate for at least 5 hours.

5. To serve, remove the tuna from the marinade; cut the fish into thin slices. Fan out the slices on a chilled serving plate. Top each with a small dollop of the West Indian Fruit Relish; drizzle a bit of the Curry Sauce over the plate. Garnish with fresh herbs, if desired. Serve with plantain or cassava chips.

....

WEST INDIAN FRUIT RELISH

Though this recipe yields about 1½ cups, you can halve, double, or triple it to make whatever quantity suits your needs. Make a lot of it, because in a pinch you can puree any leftovers in a blender or food processor to make a big-flavored sauce for fish, chicken, or grilled vegetables.

Makes about 1½ cups

¼ cup finely diced ripe papaya
¼ cup finely diced ripe mango
¼ cup finely diced pineapple
¼ cup finely diced yellow bell pepper
¼ cup finely diced red bell pepper
¼ cup finely diced red onion
½ to 1 teaspoon minced serrano or other chile pepper
1 tablespoon olive oil
1 to 2 tablespoons fresh lime juice
1½ teaspoons minced fresh mint leaves
Salt and freshly milled black pepper
Pineapple juice or sugar, if needed

1. In a bowl, toss together the fruits and vegetables. Add the oil and lime juice and toss to coat. Sprinkle on the mint and mix to distribute it throughout. Season with salt and pepper. Taste and adjust the seasoning as necessary, adding more salt and pepper, lime juice, or even a touch of pineapple juice or sugar.

2. Cover the relish and chill until needed. Serve cold or at room temperature.

....

CURRY SAUCE

This simple recipe results in an amazingly flavorful sauce that can be used sparingly on just about anything you like. Try it drizzled over fresh sweet corn—absolutely great! The Curry Oil can be kept on hand to enhance salad dressings or as the base for a quick stir-fry.

Makes about 1½ cups

CURRY OIL (MAKES ABOUT 1 CUP):
2 tablespoons fragrant curry powder
1 cup canola oil

SAUCE:
2 cups fresh orange juice
Salt

1. Make the Curry Oil: Sprinkle the curry powder into a small, nonstick saucepan or skillet and set over moderately low heat. Warm the curry just until the fragrance begins to be released.

2. Remove the pan from the heat and stir in the oil until blended. Pour the mixture into a glass jar. Cover and shake to blend again. Set the oil aside at room temperature for at least 12 hours, or until the curry powder settles to the bottom.

3. Pour off the clear curry oil into a clean jar; discard the dregs.

4. Make the Curry Sauce: Pour the orange juice into a nonreactive small saucepan and bring to a boil over moderately high heat. Cook until the juice has reduced to ¾ cup, 10 to 15 minutes. Set aside to cool.

5. Whisk the Curry Oil into the reduced orange juice until well blended. Season with salt to taste. Reserve the remaining Curry Oil for other uses.

....

ABOVE: *The ever-smiling executive chef Rex Hale loves Caribbean-style cooking and believes it will be the next food wave.*

LEFT: *Nigel and Rex at the lunchtime outdoor grill.*

CULINARY WEEK AT LA SAMANNA

The Caribbean is blessed with many beautiful islands—all within easy reach of my home on Jumby Bay. If you're feeling French, Dutch, or English, there's an island for you. But for me, St. Martin, just twenty minutes away by plane, offers the best of two worlds: Half of the island is French and the other half is Dutch (they spell it St. Maarten).

On the French side is the legendary La Samanna resort, now operated by the Rosewood Group of Dallas, Texas. Every year in early summer, Marc Ehrler, La Samanna's executive chef, plays host to other headline chefs from Rosewood properties: Dean Fearing from The Mansion on Turtle Creek in Dallas, Paul Gayler from The Lanesborough in London, Jim Mills from the Hotel Crescent Court in Dallas, Denis Meurgue from Little Dix Bay in Virgin Gorda, and the experts from other of Rosewood's global properties, including Caneel Bay in St. John and the Hotel Bel-Air in Los Angeles. It's a food lovers extravaganza: a whole week that includes talks and tastings with winemakers, specialty chefs (such as brilliant pastry chef Jacques Torres of Le Cirque), and other knowledgeable food experts. It's a culinary experience that shouldn't be missed.

During Culinary Week, La Samanna's audience of food critics, restaurateurs, and home cooks experiences a unique, five-day series of cooking classes aimed at anyone who wants to improve his or her skills in the kitchen. The atmosphere is friendly and casual, filled with the bonhomie that's found throughout the Caribbean. Many of the classes are conducted at an open-air grill by the swimming pool. Chefs pass on shopping and food-selection tips and then carry out cooking demonstrations. Here's an example of what guests got to watch, helped prepare, and then tasted and enjoyed:

··

OPPOSITE: *Five of the world's greatest chefs prove that they can have fun both in and out of the kitchen as they play at La Samanna in St. Martin.*

CHEF PAUL GAYLER'S CHILLED EGGPLANT SOUP WITH CILANTRO CHUTNEY

Here's a cooling alternative to gazpacho for the dog days of summer when chilled foods are so soothing. Make it in the cool of the evening the night before you plan to serve it or early in the morning before the heat turns sultry.

For 4 to 6

CILANTRO CHUTNEY:
1 bunch cilantro, leaves and tender stems only
1 to 2 small green chiles, seeded and chopped
3 tablespoons fresh lemon juice
¼ onion, chopped

EGGPLANT SOUP:
1½ tablespoons unsalted butter
½ large onion, chopped
1 garlic clove, minced
1 leek, well-washed, the white and light green parts only, chopped
2 eggplants, peeled and chopped
1 tablespoon curry powder
½ teaspoon ground coriander
¼ teaspoon ground cumin
4 cups vegetable or chicken stock or broth
2 tablespoons low-fat or non-fat plain yogurt
Salt and freshly milled pepper

1. Make the chutney: Combine all of the chutney ingredients in a food processor or blender and puree until smooth. Taste and adjust the seasonings. Scrape the chutney into a jar and refrigerate for up to 5 days.

2. Make the soup: Melt the butter in a nonreactive large saucepan set over moderately low heat. Add the onion, garlic, and leek, cover the pan, and sweat the mixture for 5 minutes.

3. Stir in the eggplant, curry powder, coriander, and cumin. Reduce the heat to very low, cover, and cook for 15 minutes.

4. Stir in the stock and bring the mixture to a boil. Reduce the heat and simmer until all of the vegetables are tender and soft, usually about 5 minutes.

5. Pour the soup into a food processor or blender and puree until smooth. Let cool to room temperature.

6. Stir in the yogurt and season with salt and pepper to taste. Refrigerate the soup until well chilled, at least 1 hour.

7. Ladle the soup into chilled shallow bowls and top each serving with a dollop of the cilantro chutney.

....

Paul Gayler, executive chef at London's prestigious Lanesborough Hotel and a vegetarian chef on British television, is all smiles under the warm Caribbean sun.

Dean Fearing (at right) from the famed Mansion on Turtle Creek in Dallas and British chef Paul Gayler (at left) lead a tour of the local markets during Culinary Week at La Samanna.

....

BEAUTY IS IN THE
EYE OF THE BEHOLDER

CHERYL TIEGS

♦ ♦ ♦ ♦ ♦ ♦ ♦ ♦ ♦ ♦ ♦ ♦

"HIKING IS MY FAVORITE EXERCISE.
WHEN I'M HIKING, I LOVE THE SILENCE, THE BEAUTY AROUND ME.
IT'S SORT OF MEDITATIVE—THE BREATHING, FEELING MY BODY RESPOND,
FEELING MY MUSCLES REACT. I REALLY ENJOY IT—AND THAT'S HEALTHY, ISN'T IT?"

Cheryl Tiegs was gazing at the Pacific Ocean, pondering the lunch for two. "Maybe we could go for a hike in the mountains first—it's a perfect day for it." And indeed it was—gloriously clear, slightly windy, the air warm yet crisp, though the lightweight persimmon-colored jacket she wore was just enough to take the edge off the wind's chill. "And then we'll come back and have our picnic right here on the bluffs," she added, and that decision was made. "I like to work in the mornings and get things out of the way," she remarked, "and then have a hearty lunch as my main meal of the day. Mid- to late-afternoon is when I exercise; by then, I can work off the stress of the day—and my big lunch too."

That said, the first—and fairest—supermodel of them all, Cheryl Tiegs, grabbed a basket and rounded the corner, saying, "I'll gather some wildflowers for our picnic." Cheryl Tiegs was the first of the supermodels to see the opportunity to move beyond the camera and into the business marketplace with her own line of clothing. Her business savvy is as acute as her convictions about living a healthy lifestyle.

"I'm not an extreme person," she professes. "I spend a great deal of my time trying to maintain my good health and live naturally. The way I see it, if you take good care of yourself and live right, you'll be healthy. I am rarely sick and I like

> ### PICNIC FOR TWO
>
> **NO-FAT GAZPACHO**
>
> **CRUSTY FRENCH BREAD**
>
> **NEW POTATO SALAD IN MUSTARD VINAIGRETTE**
>
> **BARBECUED CHICKEN DRUMSTICKS**
>
> **CRUDITÉS**
>
> **LEMON BISCOTTI AND CHOCOLATE BISCOTTI WITH FRESH STRAWBERRIES**
>
> *BEVERAGE: BOTTLED WATER*
>
> *WINE: GEORGES DUBOEUF 1990 POUILLY-FUISSÉ*

The fairest of them all, Cheryl Tiegs is surrounded by beauty—flowers, the ocean, and a clear blue sky.

to think it's because I make a real effort to eat right, exercise, and generally maintain my body as well as I can. I think it really pays off. I exercise almost every day—not a full workout necessarily, but I do something. Exercise just feels good to me and it makes me feel good—I hike, ride my bike, do the stadium steps nearby. Twice a week I head for the gym and do an upper-body workout with a trainer, but the rest of the time I like to exercise on my own, alone. Hiking is my favorite exercise. When I'm hiking, I love the silence, the beauty around me. It's sort of meditative—the breathing, feeling my body respond, feeling my muscles react. I really enjoy it—and that's healthy, isn't it?"

The picnic menu had been determined by Ms. Tiegs and was a compromise of sorts from what she'd have if dining alone. "I have a nutritionist I trust. But basically, I 'food-combine,'" she explained, referring to the eating plan set forth and explained in the best-selling book *Fit for Life.* "Ninety-nine percent of the time, I eat fruit only in the morning, have a big lunch, and don't combine bread with protein at any meal. So, normally, I wouldn't have bread at lunch or the biscotti or the strawberries with this meal, but they were so beautiful, I just couldn't resist."

NO-FAT CHUNKY GAZPACHO

You'll want to make this a day or two ahead of time so that the flavors can mix and mellow. Keep it chilled and serve it chilled, with or without a trio of avocado slices on top of each portion.

For 4 to 6

3 pounds (about 8 large) ripest tomatoes, peeled, seeded, pulp cut
    into chunks, juices reserved
1 large cucumber, peeled and diced (remove the seeds if you like, but
    it isn't necessary)
½ cup diced onion
½ cup diced green bell pepper
½ cup diced red bell pepper
2 whole scallions, trimmed and thinly sliced
3 garlic cloves, minced
2 tablespoons red wine vinegar
2 tablespoons dry sherry or sherry vinegar
Salt and freshly milled black pepper
1 to 1½ cups chilled tomato juice
1 to 2 teaspoons hot sauce (optional)
Thin avocado slices and minced fresh herbs, such as cilantro or
    chives, for serving (optional)

Make the No-Fat Chunky Gazpacho a day ahead; the flavor actually improves in the refrigerator.

1. In a large bowl or pitcher, stir together the tomatoes and their juices, the cucumber, onion, bell peppers, scallions, and garlic. When blended, add the vinegar, sherry, and salt and pepper to taste. Stir in just enough of the tomato juice to make the soup liquid but not soupy. Add hot sauce to taste; correct the seasonings.

2. Cover and chill for at least a day—2 is even better. If necessary, add more cold tomato juice to reach the consistency you want for serving. Serve cold, garnished with the avocados and herbs, if desired.

···

NEW POTATO SALAD IN MUSTARD VINAIGRETTE
For 4 to 6

2 pounds small red new potatoes (buy the tiniest ones you can
    find), washed
¼ cup high-quality red wine vinegar
¼ cup extra-virgin olive oil
1 tablespoon Dijon mustard
3 tablespoons snipped fresh chives
1 tablespoon chopped flat-leaf parsley
1 teaspoon salt
Freshly milled black pepper

1. Place the potatoes in a large saucepan; pour in cold water to cover by 2 to 3 inches. Set over moderately high heat and bring to a boil. Reduce the heat to low, cover the pan, and simmer for 15 to 20 minutes, or until fork-tender but not falling apart.

2. Drain the potatoes and set aside until just cool enough to handle.

3. Meanwhile, combine all of the remaining ingredients in a jar. Cover and shake well. Taste and correct the seasonings.

4. When the potatoes are cool, peel off the skins, if desired. Quarter each potato and collect the pieces in a large bowl. Shake the vinaigrette again and then pour over the still-warm potatoes. Gently toss or fold together until the potatoes are coated with the vinaigrette. Serve warm, or cover and chill, tossing occasionally.

···

BARBECUED CHICKEN DRUMSTICKS

Yum, these are good. If you prefer the lighter meat of chicken wings, substitute them, or make a combination of wings and legs. These are great hot off the grill, at room temperature, or chilled.

For 4 to 6

1 cup low-sodium soy sauce
¼ cup dry sherry
⅓ cup fresh lemon juice
⅓ cup honey
¼ cup canola oil
¼ cup Worcestershire sauce
1 to 3 teaspoons grated fresh ginger
4 pounds chicken drumsticks, any extraneous fat discarded, pieces rinsed and patted dry (see Note)

1. In a deep bowl, whisk together the soy sauce, sherry, lemon juice, and honey until the honey is thinned out by the other liquids. Add the oil, Worcestershire, and ginger to taste; whisk well.

2. Submerge the chicken drumsticks in the marinade, taking care that all are well covered. Cover and refrigerate, stirring from time to time, for 3 to 12 hours.

3. Preheat a barbecue grill or the broiler until very hot.

4. When ready to cook, remove the chicken from the marinade. Pour the marinade into a nonreactive saucepan and boil over high heat until thickened and syrupy, 3 to 5 minutes.

5. Place the drumsticks on the hot grill or under the broiler and baste with some of the reduced marinade. Cover and cook for 5 minutes. Turn the legs, baste again, cover, and cook for 5 minutes more. Uncover the grill and finish cooking until the drumsticks are browned, crisp, and cooked through. Remove from the heat and brush with another coat of the glaze. Serve hot, at room temperature, or even chilled.

NOTE: If you want to reduce the fat, remove the skin from the drumsticks before marinating. Take care while cooking, though, since the meat will be exposed directly to the heat and can dry out quickly.

ABOVE: *Simple food, sumptuously presented—a platter of New Potato Salad in Mustard Vinaigrette surrounded by Barbecued Chicken Drumsticks.*

BELOW: *A basketful of picnic essentials.*

Lemon Biscotti and Chocolate Biscotti with Fresh Strawberries.

LEMON BISCOTTI

Italian biscotti are almost always baked twice, and so are these, but it doesn't take long. These are quick and easy and amazingly refreshing.

Makes about 18

1 to 1¼ cups unbleached all-purpose flour
½ cup sugar
1 teaspoon baking powder
¼ teaspoon salt
4 tablespoons (½ stick) cold unsalted butter, cut into bits
1 large egg
Grated zest of 1 large lemon
2 tablespoons fresh lemon juice

1. Preheat the oven to 325°F. Line a baking sheet with baking parchment.

2. In a food processor, combine the flour, sugar, baking powder, and salt. Scatter the butter on top. Pulse until the mixture is crumbly.

3. Add the egg, lemon zest, and lemon juice; process for 20 to 30 seconds, until the mixture forms a dough that pulls away from the sides of the bowl and gathers around the blade. (It's all right if some of the dough remains separate.)

4. Lightly flour a work surface and your hands. Turn out the dough and knead in any bits that have separated from the mass. If necessary, lightly sprinkle with additional flour, though the dough should be a bit sticky. Shape the dough into a squarish log about 12 inches long and 1½ to 2 inches wide and high. Transfer to the prepared baking sheet.

RIGHT: *Every picnic should be this gorgeous—it's a model presentation.*

BELOW: *A basketload of fresh ingredients will be turned into crudités.*

5. Bake for 20 minutes. Remove the baking sheet to a wire rack and let cool for 15 minutes.

6. Cut the tender log of dough into ½-inch slices. Lay the slices on their sides over the parchment. Return the biscotti to the oven and bake for 5 minutes.

7. Turn the slices over and bake for about 5 minutes more, or until pale gold, fragrant, and cooked through.

8. Transfer the baking parchment to a wire rack and let the biscotti cool completely. Store in an airtight container.

CHOCOLATE BISCOTTI

This is very simple: Basically you just substitute chocolate for the lemon. Melt 1 ounce bittersweet or semisweet chocolate and let cool. Follow Steps 1 and 2 of the recipe for lemon biscotti. In Step 3, substitute the melted chocolate and ½ teaspoon vanilla extract for the lemon zest and juice. Proceed with the recipe as directed.

FREDERIQUE

◆ ◆ ◆ ◆ ◆ ◆ ◆ ◆ ◆ ◆ ◆

*"With my hectic traveling schedule, I need a workout routine that I can count on.
I chose to work with Chris because his Peak 10 program helps me balance my life and keep in shape.
This program is for anyone who wants to look and feel their best—and stay that way."*

She seems to have the patience of a saint. We're in a studio, it's the second day of shooting for a workout video, and as always with this sort of venture, a certain degree of chaos reigns. There seems to be no end to the false starts—flubbed lines, an errant sneeze, the misguided spotlight that needs to be brought into line, body microphones that squeal or whine from unknown, unheard stimuli. And yet, Frederique remains calm, unruffled, perfectly composed, but in no way disconnected from it all. She's so very, very patient. And they'll probably be at it for, oh, another eight hours or so today. And then all day tomorrow too. Amazing.

Is Frederique this decade's Grace Kelly? She may well be—there's the serenity, the cool detachment when her face is in repose, and the quick warmth that comes with even a hint of a smile. There's the long, slim but shapely body, the blonde hair, the cool blue eyes, and the attentive way she observes and listens to whatever's going on around her.

You could say that Frederique has one of the most familiar faces in America. Her cover photos for *Vogue*, *Harper's Bazaar*, *Cosmopolitan*, *Glamour*, and *Mademoiselle*, among oth-

Frederique van der Wal, as captured through the lens of photographer Antoine Verglas.

ers, and her advertising campaigns for companies such as Revlon and Guess? helped contribute to that. But without doubt, it's Frederique's work for the Victoria's Secret catalogues that brought renown among men and women alike. Indeed, thanks to the catalogues, she "visits" many homes virtually once a week, all year long.

During a break in the taping, we ask Frederique van der Wal how she does it all. "Well, obviously, I work out regularly—that's what we're doing here," she says, referring to *Frederique Presents Chris Imbo's Peak 10 Fitness* workout video. "And I eat small amounts of anything I want," she continues. "In Europe, a meal consists of small amounts of several foods; here, the portions are enormous—far too big. You don't need to eat all that food; I'm convinced you can have anything you want—in moderate amounts." And what does she like to eat? "Well, I love tuna tartare, grilled swordfish, and duck ravioli in tomato sauce, and my friend's restaurant even has a dish on the menu named for me: Artichaux à la Frederique."

Here's the recipe.

ARTICHAUX À LA FREDERIQUE

If you're in New York City, stop by Night and Day restaurant in SoHo to order the original version of this dish, created for Frederique.

For 4

4 large globe artichokes
2 lemons, halved

VINAIGRETTE:
2 tablespoons fresh lemon juice
1 tablespoon white wine vinegar
2 teaspoons Dijon mustard
1 small garlic clove, minced
¼ to ⅓ cup extra-virgin olive oil
1 tablespoon drained capers, chopped
2 tablespoons minced fresh parsley
Salt and freshly milled pepper

1. Soak the artichokes in salted cold water for about 30 minutes. Drain, rinse, and dry.

2. Half-fill a large bowl with cold water; squeeze the juice of 2 lemon halves into the water and drop in the halves. Break off and discard the stem and tough outer leaves of one of the artichokes; trim the base so it will sit flat. Lay the artichoke on its side and cut off the top inch. Snip off the sharp leaf tips with scissors or a knife; rub all of the cut surfaces with a lemon half. Drop the trimmed artichoke into the bowl of acidulated water. Trim and soak the remaining artichokes.

3. Set up a steamer large enough to hold all of the artichokes in one layer. Make sure that neither the pot nor the steamer tray is made of aluminum; it will react with the artichokes and change their color and flavor. Bring about 1 inch of water to a boil in the bottom of the steamer. Squeeze the juice of the remaining lemon half into the pot. Drain the artichokes and stand them on the steaming rack. Cover and steam until a leaf from the base can be plucked off easily, 35 to 45 minutes, depending on the size of the artichoke. Drain the artichokes upside down until just cool enough to handle.

4. Meanwhile, make the vinaigrette: In a jar, combine all of the dressing ingredients. Cover tightly and shake to mix very well. Taste and season with salt and pepper as needed. Cover and shake again. Set aside until needed.

5. Gently spread the artichoke leaves apart and pull out the tender center leaves in one piece. Scoop out the choke with a small spoon. Reshake the vinaigrette and then spoon some of it into the center of each artichoke. Serve at once.

RIGHT: *Artichaux à la Frederique.* CENTER: Frederique Presents Chris Imbo's Peak 10 Fitness *is a video that offers a 10-week personal training program developed by Chris Imbo, personal trainer to a number of New York City–based luminaries. The Peak 10 program guides viewers to better health by emphasizing a commitment to exercise and a better understanding of dietary considerations.* BOTTOM: *Frederique and Chris Imbo work it out for the cameras.*

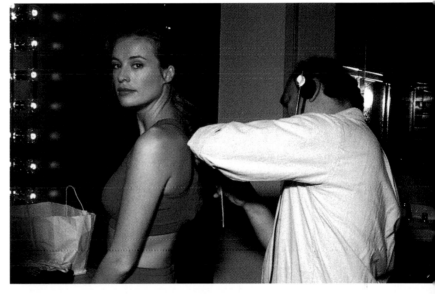

NICOLE MILLER

"I REALLY TRY TO ACHIEVE A GOOD NUTRITIONAL BALANCE—PROTEINS, GRAINS, AND FRUITS AND VEGETABLES. I'M PERMANENTLY ON A DIET."

"Small but mighty" might be just the phrase to describe Nicole Miller. This remarkable clothing and fabric designer may be small in stature but she's enormous in virtually every other way. Her designs, many of them centered on a food or drink motif, have become legendary, worn by men, women, and children as casual day-to-day wear and formal attire as well. She's the first designer we can think of who has so thoroughly and completely injected a sense of humor into mainstream fashion as we know it today.

The minute Nicole Miller said, "My mother is French," a lot of puzzle pieces started fitting into place. "She was—and is—an excellent cook. Nowadays, she's totally committed to eating for good health, and she's very strict about it. I'm not that extreme, though I'm careful about what I eat, but when we were growing up, we ate everything. My sister used to have a bakery and now she has a restaurant, The Boiler Room, in Great Barrington, Massachusetts. I guess you could say the whole family is into food."

"I'm constantly amazed by the way people eat," she continues. "They read that fish is good for you and then that's all they eat. They don't realize the bad things—such as a buildup of mercury in the body—that can come from it. I like fish, but in moderation—once or twice a week. I really try to achieve a good nutritional balance—I'm permanently on a diet."

Well, she doesn't look as if she needs to lose weight. "Well, no, but I have to work at it. I used to go to Equinox [a local gym] four times a week, but I've had to cut back to three times. I don't like classes much—I go by myself and have my own little routine. If time is short, I do a half-hour run on the treadmill. When I have more time, I do weights and machines as well."

Nicole's kitchen is relatively small in comparison to her huge loft. "I really want to re-do my kitchen, but the guy next door keeps changing his mind about whether he wants to move to Paris and sell his apartment to me so I can expand or whether he wants to stay in New York. I love to cook, but I don't have any time for it during the week. I've become a weekends-only cook, but I truly love it. I make elaborate Saturday night dinners for my boyfriend."

Is she the sort of cook who tastes all day and then isn't hungry at mealtime? Her answer is at first adamant and then almost shy: "Well, no, I'm not a taster or a closet eater. I do have one food weakness though—potato chips. Not fancy ones, mind you, just plain old potato chips from a bag. But I try to be good even with them. I tape the bag shut and hide it in the back of the closet."

THE MENU

◆ ◆ ◆ ◆ ◆ ◆ ◆

BRUNCH

for six

GRILLED VEGETABLE CROSTINI

SWORDFISH SALAD

CARAMELIZED ONION, OLIVE, AND SUN-DRIED TOMATO CRUSTLESS QUICHE

ANGEL FOOD FRUIT TART

The designer at home—Nicole Miller in her loft in lower Manhattan. The Calder-like "octopus mobile" lamp was made in the 1950s by Serge Mouille.

GRILLED VEGETABLE CROSTINI
For 6 to 8

*2 large zucchinis, trimmed and cut on the diagonal into ¼-inch-
thick slices*

*3 large portobello mushrooms or 8 cremini mushrooms, washed,
stems removed, caps sliced*

Olive oil

½ cup tapenade (black olive spread)

8 slices whole-grain or pumpernickel bread

*3 red bell peppers, roasted, peeled, and seeded, each cut into 4 or 5
large pieces*

Arugula and cherry tomatoes, for garnishing the platter

1. Preheat a stovetop grill or grill pan over moderately
high heat.

*Brunch is served—Grilled Vegetable Crostini, Swordfish Salad, and
Caramelized Onion, Olive, and Sun-Dried Tomato Crustless Quiche
await the gang.*

2. Very lightly brush both sides of each zucchini and
mushroom slice with oil. Working in batches, arrange the
vegetables in a single layer and grill until softened on one side,
about 3 minutes.

3. Turn the slices and grill the other side until tender
and/or lightly browned, 2 to 3 minutes more. Continue until
all of the vegetables are grilled.

4. Toast the bread. Cut each slice in half.

5. Spread each piece of toast with a thin layer of the tapenade. Arrange a piece of each vegetable—zucchini, mushroom, and roasted pepper—on top. Transfer to a platter and
garnish the dish. Serve warm or at room temperature.

RIGHT: *The gang's all here—conversation and wine flow freely.*

BELOW: *Nicole's signature style as designed for a limited bottling of Korbel's Brut Rosé sparkling wine.*

SWORDFISH SALAD

For 6 to 8

1½ pounds thinly sliced (½ inch) swordfish steaks, any bones removed

1 tablespoon olive oil

Salt and freshly milled pepper

1 large bunch arugula or watercress, washed and dried, large stems removed

½ cup coarsely chopped parsley

1 medium-large red onion, half of it diced, the other half sliced and separated into rings

¼ cup drained capers

¼ cup balsamic vinegar or red wine vinegar

1½ teaspoons anchovy paste

1 garlic clove, minced

¼ cup extra-virgin olive oil

1. Preheat the broiler or a stovetop grill.

2. Rub both sides of the swordfish with the olive oil; sprinkle liberally with salt and pepper. Arrange the fish on a broiler pan or the grill and cook until just opaque in the center, 2 to 3 minutes on each side. Set aside to cool to room temperature.

3. Meanwhile, toss together the salad greens, parsley, diced onion, and capers in a large serving bowl. In a jar, combine the vinegar, anchovy paste, garlic, and extra-virgin oil with 3 tablespoons water. Cover tightly and shake very well. Taste, season with salt and pepper, and shake again.

4. Cut the fish into large chunks. Shake the dressing and pour half of it over the salad ingredients; toss. Add the swordfish and onion rings, pour on the remaining dressing, and gently toss again. Serve at room temperature.

CARAMELIZED ONION, OLIVE, AND SUN-DRIED TOMATO CRUSTLESS QUICHE

If you're not a whiz with pastry or you simply can't be bothered, this is the quiche for you—it has no crust. You can caramelize the onions hours or even a day or so ahead of time, so that putting the quiche together will be a cinch.

For 6

2 tablespoons unsalted butter
3 large sweet onions, thinly sliced
Large pinch of sugar
4 whole eggs
6 egg whites
1 cup cured black olives, pitted and torn into bits
½ cup loose sun-dried tomatoes (not oil-packed), chopped
8 ounces low-fat fresh goat cheese, crumbled or thinly sliced and chopped
Salt and freshly milled pepper
2 to 3 tablespoons snipped fresh chives or basil

1. Melt the butter in a large sauté pan or saucepan over moderately high heat. Add the onions and cook, stirring, until wilted and softened, about 5 minutes.

2. Sprinkle on the sugar, reduce the heat to moderately low, and partially cover the pan. Cook, stirring from time to time, until the onions greatly reduce in volume and caramelize to a golden brown color, 15 to 20 minutes. If the onions begin to stick, add a bit of water or stock and let evaporate. Set the onions aside until needed. (If making ahead, let cool, cover, and refrigerate until needed. Let come to room temperature before using.)

3. Preheat the oven to 350°F. Lightly oil or spray a 10-inch pie plate or quiche mold.

4. In a large bowl, beat the eggs with the egg whites just until the yolks are broken up and blended with the whites. Add the caramelized onions, olives, sun-dried tomatoes, and goat cheese; season with salt and pepper. Stir in the chives. Pour the mixture into the prepared baking dish.

5. Bake the quiche until firm in the center and golden on top, about 30 to 35 minutes.

6. Remove the quiche to a rack to cool and set for at least 10 minutes. Serve the quiche warm or at room temperature.

· ·

ANGEL FOOD FRUIT TART

Here's an excellent dessert that you can pull together from scratch when you have time and feel energetic, or you can depend on a store-bought angel food cake when you're busy. Also, making several at once is easy as can be. The virtue of angel food cake is that it is fat-free. If you choose, substitute another type of cake and whatever fruits are abundant and ripe—bananas, grapes, tangerines, pineapple, and papaya are all good choices.

For 6

1 angel food cake or another type of white cake
2 to 3 kiwifruits, peeled and sliced
1 pint ripe strawberries, hulled and sliced
2 to 3 large ripe peaches or nectarines, peeled, stoned, and sliced
1 cup hot water
1 envelope (1 tablespoon) unflavored gelatin
½ cup strained low-calorie apricot preserves

Angel Food Fruit Tart—just before it disappeared.

1. Cut a horizontal 1-inch-high slice off the top of the cake; if you are using an angel food cake, you'll have a big ring with a hole in the center; otherwise, it will be a flat layer. Set the layer in a pie plate or shallow dish.

2. Decoratively arrange the fruit over the cake.

3. Pour the hot water into a nonreactive small saucepan and set over low heat. Sprinkle on the gelatin and let soften for 1 minute. Stir until the gelatin dissolves and the mixture is hot. Stir in the preserves and heat until melted and syrupy.

4. While still warm, drizzle the syrup over the fruits and brush or smooth into a layer that coats completely. Loosely cover the tart with plastic wrap. Chill for at least 1 hour. Cut into wedges to serve.

TOP LEFT: *Nicole Miller's collection of farm animals, iguanas, and a flamingo stand in the corner of her open, spacious loft apartment. Plenty of natural light shines through the huge arched windows.*

TOP RIGHT: *A close-up of one of the iguana sculptures in Ms. Miller's collection.*

RIGHT: *More of Nicole's collection of art—a collage, a sculpture, and a giant "cutout doll" of the designer herself looking very much like a slim and shapely mermaid.*

VENDELA

• • • • • • • • • • •

"I LOVE TO EXERCISE, BECAUSE THEN I CAN FORGET ABOUT EVERYTHING ELSE."

Supermodel Vendela Kirsebom is a veritable *smörgåsbord* of Swedish delights. Her natural beauty is enhanced by no small smattering of intellect—she's well educated and fluent in three languages, has traveled much of the world, is wildly successful at her work, *and* is studying acting and dance to further expand her abilities. But it's that face and that body that have made Vendela a household presence in magazine articles, photo essays, and advertisements, as well as on television in guest appearances and as a reporter.

Hectic as her lifestyle may be, Vendela is adamant about keeping fit and healthy. "It's part of the job," she says. "I work out with a trainer at a gym five days a week, and then on weekends I run at the track of a nearby university or get in some serious workout time on my mountain bike. I love yoga too—both as exercise and as a method of relax-

ation." Her four pages in the 1995 *Sports Illustrated* Annual Swimsuit Issue (and the calendar and TV special it spawned) are proof that her time and trouble truly pay off.

By all appearances Vendela is as capable in the kitchen as she is on the runway or in front of a camera. Her recipe for Spaghettini à la Vendela couldn't be tastier or simpler to prepare, and yet it is sophisticated—good evidence of the Italian way of cooking and eating. "After graduating from school, I moved to Italy to begin my modeling career with Ford Europe. The foods I ate there have inspired my love of using great ingredients and letting the good fresh flavors of the foods come through. I strongly believe in eating healthful foods and also in taking the necessary steps to ensure I'm living an overall healthy lifestyle."

SPAGHETTINI À LA VENDELA

Although Vendela gave us her recipe for a cooked marinara sauce, she also included this uncooked summer version. If you use the best, most flavorful tomatoes you can find, it's spectacular at any time of year. Fresh-made smoked mozzarella can be used for an intriguing flavor.

For 4

1 pound spaghettini
4 large, very ripe tomatoes, peeled, seeded, and chopped (about 2 cups)
¼ cup extra-virgin olive oil
Pinch of salt
Pinch of sugar
Freshly milled black pepper
4 to 6 ounces fresh-made mozzarella cheese, cut into ¼-inch dice
10 large basil leaves, cut into thin shreds

1. Bring a large pot of salted water to a boil over high heat. When the water boils, add the spaghettini and stir well. Bring the water back to a boil, reduce the heat to moderate, and cook the pasta until just al dente; the timing will vary by brand.

2. Meanwhile, combine the tomatoes, oil, salt, and sugar in a bowl. Toss to blend well. Season with pepper to taste; correct the seasonings, if necessary.

3. When the pasta is done, drain well. Mound the pasta on a serving dish. Pour the sauce over the pasta, scatter the cheese and basil over the top, and serve immediately, while the pasta's still hot.

ABOVE: *Spaghettini à la Vendela—a brilliantly fresh and flavorful dish. Best of all, the sauce requires no cooking at all.*

LEFT: *Supermodel Vendela—doin' what comes naturally.*

VERA WANG

◆ ◆ ◆ ◆ ◆ ◆ ◆ ◆ ◆ ◆ ◆ ◆

"IN THE WEEKS JUST BEFORE A WEDDING, EVERYONE INVOLVED IS OVERSTRESSED AND HARRIED. I WANTED TO PROVIDE A SMALL, INTIMATE RESPITE FROM THE CHAOS, AND I DON'T KNOW A NICER WAY TO DO THAT THAN TO SERVE UP A LUNCH THAT IS HEALTHFUL AND SOOTHING AND CALM."

Even though you keep murmuring over and over to yourself, "This is not a fairy tale; this is not a fairy tale; this is real, not faux; this is real, not faux," a dreamlike quality remains and it emanates directly from Vera Wang. She's the world's foremost creator of wedding gowns and bridesmaid's dresses, and her designs bespeak a classic simplicity that has become the Vera Wang hallmark. The quality and fineness of her materials and workmanship have become legend. Ms. Wang will settle for nothing less than perfection, and—somehow—she achieves it more consistently than other, less watchful souls.

Vera Wang's home on Manhattan's Upper East Side is a perfect example of her style and lifestyle. The high-ceilinged ivory marble entrance foyer is a study in balance and restraint. From the doorway of the beautiful formal dining room, you see a slim, small-boned woman moving about the room and eyeing the table from several viewpoints. "This looks like the correct spot to me," she says, turning to explain. "I'm trying to figure out where the sun will be at lunchtime." No detail—past, present, or future—escapes Vera Wang's attention, especially when it comes to the comfort of her guests.

The dining room is awash with light now, and the rich color of the painted walls is echoed in the fabrics used for the window treatments. The shiny herringbone wood floors are

> ## PRE-WEDDING LUNCH
> *for six*
>
> CHAMPAGNE
>
> MIXED BABY GREENS WITH AGED GOAT CHEESE
>
> COLD POACHED FILLETS OF SEA BASS WITH DILLED YOGURT SAUCE
>
> SORBET–FROZEN YOGURT BOMBE: RASPBERRY, MANGO, AND VANILLA

Vera Wang puts the final touches on the spectacularly set luncheon table just moments before her guests arrive.

uncovered for this occasion, and a massive, white Steinway grand piano stands at one end of the room. Fine paintings, antique Chinese vases, and breathtakingly graceful, museum-quality furniture are placed just so. The signed Hepplewhite commode that stands between the windows is in flawless condition, as is the gilt-framed mirror that hangs above it. And Vera Wang takes it all in at once—the mistress of all she surveys.

The capacious table is about to be set. First comes the round, pale blue silk velvet underskirt, so oversized that it pools luxuriously on the floor. It is topped with a pristine white piqué overlay that is utterly free of creases or wrinkles. (And you wonder, how do people do these things?) Next, the huge bouquet of flowers—tall delphiniums varying in tones from grape to lavender to palest pink to almost white—are placed in the center, while four pink and lavender ribbon-bedecked small boxwood topiary balls nestle beneath. (For contrast, a matching arrangement of flowers is positioned atop the Hepplewhite commode just opposite the table.) With due ceremony a quartet of matching seventeenth-century silver candlesticks, each fitted with a tall white taper, take their stately places, and already the table has been transformed into an excellent study for a still-life painter.

Ms. Wang's majordomo enters, bearing the Limoges "Am-

ABOVE: *A close-up look at a single place setting—a contemporary but classic combination of finery.*

bassador" dinner plates and bread plates, swiftly followed by Tiffany & Company's "King James" flatware, and the gold-rimmed Baccarat crystal water glasses and wineglasses. Tiny round silver trays are mounded with almonds coated in edible silver and gold, and the union adds perfectly to the metallic and crystal gleam. Diminutive silver saltcellars and pepper shakers are strategically placed, and Ms. Wang sits down to ponder the place cards and seating arrangements.

While the faggot-edged white linen napkins are being tied with wired silver ribbons, Ms. Wang fits each card into its tiny silver shell-shaped holder and distributes them around the table. And then, with an elfin gleam in her eye, Vera Wang extracts six ribbon-embellished Tiffany-blue boxes from the sideboard and nestles one just to the right of each place setting. She's not saying what they contain, claiming instead that they are "just a bibelot to let my guests know I'm thinking of them." But she's perfectly aware that trinkets from Tiffany are always exciting, and she grins at her little secret.

RIGHT: *The glittering gleam of a pristine tabletop—perfection awaits the bride-to-be and the ladies of her wedding party.*

The occasion for this luncheon is to celebrate the upcoming wedding of a friend with a few members of her bridal party. The menu she had chosen would be ideal for entertaining, since most of the dishes could be prepared well in advance—an excellent plan for any host or hostess. The other goal was equally well met: this luncheon would be light but filling and satisfying, yet could not—under any circumstances—be responsible for any last-minute alterations to the bride's dress. (If anyone knows about that sort of problem, Ms. Wang is an expert.)

The luncheon will commence with tall flutes of well-chilled Champagne as her guests arrive. After they are seated (and presumably after they have opened their Tiffany boxes), the first course salad will be presented. Following that will be the chilled sea bass entrée in dilled yogurt sauce, and after that, the pièce de résistance, a three-flavored bombe made from sorbets and fat-free frozen yogurt.

Take a page from this talented and stylish woman's book next time you want to treat the bride-to-be or celebrate a special event. This menu is as adaptable as it can be—an excellent, healthful, low-fat meal that's well suited to any occasion.

The light first course—Mixed Baby Greens with Aged Goat Cheese.

MIXED BABY GREENS WITH AGED GOAT CHEESE

It doesn't matter whether you buy a domestic goat cheese or an imported one for this salad—just make sure it's a good one. We suggest serving the salad with the entirely edible rind, although some of your guests might remove it.

For 6

1½ tablespoons white wine vinegar or tarragon vinegar

1 tablespoon Dijon mustard

Salt and freshly milled black pepper

½ cup extra-virgin olive oil

12 ounces mesclun (mixed baby greens), washed and dried

8 to 12 ounces aged goat cheese, at room temperature,
    cut into 12 slices

1. In a jar, combine the vinegar, mustard, salt and pepper to taste, and the oil. Cover tightly and shake well. Taste and correct the seasonings; cover, and set aside at room temperature until needed.

2. Just before serving, shake the dressing to remix. Pour it over the mesclun and toss to coat. Divide the greens among 6 salad plates. Arrange 2 slices of the cheese over each serving.

COLD POACHED FILLETS OF SEA BASS WITH DILLED YOGURT SAUCE

This method of poaching fish follows Chinese methods and produces perfect results.

For 6

2 cups dry white wine
3 shallots, chopped
2 scallions, trimmed, halved lengthwise, and cut into thirds
1 bay leaf
8 peppercorns
1 teaspoon salt
1½ teaspoons dried dill weed
½ lemon, chopped
6 fillets (each 4 to 6 ounces) sea bass or other non-oily, flaky white fish

DILLED YOGURT SAUCE:
1½ cups low-fat plain yogurt, drained in a strainer for 20 minutes
½ teaspoon grated lemon zest
⅓ cup finely snipped fresh dill
Salt and freshly milled pepper

1. Combine the wine, shallots, scallions, bay leaf, peppercorns, salt, dill, lemon, and 8 cups of water in a nonreactive large saucepan. Set over high heat and bring to a boil. Reduce the heat to moderately low, cover the pan, and simmer the poaching liquid for 15 minutes.

2. Meanwhile, choose a large, shallow, heatproof dish (or two) that's large enough to hold the fillets flat in a single layer (the largest size rectangular Pyrex dish is perfect; you don't want to use an aluminum pan, although stainless steel is all right). Arrange the fillets in the dish. Clear some space in the refrigerator; you'll need enough room for the dish while the fillets cool.

3. Bring the poaching liquid back to a boil. Pour it through a strainer over the fish fillets, covering them completely. Lift one end of each fillet to make sure some liquid gets underneath. Cover the dish with foil and let the fillets poach for 5 minutes. Check the fish with the tip of a knife; it should be opaque to the center. If not, cover and let sit for 2 to 3 minutes longer.

4. Pour off all of the poaching liquid. (You can reserve it and freeze for later use, if desired.) Remove any skin from the fillets while they are still warm. Cover the dish with plastic wrap, and refrigerate until chilled through.

5. Make the sauce: Whisk together all of the sauce ingredients in a small bowl. Taste and season with salt and pepper. Cover and chill. Check the seasonings and adjust, if necessary, before serving.

6. Place a fish fillet on each of 6 dinner plates. Nap with some of the dilled yogurt sauce and serve cold or at cool room temperature.

••

OPPOSITE: *Cold Poached Fillets of Sea Bass with Dilled Yogurt Sauce—an entrée that's filling and good for you but light and almost fat-free.*

SORBET—FROZEN YOGURT BOMBE: RASPBERRY, MANGO, AND VANILLA

Two tips for easy bombe making: Before you start the bombe, clear space in the coldest part of your freezer so the layers will set efficiently, and start far enough ahead of time—several days isn't out of the question, though it will take just minutes at any one time—to ensure that the finished bombe has plenty of time to freeze solid.

We used flavors that have highly contrasting colors, but this lovely bombe is equally beautiful when made with three pastel shades—say, lemon and mandarin ices with pale peach or key lime yogurt.

For 6; fills one 4-cup/1-quart mold

1 pint raspberry sorbet
1⅓ cups mango sorbet
⅔ cup vanilla frozen yogurt
Fresh fruit and mint sprigs, for garnish

Spoon the first layer of softened sorbet in an even layer over the bottom and sides of the chilled mold; an offset spatula can make this process easier. Place plastic wrap directly on the surface of the sorbet, and freeze until very well set, at least 1 hour.

Add the second layer as you did the first. To finish filling the mold, spoon in the sorbet or frozen yogurt and fill the mold completely. Cover with plastic wrap, pressed directly onto the surface. If the mold has a lid, set it in place. Freeze the bombe for at least 4 hours, or overnight.

1. Choose a decorative mold (with or without a lid, although a lid can come in handy) and determine its capacity by filling it with water and pouring the water into a large measuring cup. You want to be sure you have enough sorbets and yogurt to fill that particular mold. If your mold is larger than 4 cups, you'll have to adjust the proportions accordingly. If desired, coat or spray the mold with oil, and then line it with 1 or 2 long sheets of plastic wrap, taking care to fit the wrap seamlessly into all of the mold's nooks and crannies and making sure that both ends extend way beyond the edges of the mold. Lined or not, chill the empty mold until very cold.

2. Soften the sorbet for the outer layer of the bombe until just malleable but not melting. Spoon it into the cold mold and smooth into an even layer over the bottom and sides; an offset spatula can make this process easier. Place plastic wrap directly on the surface of the sorbet, and freeze until very well set, at least 1 hour.

3. Soften the sorbet for the second layer as you did before. Remove the mold from the freezer, remove the plastic wrap cover, and spoon in the sorbet for the second layer. Quickly smooth into an even layer, following the contours of the mold. Press plastic wrap directly on the surface and freeze until both layers are very well set, at least 2 hours.

4. Usually, the sorbet or frozen yogurt for the inner layer can be slightly less malleable than the previous two. Remove the mold from the freezer, remove the plastic wrap, and spoon in the sorbet or yogurt, filling completely. Cover with plastic wrap, pressed directly onto the surface. If the mold has a lid, set it in place. Freeze the bombe for at least 4 hours, or overnight.

To unmold the bombe, dip a large towel into hot water. Quickly wring it out and wrap the towel, turban-style, around the mold; wait for 30 to 60 seconds. Run a thin knife around the inside edge, and invert the mold onto a plate.

Lift the mold away from the bombe with one easy tug.

A festive and colorful dessert—Sorbet–Frozen Yogurt Bombe: Raspberry, Mango, and Vanilla.

5. To unmold and serve: If you lined the mold with long sheets of plastic wrap before you started filling it, grasp opposite sides and wiggle the wrap slightly to loosen it (you might have to do this on two opposite sides). Invert a plate over the top of the mold and invert the two together. Lift off the mold; carefully peel off the plastic. If you didn't line the mold, loosen it by using a large towel that's been dipped in hot water. Wrap the towel, turban-style, around the mold; wait for 30 to 60 seconds. Run a thin knife around the inside edge, and invert the mold onto a serving plate. Slice the bombe and garnish with fruit and mint sprigs.

FABIO

• • • • • • • • • • •

"AS FOR BEING FIT, I HAVE TO WORK AT IT LIKE ANYBODY ELSE.
BUT I BELIEVE YOU'VE GOT TO START WITH THE RIGHT MOTIVATION. YOU'VE GOT TO BELIEVE
IN YOURSELF—YOU DESERVE TO BE HEALTHY AND FIT. WITHOUT THAT, THE REST FALLS APART."

Fabio—the fabulous, the fabled, the fab—is a big (6´3´´, 220 pounds), big-deal, big-time success. And as any one of his fans will tell you, this guy can really "cook"—he's blessed with all of the necessary ingredients: brawn, biceps, and a behemoth body. But it wasn't always that way; he worked to get where he is, and he's more than willing to share the secrets of how he does it.

Born in Milan in 1961, Fabio was injured in a skiing accident at age sixteen. Part of his therapy required weightlifting, and while working out in a gym, he was spotted by a photographer who suggested that he model. It wasn't until Fabio was twenty-five that he posed for the cover of a romance novel—the first of the more than 999 that followed. Readers responded like never before, and Fabio became a worldwide sensation.

Not content to model forever, Fabio has branched out enormously: He walked off the covers of novels onto video-

> ## THE RECIPES
>
> ◆ ◆ ◆ ◆ ◆ ◆ ◆
>
> ACORN SQUASH AND APPLE PUREE
>
> GLAZED SWEET POTATOES
>
> CHICK–PEA SOUP

Fabio on life: *"I've lived my whole life based on eating right and good exercise. To me, it is important. I think it should become a top priority for everybody."*

tape, TV, telephone, the pages of his own magazine, and appearances as a national spokesperson for the American Cancer Society. *Fabio Fitness*, his first workout video, was directed specifically at weight training for women. Late last year his quarterly magazine, *Fabio's Healthy Bodies—Lifestyles of the Fit & Famous*, hit the newsstands, followed this year by his internationally syndicated cable TV show, "Fabio's Healthy Bodies Magazine on Television." A newsletter, several books, and a line of fitness products are also in the works. And for all those fans who want the opportunity to hear Fabio's deep, Italian-accented voice, that, too, is possible via the *Fabio's Healthy Bodies Magazine* Fitness and Nutrition Line, a 900 number that offers advice and information on health, diet, and exercise. Each call will conclude with this admonishment from Fabio himself: "Mother was right. Eat your vegetables." Certainly, Fabio does, and he shares these vegetarian recipes with us.

"I'll take healthy, natural foods over processed ones any day, and I won't eat sweets or use oil or butter."—Fabio

ACORN SQUASH AND APPLE PUREE
For 2

1 acorn squash, halved, seeds and strings discarded
1 apple, such as Golden Delicious, peeled, cored, and cut into 1-inch cubes
1½ teaspoons butter or margarine
Freshly grated nutmeg
Salt and freshly milled pepper

1. Arrange the squash, cut side down, in a microwave-safe dish. Prick the skin all over with the tip of a sharp knife. Cover tightly and microwave on HIGH power for 10 minutes.

2. Put the apple in a 1- or 2-cup glass measuring cup, cover, and microwave on HIGH power until tender, 4 to 6 minutes.

3. Meanwhile, scoop out the squash pulp; discard the skin. Pour off any liquid that accumulated while the apple was cooking. Force the squash and apple through the medium disk of a food mill into a bowl, or puree in a food processor or blender.

4. Add the butter and nutmeg, and season with salt and pepper to taste. Serve hot.

GLAZED SWEET POTATOES

This low-fat, high-fiber recipe provides a rich source of vitamin A from the sweet potatoes, and vitamin C from the orange and lemon juices.

For 4

1 pound sweet potatoes, peeled and cut into ½-inch-thick slices
1 tablespoon cornstarch
1 tablespoon firmly packed brown sugar
¾ cup fresh orange juice
2 tablespoons fresh lemon juice

1. Preheat the oven to 425°F.
2. Lightly coat or spray a 1-quart casserole with vegetable oil. Arrange the sweet potato slices in the casserole.
3. In a small bowl, combine the cornstarch, brown sugar, orange juice, and lemon juice. Stir to blend well. Pour the mixture over the sweet potatoes, coating them as evenly as possible.
4. Cover the casserole and bake until the sweet potatoes are tender and the glaze has thickened, about 40 minutes. Serve hot.

Front and center is Fabio's Chick-Pea Soup; in the background, thick slices of his Glazed Sweet Potatoes encircle a mound of Acorn Squash and Apple Puree.

CHICK-PEA SOUP

This hearty soup is a meal in itself—it doesn't require long cooking, and you can vary it by using whatever vegetables you have available. Serve it with warm whole-grain rolls or bread.

For 4

2 tablespoons olive oil
1 large onion, chopped
2 to 3 garlic cloves, minced
2 cups peeled, chopped sweet potatoes (or substitute carrots or
* winter squash, such as acorn or butternut)*
3 cups chicken broth or vegetable broth
1 bay leaf
1 teaspoon dried basil
½ teaspoon dried thyme
¼ teaspoon paprika
Salt and freshly milled pepper
1 large ripe tomato, chopped

10 ounces fresh green beans, topped, tailed, and cut into 2-inch
* lengths, or 1 package (10 ounces) frozen green beans, thawed*
* and cut into 2-inch lengths*
1 can (12 to 16 ounces) cooked chick-peas, drained

1. Warm the oil in a nonreactive large saucepan over moderate heat. Add the onion, garlic, and sweet potatoes and sauté for 5 minutes.
2. Stir in the broth, bay leaf, basil, thyme, paprika, and salt and pepper to taste; bring to a boil. Reduce the heat to moderately low, cover, and simmer until the vegetables are tender but not mushy, about 15 minutes.
3. Stir in the tomato, green beans, and chick-peas. Simmer, uncovered, until tender, about 10 minutes more. Serve hot.

NIKI TAYLOR

◆ ◆ ◆ ◆ ◆ ◆ ◆ ◆ ◆ ◆ ◆

*"FOOD IS FUN. I'M ALWAYS LEARNING MORE AND EXPERIMENTING.
RIGHT NOW, I'M PARTICULARLY FOND OF THAI AND OTHER ASIAN FOODS. THE FLAVORS ARE CLEAN,
THE DISHES ARE NATURALLY HEALTHFUL AND BALANCED, AND I JUST LOVE THEM."*

No doubt you've seen her on some of her more than 170 magazine covers, in television commercials, as a Cover Girl cosmetics spokesperson, or hosting a few of Robin Leach's "Lifestyles" TV segments on celebrities and fashion. She's Niki Taylor, Florida-born and -bred supermodel, who seems well on the road to having it all. Her career started at the tender age of fourteen, when she was chosen as the cover girl for *Seventeen*. "It was my first big break," she says. "I remember it as if it were yesterday." Now, just six years later, she has managed to amass a most impressive portfolio, and she did it while attending high school full-time. "I don't know how I did it; it really took masterful planning to build a schedule that let me work and go to school without falling behind. I was busy every minute, but I loved it, I simply loved it." Since then, she has married and at the end of 1994 became a mother—twice—to identical twin boys, Jake and Hunter.

While she is not reclusive à la Garbo, you won't often find Niki at opening celebrations for hot, new, trendy restaurants and clubs all over the world. She maintains a low profile when she's not working, preferring to stay close to home, with her husband and her sons, and near her mother—all in southern Florida. Though she is fully capable of tranforming her look into an array of personalities for the camera lens, Niki is a rather shy, unassuming, all-American girl who is most content when she's out of the limelight.

"I love being at home," she says, "puttering in the kitchen, cooking fresh organic fruits and vegetables into purees for the boys' meals, trying out new recipes and new ingredients. South Florida has so much wonderful food available—from the best citrus to great tomatoes year-round, to exotic fruits you've never seen before—and I like to buy some of each and then go home and play in the kitchen. Food is fun. I'm always learning more and experimenting. Right now, I'm particularly fond of Thai and other Asian foods. The flavors are clean, the dishes are naturally healthful and balanced, and I just love them."

In addition to being blessed with great natural beauty, Niki is lucky in that she can indulge her appetite without apparent ill effects. "I'm fortunate because I don't have to be too careful with what I choose to eat. But I really don't have cravings for the 'bad' things. Maybe it's my metabolism, or maybe it's the fact that I work out with a trainer at a nearby gym five days a week. I just know that being fit and trim feels good and is good for me."

ORIENTAL CHICKEN SALAD WITH TOASTED SESAME SEEDS

This dish has it all: a variety of textures and flavors that you can adapt to whatever is fresh in the market. The chicken for this main-course salad can be roasted, poached, sautéed in a nonstick skillet, or left over from last night's dinner—absolutely any way will do.

For 4

DRESSING:
1 tablespoon rice vinegar or white wine vinegar
1 tablespoon fresh lemon juice
1 tablespoon light soy sauce
1½ teaspoons minced fresh ginger
1 teaspoon Dijon mustard
¼ cup vegetable oil
2 tablespoons Asian sesame oil
Salt and freshly milled pepper

4 ounces snow peas, topped and tailed
1 can or jar (6 to 8 ounces) baby corn, drained
1 head soft leaf lettuce, washed and dried
1¼ pounds boneless, skinless chicken breasts, cooked, cooled, and
*   sliced*
1 red bell pepper, thinly sliced
⅓ cup sliced scallions
1 tablespoon sesame seeds, toasted
Flat-leaf parsley or cilantro sprigs, for garnish

1. Make the dressing: In a jar, combine all of the dressing ingredients; add salt and pepper to taste. Cover tightly and shake until well mixed. Taste and correct the seasonings, if necessary.

2. Bring a small saucepan of salted water to a boil. Add the snow peas and baby corn and boil for 1 minute. Drain and re-fresh under cold running water. Pat the vegetables dry.

3. Divide the leaf lettuce among 4 dinner plates. Arrange the chicken, snow peas, baby corn, and bell pepper over the lettuce in an attractive pattern. Sprinkle on the scallions and sesame seeds; drizzle on the dressing. Garnish with the parsley or cilantro sprigs and serve.

THE SPOTLIGHT SHINES BRIGHT

ALAN AND GINA THICKE

◆ ◆ ◆ ◆ ◆ ◆ ◆ ◆ ◆ ◆ ◆

"BEFORE GINA, MY FOUR BASIC FOOD GROUPS WERE SUGAR, SALT, FAT, AND CAFFEINE.
I'M NOW A SEMI-VEGETARIAN—I ONLY EAT ANIMALS THAT EAT VEGETABLES."
—ALAN THICKE

They are as charming and friendly as the day is long—and twice as nice. He is Alan Thicke, Canadian-born actor, producer, songwriter, screenwriter, and newspaper columnist; he is Jason Seaver, TV's most adorable dad on "Growing Pains," and also doing a true star turn as the thick, eccentric egotist Dennis Dupree on "Hope and Gloria." She is Gina Thicke, a broadcast journalist and a native of South Carolina. Gina was named Miss World 1991—only the second American to win in the pageant's forty-one-year history. Alan and Gina met when they co-hosted the 1992 Miss World pageant, and after a year of courtship Mr. Thicke proposed a new title for Gina—Mrs. Thicke.

The wedding was held at Greer Valley Ranch, their eleven-acre spread, situated in a canyon in the heart of the Santa Barbara farm country. Gina laughs when she adds, "Nobody seems to mind that he took it upon himself to name the valley after his mother's family." This is the place—backdrop provided by Mother Nature and the Santa Ynez Mountains—where the Thickes escape from their busy work lives in Los Angeles.

As Gina describes it, "It's such a great place—we're comfortable there, we have horses, a pool, and tennis courts, a marvelous antique-y 'country' kitchen, and the world's best neighbors. We have an 'open-door policy' with them; we can

> ### THE MENU
> ◆ ◆ ◆ ◆ ◆ ◆ ◆
> *Early-evening dinner for two*
> **GINA'S VEGETARIAN CHILI**
> **BUTTERMILK CORNMEAL MUFFINS**

Home, home on the ranch—Alan and Gina Thicke enjoy a healthful, home-cooked meal on their front porch, deep in the heart of Santa Barbara's farm country.

cut whatever we want from their huge organic garden, their kids use our pool, and you don't even have to call and ask permission, you just do it. I tell Babaloo [the Thickes' pet Dalmatian] that he's going to camp and we go there."

Even though weekends at Greer Valley Ranch aren't as frequent as they'd like, Alan and Gina seem to stay busy when they're there. "We both ride a lot—great trail rides through the canyons and mountains," says Gina. "Our favorite ride is on the beach—just five miles away. Alan's big on hammock time too—it's big and old and well broken in, not stiff." But hammock time doesn't keep a person fit and healthy and looking terrific, does it? "No way," says Gina. "We have a full gym in L.A. that goes practically unused. I'm a StairMaster groupie, so I use it and play a lot of tennis. Alan's more into activities and sports to stay fit—he plays hockey regularly in a league and tennis all of the time.

"One of the things that most appealed to me about Alan when we were dating was his relationship with his family. His sister is a great cook; his brother's wife is the baker of the family; and I, well, I'm still learning. I really enjoy cooking for the two of us, but I admit, in the beginning, I was a bit intimidated when I had to cook dinner for Brennan and Robin [Alan's sons, ages nineteen and seventeen, respectively].

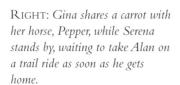

LEFT: *Alan is interrupted while putting in some "hammock time" but he looks more than willing to share the space. The site of the Thickes' outdoor wedding ceremony is just a tree or two away. The couple honeymooned at Jumby Bay Island, Antigua* (see p. 24).

RIGHT: *Gina shares a carrot with her horse, Pepper, while Serena stands by, waiting to take Alan on a trail ride as soon as he gets home.*

At first, I thought that they wanted meat and potatoes—and lots of it—but lately, now that they're more grown up and far more health-conscious, they've started saying things like, 'Now, Gina, let's watch the red meat—what about some light pasta or chicken some of the time?' That's fine with me—that's what I like to cook and eat anyway."

Does Mr. Thicke lend a hand in the kitchen? "Well, I suppose you could put it that way," Gina replies affectionately. "He likes to pick and sneak bites when I'm not looking. You know, he runs his finger around the base of the cake—that sort of thing. Sometimes I just have to slap his hands.

"Alan's not much of a cook himself," Gina adds, making the point that he's cooked for her just once in two years. She continues, "But, bless him, he's a good eater. He loves food—he'd eat twenty-four hours a day if he could." But neither of them can. Gina's fiercely determined to make sure their lifestyle is a healthy one. "Our meals are light—there's always a salad, and the main course is usually easy—pasta or vegetables, chicken or fish. We both like spicy foods—I make vegetarian pizza all of the time. For dessert we have fruit salad or a sorbet. I try to keep ready-to-eat fruit and vegetables in the fridge—already washed, cut up, and ready to go—for snack attacks. And I love to use herbs. I keep a huge planter of herbs—my 'herb bowl'—near the kitchen, so it's easy to snip some cilantro or basil or rosemary and use it immediately." But, she admits, if left to his own devices, Alan would probably eat Häagen-Dazs and popcorn—his favorite foods—all day long.

. . . .

TOP: *Gina Thicke among the cabbages—the prettiest Cabbage Patch Kid there ever was.*

RIGHT: *"It's what I call a 'Kentucky ranch,'" says Gina. "You know, green and white, big and comfortable." The house was built in 1934.*

GINA'S VEGETARIAN CHILI

For someone who says, "I'm not much of a 'from scratch' kind of cook," Gina Tolleson Thicke certainly puts together a tasty bowl of chili. Her instincts are good; she uses the best, freshest ingredients she can find in the garden. Serve this with your favorite green salad.

For 4 to 6

2 teaspoons vegetable oil
1 large garlic clove, minced
1 large onion, diced
1 carrot, scrubbed, trimmed, and thinly sliced
3 cups cooked pinto beans, drained of all liquid
1 cup diced ripe tomatoes with their juices
1 can (28 ounces) Italian plum tomatoes, tomatoes diced, juices reserved
1 can (8 ounces) tomato sauce
1½ cups fresh corn kernels
1 zucchini, trimmed, halved lengthwise, and sliced
1 yellow squash, trimmed, halved lengthwise, and sliced
1 to 2 jalapeños or mild green chiles, minced

1 tablespoon chili powder
1 tablespoon paprika
2 teaspoons ground cumin
1 teaspoon salt
Chopped fresh cilantro, for serving

1. Warm the oil in a nonreactive large pot over moderate heat. Add the garlic, onion, and carrot and sauté until softened, about 5 minutes. Stir in the pinto beans, fresh tomatoes, canned tomatoes with their juices, tomato sauce, and corn; bring to a simmer and cook for 5 minutes.

2. Stir in the zucchini, yellow squash, chiles, chili powder, paprika, cumin, and salt. Bring the mixture to a simmer. Reduce the heat to low, partially cover, and simmer for 45 minutes.

3. Taste the chili and add chiles or salt as needed. Ladle into bowls and sprinkle with the cilantro. Serve with tortilla chips and cornmeal muffins.

LEFT: *Festive, casual, relaxing—the three most important ingredients.*

RIGHT: *Gina's handiwork with the vegetables for her chili—purloined (with permission) from the neighbor's organic garden.*

BUTTERMILK CORNMEAL MUFFINS

No Southern-born lady would think of cooking up a chili dinner without offering some form of corn bread to go with it. These buttermilk cornmeal muffins are just the ticket.

Makes 1 dozen

1½ cups yellow cornmeal
½ cup sifted unbleached all-purpose flour
2½ teaspoons baking powder
1 teaspoon salt
1¼ cups buttermilk
1 large egg
1 tablespoon vegetable oil
2 to 3 tablespoons chopped jalapeño or other chiles (optional)

1. Preheat the oven to 400°F. Lightly spray or oil a 12-cup muffin tin.

2. In a mixing bowl, stir together the cornmeal, flour, baking powder, and salt. In a small bowl, use a fork to mix together the buttermilk, egg, oil, and chiles. Pour the wet ingredients over the dry ingredients and stir with the fork until just combined.

3. Spoon the batter into the prepared muffin tin, filling each cup about two-thirds full. Bake until the muffins are lightly browned on top and springy to the touch, 15 to 20 minutes. Serve hot, or remove from the pan and cool on a rack.

A colorful, tasty, and healthful meal that's sure to keep the Thickes thin.

KENNY ROGERS

◆ ◆ ◆ ◆ ◆ ◆ ◆ ◆ ◆ ◆ ◆

"I BELIEVE NONFRIED CHICKEN IS THE WAVE OF THE NINETIES, AND
WORKING WITH FOLKS WHO MADE FRIED CHICKEN A BILLION-DOLLAR BUSINESS
GIVES ME CONFIDENCE THAT WE'RE DOING IT RIGHT."

Kenneth Ray Rogers, better known to most of us as Kenny Rogers, is an award-winning singer, songwriter, musician, actor, producer, philanthropist, and businessman, and since 1991, a restaurateur. And since he's doesn't do things halfway, when Houston-born Rogers was convinced that a chain of wood-fire-roasted-chicken restaurants was a notion whose time had come, he jumped in feet first and with his baby-blue eyes wide open, he put his name on it. This is no mere endorsement for the food at Kenny Rogers Roasters—he's a co-owner and partner in the venture.

Well, Kenneth Ray is in good company. Partner John Y. Brown, former governor of Kentucky and the man who has been credited with building the worldwide success of KFC, joins Rogers in his enthusiasm for their gamble's growing popularity. Since the chickens are marinated in a secret mix-

> ## THE RECIPES
> ◆ ◆ ◆ ◆ ◆ ◆ ◆
> ### CHICKEN FAJITAS
> ### FRESH TOMATO-CUCUMBER SALSA
> ### FIRE AND ICE CHILI

All dressed up and in the holiday spirit, Kenny Rogers's Christmas concerts are an ever-popular event.

ture of citrus, herbs, and spices, threaded onto a rotisserie spit, and then slow-roasted over a hardwood fire, their fat melts off in the fierce heat. It is a healthful, if ancient, method of cooking. From the looks of it, Rogers and Brown have another hit on their hands. Started in Florida, the chain now dots the map, with locations countrywide as well as in Canada, Singapore, Greece, Kuala Lumpur, and elsewhere.

And as Kenny says, "You might wonder why I've gotten into the food business. Well, you know I like to sing. What you might not know is how much I like to cook and enjoy good food. But enjoying good food today also means trying to eat healthy. That's why I decided to open my own restaurants with homemade recipes that are as good to eat as they are good for you." When you're cooking at home, though, be sure to give these recipes from Kenny's own file box a try.

CHICKEN FAJITAS
For 4

¼ cup canola oil
2 tablespoons white wine vinegar
2 tablespoons fresh lime juice
1 yellow onion, finely chopped
1 garlic clove, crushed
1 tablespoon Louisiana hot sauce
Dash of Tabasco sauce
½ teaspoon ground cumin
½ teaspoon salt
¼ teaspoon coarsely milled black pepper
4 skinless, boneless chicken breast halves
8 soft flour tortillas, warmed
Fresh Tomato-Cucumber Salsa (recipe follows), for serving
Low-fat sour cream, for serving
Shredded iceberg lettuce, for serving

1. In a large bowl, combine the oil, vinegar, lime juice, onion, garlic, hot sauce, Tabasco, cumin, salt, and pepper. Add the chicken to the marinade and turn to coat well. Cover and refrigerate for 6 hours.

2. Prepare a charcoal grill, adding mesquite wood briquettes, or preheat a stovetop grill.

3. When the grill is very hot, grill the chicken breasts until cooked through, 3 to 5 minutes on each side.

4. Cut the chicken across the grain into ½-inch-wide slices. Serve with warmed tortillas, salsa, sour cream, and lettuce.

....

FRESH TOMATO-CUCUMBER SALSA
Makes about 2 cups

2 ripe tomatoes, cut into ¼-inch dice
1 small onion, cut into ¼-inch dice
1 cucumber, cut into ¼-inch dice
1 green bell pepper, cut into ¼-inch dice
¼ cup chopped cilantro
Fresh lime juice, salt, and freshly milled pepper, for seasoning

Combine all of the ingredients in a bowl. Season to taste. Cover and refrigerate until chilled.

....

Kenny Rogers' Chicken Fajitas surrounded by all the fixin's. Serve yours with black beans, sliced scallions, sour cream, and the best homemade flour tortillas you can find.

Kenny Rogers, restaurateur.

FIRE AND ICE CHILI

For 8 to 10

1 can (20 ounces) pineapple chunks in syrup, drained, syrup
    reserved

1 can (28 ounces) whole plum tomatoes, drained, chopped, juices
    reserved

1 can (6 ounces) tomato paste

1 can (4 ounces) green chiles, drained and diced

3 garlic cloves, crushed or minced

2 yellow onions, chopped

1 green bell pepper, cored, seeded, and chopped

¼ cup chili powder

4 teaspoons ground cumin

1 tablespoon diced jalapeño chiles (double the quantity for more
    fire)

2 teaspoons salt

2 tablespoons olive oil

2 pounds lean, boneless pork butt, trimmed of all fat, cut into 1-
    inch cubes

Sliced scallions, shredded cheddar cheese, and low-fat or no-fat sour
    cream, for serving

1. In a large bowl, combine the reserved pineapple syrup, the tomatoes and their juice, the tomato paste, green chiles, 2 cloves of the garlic, 1 of the onions, the bell pepper, chili powder, cumin, jalapeños, and salt. Set aside.

2. Heat the olive oil in a nonreactive large saucepan or stockpot over moderately high heat until almost smoking. Working in batches if necessary, add the pork and cook, turning, until browned on all sides.

3. Stir in the remaining garlic and onion; cook, stirring, until the onion is soft, 3 to 5 minutes.

4. Stir in the tomato mixture and bring to a boil. Cover the pan, reduce the heat to moderately low, and simmer for 2½ hours.

5. Stir in the pineapple chunks, cover, and simmer for 30 minutes more. Serve with the condiments.

....

A bowl of Fire and Ice Chili with Fresh Tomato-Cucumber Salsa and tortilla chips on the side.

LEEZA GIBBONS

◆ ◆ ◆ ◆ ◆ ◆ ◆ ◆ ◆ ◆ ◆

"I TRY TO MAKE EATING LIGHT, LOW-FAT FOODS AND
REGULAR EXERCISE A VERY NATURAL PART OF EVERY DAY."

Leeza Gibbons seems to have her head on straight—and that's a major compliment for a woman who wears so many hats. She's a wife to actor/artist husband Stephen Meadows; she's a mother to Lexi, age six, and Troy, age three; and she's all over the airwaves. She has a nationally syndicated daily radio show, "Entertainment Report," and two weekly shows, "Entertainment Tonight on the Radio" and "The Top 25 Countdown with Leeza Gibbons." But there's more—Leeza wears a whole wardrobe of TV hats as well.

After working at a number of regional TV stations—in Texas, South Carolina, and New York—Leeza first "met" most of us when she was a reporter for TV's mega-successful "Entertainment Tonight." We watched as she grew into a co-anchor spot on "ET," and we've seen her in all sorts of situations—with Jerry Lewis on the Labor Day Telethon, as host of the TV special "Hollywood Gets MADD," and as the calming influence for anxious contestants in the Miss Universe and Miss USA pageants.

Most recently, we know her as host and executive producer of "Leeza," her NBC-TV daytime talk show. Leeza's goal for "Leeza" is to deal with subjects in a singularly unsensational way: "I won't offer a forum for hate, and I'm not interested in being a referee. I want to create a sane, positive setting where we can communicate without the audience jeering." But that can't be easy in the competitive world of "talk TV."

So how does Leeza cope? Well, sometimes she gives in—but just a bit: "I think I'm like most women—chocolate is my most powerful enemy. What I usually do, though, is give in to it and have a smidgen. That way the chemical in the chocolate can do its thing on my brain, and I can get past the craving and get on with it. I find forbidden foods become far too powerful, and that gives them too much control over our lives. French fries and other salty carbohydrates are also a weakness. I try never to eat in my car, and if I stick to that rule, I can usually win over a french fry attack."

Then there's her other ploy: Leeza's learned to work off anxiety and unwind physically by exercising. Whether it's a quick power walk in the studio parking lot or an at-home session on the climbing machine, treadmill, or StairMaster, Leeza gives some time every day to exercise. "My favorite workout is in the morning when my kids are playing in the play area right next to my gym equipment. I can have the morning shows on TV, and between my time on the treadmill and weights, I can play with the kids, get some news, and check exercise off my list for the day. It's the ultimate 'time-share.' We have a good time, and that way, my children view exercise as a natural part of our day."

LUNCH ON THE SET

◆ ◆ ◆ ◆ ◆ ◆ ◆

Recipes from Frisée Catering, Santa Monica, California

for four to six

ORANGE-BASIL SHRIMP KEBABS

STEAMED COUSCOUS

GREEN BEANS WITH LEMON-PEPPER VINAIGRETTE

ORANGE-BASIL SHRIMP KEBABS

Here's a simple formula for healthful kebabs; the quantity of protein is within recommended limits, you can use a wide variety of firm vegetables, and the marinade is delicious over chicken or fish as well.

For 4 to 6

1 long, thin zucchini, trimmed, halved lengthwise, and cut into ¾-inch chunks
1 red bell pepper, cut into 1-inch squares
18 jumbo shrimp, peeled and deveined
1 yellow bell pepper, cut into 1-inch squares
Juice of 1 orange
1 tablespoon rice wine vinegar
2 tablespoons chopped basil leaves
1 teaspoon minced garlic
1 teaspoon freshly milled black pepper
½ teaspoon salt
¼ cup olive oil

1. If possible, soak 6 long (9 inches or so) bamboo skewers in a bowl of cold water.

2. Assemble the kebabs: Thread each skewer with a chunk of zucchini, a square of red bell pepper, a shrimp, and a square of yellow bell pepper, and then repeat the sequence, using 3 shrimp on each kebab.

3. In a bowl, whisk together the orange juice, vinegar, basil, garlic, pepper, salt, and oil until emulsified. Pour the marinade into a nonreactive shallow baking dish. Arrange the skewers in the marinade in a single layer. Turn to coat all of the ingredients on all sides. Set aside for 1 to 2 hours.

4. Prepare a barbecue grill or stovetop grill, or preheat the broiler.

5. Grill or broil the kebabs, brushing with some of the marinade, for about 3 minutes on each side, or until the shrimp are cooked through. Serve with steamed couscous and green beans.

····························

GREEN BEANS WITH LEMON-PEPPER VINAIGRETTE

Since the proportions in this simple vinaigrette are two parts lemon juice to one part oil, you can easily adjust the amount to your needs. If you like your dressing a bit piquant, add the pepper flakes and let the flavors develop for a while.

Leeza enjoys a quick, healthful "dressing room" lunch of Orange-Basil Shrimp Kebabs, steamed couscous, and Green Beans with Lemon-Pepper Vinaigrette between tapings of the "Leeza" show. Now, don't cheat—dessert comes last.

For 4 to 6

1½ pounds green beans or sugar snap peas, topped and tailed
½ cup fresh lemon juice
¼ cup extra-virgin olive oil
Sea salt and freshly milled black pepper
½ to 1 teaspoon dried red pepper flakes

1. Steam the beans until just crisp-tender; they should retain some crunch.

2. Meanwhile, in a jar, combine the lemon juice, oil, and salt and pepper to taste. Cover and shake until well mixed.

3. While the beans are still hot, pat them with paper towels to dry them a bit so the vinaigrette will cling better. Pour the vinaigrette over the beans and toss to coat. Sprinkle with the pepper flakes, to taste. Serve warm or at room temperature.

····························

GLADYS KNIGHT AND KENYA LOVE

◆ ◆ ◆ ◆ ◆ ◆ ◆ ◆ ◆ ◆

"WE ALWAYS KNEW THAT MOM WAS A SUPERSTAR IN THE EYES OF THE PUBLIC,
BUT TO US, SHE WAS A MOTHER WHO TAUGHT US WHAT WAS REALLY IMPORTANT IN LIFE—FAMILY, AND
KEEPING HEALTHY ENOUGH TO ENJOY EVERY MOMENT THAT GOD SENDS US."
—KENYA NEWMAN LOVE, GLADYS KNIGHT'S DAUGHTER

Gladys Knight and her daughter, Kenya Love, are relaxing in a friend's New York apartment. Gladys is working one of her ever-present crossword puzzles without missing a syllable of the conversation that's going on around her. As she works—in ink—she interjects comments here and there, asks questions, admonishes Kenya, who's on the telephone, to "tell Gram hi for me and that I'll see her on Sunday," and generally, hangs out until her special leg of lamb is due to come out of the oven. If you've ever seen her on the concert stage or in an interview on television, you have seen the very same Gladys Knight, who has snuggled her fit, red-cashmere-clad body into the corner of a sofa. When she occasionally calls out, "What's a seven-letter word for _____?" she is answered with a chorus of possibilities, looks up, smiles that big smile, and says, "Thank you, people."

It's fairly easy to get Gladys talking—especially if the subject is her family or food. "Food and family go together naturally," says Gladys. "I learned the importance of both of them when I was a very young girl. My father worked two jobs, and when he got home at one or two o'clock in the morning, he had a habit of waking up all of the children— much to my mother's chagrin—getting us up out of bed and down to the kitchen so he could spend some time with us.

> ## THE MENU
>
> ◆ ◆ ◆ ◆ ◆ ◆ ◆
>
> *for six to eight*
>
> ROAST LEG OF LAMB À LA GLADYS
>
> VEGETABLE CASSEROLE
>
> GREEN SALAD WITH HONEY-MUSTARD DRESSING
>
> KENYA'S NO-FAT OATMEAL-RAISIN COOKIES

A mother-daughter combo you'd swear were sisters—Gladys Knight and Kenya Newman Love.

He always brought home our favorite sandwiches—they were called 'splits'—sort of a po' boy type of treat—and we'd all sit there around the kitchen table and eat and talk and catch up with each other. It was his way of teaching us 'healthful' family values, and we loved it."

Family remains key to Gladys Knight, and her relationship to all its thirty-five family members is intimate; hoots of laughter accompany reminiscences of Easter, Thanksgiving, and family birthday parties. "There are kids running all over the place, it's utterly chaotic, and we just love it. Mom couldn't help putting family first even if she tried," adds Kenya. "Gram wouldn't have it any other way." Gram is Gladys's mother, Elizabeth Knight, "the real hub of the family." Kenya laughs as she talks about Gram: "She's a real character—very strong-willed—and she likes to be involved in *everything*."

Much of the Knight clan lives in Las Vegas, near—or in Gram's case, with—Gladys. Jimmy Newman, her elder son, is Gladys's manager, and Shanga Hankerson, the younger, attends the University of San Diego on a football scholarship. Kenya, herself a mother of two—Aria and Aaron—is owner of Kenya's Gourmet Bakery in Las Vegas. (In fact, Gladys's management company, Shakeji, Inc., is a word made up from her kids' names.)

TOP: *Kenya serves Roast Leg of Lamb to . . . its creator.*

ABOVE: *Kenya Newman Love in her Las Vegas bakery, which features "Cakes of the Stars," including the favorites of Patti Labelle, Natalie Cole, Dionne Warwick, and Kenya's mother, Gladys Knight.*

Talk to Kenya or Gladys and food is always a hot topic. Kenya's bakery is also a café that offers light, healthful meals, fresh-baked breads (Gladys's favorite is the Basil Bread), as well as some of the best sweet treats that "Sin City" has to offer. A good deal of emphasis is put on healthful eating; the bakery's line of low- or no-fat goodies is very popular. (If you like chewy cookies, they don't get any better than Kenya's Oatmeal-Raisin Cookies—the recipe is on page 86—and they contain not a jot of fat.) Another inspiration, "Cakes of the Stars," was an overnight sensation. The line consists of four one-pound loaf cakes: the tropical, fruity Gladys Knight Pineapple Passion; the super-moist pound-cake-style Patti Labelle Sock-It-to-Me Cake; the citrusy, lemon-glazed Natalie Cole Luscious Lemon Cake; and the deep, deep, chocolate, chocolate Dionne Warwick Classic Chocolate. (Though these cakes are currently available by mail-order, plans are in the offing for national distribution.)

Running the bakery is a full-time, hectic job in and of itself. But Kenya manages to work out at least twice a week—"mostly with weights, the treadmill, and the bike—I don't like those steps." In addition, she plays USTA tennis, and though she's not yet through her first year of competition, she's already Las Vegas's number-one player in her category. She says, "Finding time is the hardest thing I do. It's so hard to fit everything in." Gladys, meanwhile, trots around the globe singing to her millions of dedicated fans with, and sometimes without, her personal trainer and nutritional adviser, Al Claiborne, in tow. "Dashing from city to city can make you tired and lazy," Gladys admits, "but Al knows exactly how I should eat and exercise in order to cope with my schedule and my love of good food."

Laughter seems to be an essential ingredient to a healthy lifestyle for this mother and daughter who could pass as sisters on any day of the week. Whenever they are together, they tend to giggle like teenagers at the drop of a hat. "There's always something to smile about," says Gladys, "and a sense of humor is very important to keeping a sound body, mind, and soul." And soul, of course, is something that Gladys Knight knows all about.

ROAST LEG OF LAMB À LA GLADYS

Gladys Knight is a *very* purposeful cook—she just doesn't mess around. And when you want to make this lady happy, just set a beautiful leg of lamb in front of her and watch what happens.

For 6 to 8

1 leg of lamb (6 to 8 pounds, with fat on one side)
Seasoning salt
Vegetable salt
Garlic salt
Onion salt
Dried dillweed
Freshly milled black pepper
Sweet Hungarian paprika
1 large onion, cut into thick slices, separated into rings
3 celery ribs
1 extra-large roasting bag

1. Preheat the oven to 325°F.
2. Place the lamb on a cutting board. Begin sprinkling it liberally with all of the dried seasonings, rubbing them in and adding more until the meat is well coated all over. Place the lamb, fat side up, in the roasting bag; scatter the onion and celery around it. Close the bag securely. Use the tip of a sharp knife to cut a few slits in the top of the bag.
3. Place the bag in a large roasting pan. Roast for 2 to 2½ hours, or until a meat thermometer registers 160° for medium or 175° for well-done.
4. Remove the lamb from the oven and let rest for 15 to 20 minutes before carving. Serve with the roasting juices just as they are.

••••••••••••••••••••••••••••••••••••••

Roast Leg of Lamb à la Gladys—in all its glory.

GREEN SALAD WITH HONEY-MUSTARD DRESSING

There's no fat in this salad dressing except any traces that might be in the mustard. You'll like it on any combination of greens and other salad ingredients.

For 6 to 8

4 cups washed, dried, torn-up soft salad greens
2 cups washed, dried, torn-up soft red salad greens
¼ cup mild honey
¼ cup mild Dijon mustard

1. Combine the greens in a large salad bowl. Cover and chill until needed.
2. Mix together the honey and mustard and stir very well. Pour the dressing over the salad greens and toss to coat well.

••••••••••••••••••••••••••••••••••••••

VEGETABLE CASSEROLE

Again, Gladys Knight is a demon of efficiency in the kitchen, making quick work of layering the ingredients for this creamy casserole. You'd think she had to catch a midnight train to Georgia.

For 6 to 12

2 tablespoons vegetable oil
1 garlic clove, minced
1 onion, chopped
2 large bags (each 1 pound) frozen mixed vegetables, such as a
    combination of broccoli, carrots, water chestnuts, French-cut green
    beans, and mushrooms
Salt and freshly milled pepper
1 quart (4 cups) part-skim ricotta cheese
3 cups shredded part-skim mozzarella cheese (12 ounces)
2 pints (4 cups) non-fat cottage cheese
1½ cups shredded Jack cheese (6 ounces)
1½ cups shredded cheddar cheese (6 ounces)
3 slices whole wheat bread, toasted until crisp, torn into crumbs

1. Preheat the oven to 350°F. Lightly oil or spray a large rectangular baking dish.

2. Warm the oil in a large sauté pan over moderate heat. Add the garlic and onion and sauté until wilted, about 3 minutes. Add the frozen vegetables and cook, tossing, until warmed through. Season the vegetables with salt and pepper to taste. Turn off the heat.

3. Spread half of the ricotta cheese over the bottom of the baking dish. Sprinkle with 1 cup of the mozzarella, and top that with a layer of half the cottage cheese. Mix together the Jack and cheddar cheeses; sprinkle on 1 cup of the mixed cheeses. Spread half of the vegetable mixture over the top; sprinkle on 1 cup of the mozzarella. Repeat the layering, using the remaining ricotta, the remaining mozzarella, the remaining cottage cheese, 1 cup of the mixed cheeses, and the remaining vegetables. Top with the remaining 1 cup mixed cheeses. Evenly sprinkle the toasted crumbs over the top.

4. Bake until the cheeses are bubbly and the casserole is browned on top, 1 to 1¼ hours. Serve hot.

KENYA'S NO-FAT OATMEAL-RAISIN COOKIES

Yes, these are remarkably chewy and good and they contain NO fat or cholesterol! You'll love them.

Makes about 3 dozen

3 cups old-fashioned rolled oats
2 cups unbleached all-purpose flour
1 cup firmly packed brown sugar
1 teaspoon baking soda
1 teaspoon baking powder
1 teaspoon salt
1½ teaspoons ground cinnamon
1½ cups unsweetened applesauce
½ cup light corn syrup
3 egg whites
2 teaspoons vanilla extract
2 cups raisins

1. Preheat the oven to 350°F. Have ready 2 nonstick baking sheets, or line 2 baking sheets with baking parchment.

2. Combine the oats, flour, sugar, baking soda, baking powder, salt, and cinnamon in a large mixing bowl. Add the applesauce, corn syrup, egg whites, and vanilla and beat until all of the dry ingredients are moistened. Add the raisins and beat together until uniform; the mixture will be very moist.

3. Use an ice cream dipper or large spoon to scoop large blobs of the batter onto the baking sheets; the cookies will spread out during baking, so do not crowd the baking sheet. Bake until set and just lightly browned, 10 to 12 minutes. Let cool on the baking sheets for several minutes; remove to a rack to cool completely.

4. Continue making cookies until all of the batter is baked. Store the cookies in an airtight container so they stay moist and chewy.

OPPOSITE: *Kenya puts her mother through the simple procedure that results in Kenya's chewy No-Fat Oatmeal-Raisin Cookies.*

DIAHANN CARROLL AND VIC DAMONE

• • • • • • • • • • • •

"WHILE THE PASTA IS COOKING, TASTE THE WATER.
THIS IS VERY IMPORTANT—IF THE WATER TASTES FLAT, THE PASTA WILL BE FLAT."
—VIC DAMONE

They are a classic couple: He's known as "the singer's singer," and she's absolutely astoundingly versatile—as an actress in films, TV, and on Broadway, as a Grammy-nominated singer, and as a nightclub headliner. And no matter which of their homes they're in at the time—Beverly Hills, New York City, or Palm Springs—just guess where you'll find Vic Damone. This gourmet cook spends much of his time enthusiastically dabbling in the kitchen—any kitchen.

"I'm from the old school," says Damone. "I cook the way my mother cooked when I was just a boy growing up in Brooklyn. She never gave me any formal lessons; I just do it—I follow her example. She never measured anything, so I never measure anything. My theory is that if it tastes right, it *is* right. You have to choose the best ingredients and then be nice to them. Don't add too many things that will take away from their natural goodness. You have to taste all of the time, you need to stay on top of what's happening and fine-tune it until it's right. You'll know it when you taste it."

Diahann Carroll, certainly one of Hollywood's greatest beauties, smiles when she says, "Vic's the cook in the family. I wouldn't dream of interfering with that. He made dinner for me on our very first date, and he hasn't stopped since." And though their meals are healthful—"I try to eat to live, not live to eat, but it's not easy," she says—staying fit is a major priority. She works out regularly with a trainer—stretching, toning, cardiovascular conditioning—and enjoys swimming and tennis. "Exercise can be grueling, but you have to do it to get results. And ultimately, looking good makes you feel good too."

Vic Damone's Penne con Pomodori—the centerpiece of the first dinner he cooked for Diahann. Combined with a bottle of Château Margaux, it's sure to please your date too.

PENNE CON POMODORI
For 2

Virgin olive oil
4 garlic cloves, minced
10 to 12 big, fat, ripe plum tomatoes, peeled, seeded, and coarsely chopped
12 large basil leaves, cut into chiffonade (see page 23)
Coarse (kosher) salt and freshly milled black pepper
½ pound penne
Freshly grated Parmesan cheese

1. Pour in enough olive oil to cover the bottom of a non-reactive deep sauté pan or saucepan. Place over moderately high heat until the oil begins to shimmer. Add the garlic and sauté until golden brown, 3 to 5 minutes.

2. Stir in the tomatoes, half of the basil, and generously season with salt and pepper. Reduce the heat to moderately low, partially cover the pan, and cook, stirring from time to time, until the tomatoes fall apart and the flavor of the sauce begins to develop, at least 30 minutes. If the sauce gets dry at any point, stir in some red wine, tomato juice, stock, or water—just enough to moisten it. Taste the sauce: If the tomatoes are too acidic, stir in a pinch of sugar or balsamic vinegar.

3. When it's time to get serious about dinner, bring a large quantity of water to a boil in a pasta pot. Add a little olive oil and season the water with salt and pepper. Stir in the penne, bring the water back to a boil, and reduce the heat to moderate. While the pasta is cooking, taste the water: This is very important—if the water is flat, the pasta will be flat. Add salt, pepper, or Italian seasoning if the water is flat. When the pasta is almost, but not too, done, drain it.

4. Throw the pasta into the sauce and stir together for a minute. Divide between 2 pasta plates and sprinkle with the remaining basil. Serve with freshly grated Parmigiano Reggiano. Add a nice bottle of wine—we had Château Margaux.

MATT LAUER

◆ ◆ ◆ ◆ ◆ ◆ ◆ ◆ ◆ ◆ ◆ ◆

"MR. LAUER IS A SMOOTH TALKER WHO HAS SOMEHOW AVOIDED BECOMING A SMOOTHY."
—FROM *THE NEW YORK TIMES*, AUGUST 21, 1994

Matt Lauer became an overnight sensation after just fifteen years of paying his dues. But you could say that 1994 was Matt Lauer's big year: NBC's "Today" show watchers all over America took to his looks and style and loved the way he got on so well with Bryant Gumbel and Katie Couric; everyone in the New York market thought he was just great with Sue Simmons on WNBC's "Live at Five"; *People* magazine named him one of its "Fifty Most Beautiful People" in 1994. Clearly, Matt Lauer had arrived.

During his fourteen years of apprenticeship at television stations in Huntington, West Virginia; Richmond, Virginia; Providence, Rhode Island; Philadelphia; Boston; and New York, and for networks as various as NBC, ABC, HBO, and Lifetime, Matt Lauer did it all—produced, reported, hosted, co-anchored, and anchored. Indeed, he worked with Robin Leach as co-host of ABC-TV's daytime series "Fame, Fortune and Romance." There's something about him that's accessible and likable; for one thing, he's disarmingly up-front and honest: "I'm really not all that careful about what I eat. Sometimes I go to a diner or coffee shop and eat greasy eggs for breakfast. And sometimes I'll have a steak for dinner. But then the next day, my body will lead me to something else I need, usually something light, that kind of counterbalances the steak. I'll have a 'cleansing day.' It's amazing that your

---

THE RECIPES

◆ ◆ ◆ ◆ ◆ ◆ ◆

HOMEY WHOLE WHEAT LOAVES

MIXED FRUIT SALAD WITH
GINGER-HONEY DRESSING

Matt Lauer sometimes enjoys a light, "after work" breakfast between the "Today" show and returning to his office in New York's Rockefeller Center.

body knows how to send those signals and take care of itself."

So, Matt Lauer is luckier than most of us—or maybe just smarter, since he listens to his body. At age thirty-six, he's slim, fit, fresh, unaffected, and quick to smile. We caught him at a quick breakfast at the American Festival Cafe at Rockefeller Center. He'd been up since 4:15 A.M., done his news anchoring duties on the "Today" show, and was taking a brief break before he tackled the work that awaited him in his office at NBC. Even though in terms of hours since awakening, it was more like his lunchtime, Matt ordered simple breakfast fare—orange juice, fruit salad, whole wheat toast, and just one cup of coffee.

As ice skaters twirled and dipped in the background, beyond his right shoulder, Matt Lauer almost blushed when asked about all those female fans who heft those giant, hand-printed signs that declare "We Love Matt" outside the ground-floor "Today" show studio. "It's amazing, isn't it?" We think so, but we've got to agree with *Us* magazine when they featured Lauer as one of the ninety-four stories that rocked 1994: "Lauer Power—Imagine a warm Bryant Gumbel, a not-so-perky Katie Couric and a Willard Scott with dignity, and you get Matt Lauer, the best thing to happen to the morning since Cody Gifford was potty trained."

ABOVE: *These Homey Whole Wheat Loaves are good for sandwich building or morning toast.*

BELOW: *Matt Lauer lends a hand in making Ivana Trump's Cooks for Kids II a hugely successful event.*

HOMEY WHOLE WHEAT LOAVES

Making down-home-tasting whole wheat bread can be a real workout—if you don't take the easy route and use a heavy-duty electric mixer. Since this recipe yields enough dough for two loaves, the kneading time is relatively long. But your biceps will thank you for it.

Makes 2 loaves

2 envelopes or 1½ tablespoons active dry yeast
2 tablespoons firmly packed brown sugar
2½ cups lukewarm (105°–115°) water
2 teaspoons salt
2 tablespoons canola or other vegetable oil
2 cups whole wheat flour
3½ to 4½ cups unbleached all-purpose flour or bread flour

1. In a large mixing bowl, combine the yeast, sugar, and ½ cup of the warm water. Stir to dissolve the sugar and yeast; set aside until foamy, 5 to 10 minutes.

2. Pour in the remaining 2 cups warm water, the salt, oil, whole wheat flour, and about 2 cups of the white flour. Stir by hand or beat on slow speed until well combined, 2 to 3 minutes.

3. Begin adding the remaining 1½ to 2½ cups flour, about ¼ cup at a time. *If you are working by hand:* When the dough becomes too stiff to stir, turn it out onto a lightly floured surface. Continue to add the remaining flour, kneading it in until the dough is smooth, elastic, and only slightly sticky to the touch, about 10 minutes. *If you are using a heavy-duty mixer:* Scrape the dough off the beater and switch to the dough hook. Slowly add the flour, stirring on low speed so the flour doesn't fly around, and beat until the dough is homogenous and pulls away from the sides of the bowl, at least 4 to 5 minutes. Stop the mixer and feel the dough: It should be soft and smooth, yet spongy. If it isn't, continue kneading. Turn out the dough onto a lightly floured surface and knead for a minute or two by hand.

4. Lightly oil a large bowl. Put the dough into it and turn to coat the top with oil. Cover the bowl with plastic wrap and/or a clean towel. Set aside in a warm, draft-free place until the dough doubles in bulk, 1 to 1½ hours.

5. Oil two 9-x-5-inch loaf pans. Punch down the dough; turn out onto a lightly floured surface and divide in half. Pull each half into a slightly oblong loaf shape and fold the short ends under. Fit each loaf, seam side down, into a loaf pan.

Cover each pan with plastic wrap. Set aside in a warm draft-free place until almost doubled again, 45 to 60 minutes.

6. About 30 minutes before you plan to bake the breads, move an oven rack one-third of the way down from the top of the oven and preheat the oven to 375°F.

7. Place the loaf pans several inches apart in the upper third of the oven. Bake the loaves for about 25 minutes, or until the tops are golden and the bottoms sound hollow when tapped. Remove the loaves from the pans and let cool on a wire rack.

ABOVE: *The Ice Rink at Rockefeller Plaza is a pleasure at any time of day; here skaters are gliding through their early-morning workouts.*

MIXED FRUIT SALAD WITH GINGER-HONEY DRESSING

This is as good as part of your breakfast as it is for a midday treat or dessert.

For 4

GINGER-HONEY DRESSING:
⅓ cup mild honey
2 teaspoons minced or grated peeled fresh ginger
1 cinnamon stick, cracked
1 large strip orange zest
1 large strip lemon zest

2 navel oranges, peeled and sectioned, any juices reserved
2 kiwifruits, peeled and sliced
1 cup strawberries, hulled and halved
1 cup green grapes, washed
1 cup raspberries, rinsed
½ cup blueberries, rinsed
4 mint sprigs, for garnish

1. Combine all of the dressing ingredients with 1 cup water in a small saucepan; bring to a boil. Reduce the heat to moderately low and simmer until fragrant, about 5 minutes.

2. Meanwhile, combine all of the fruits in a serving bowl.

3. Strain the dressing through a fine sieve; discard the solids. Pour the dressing over the fruit and gently toss to combine. Divide the fruit and dressing among 4 bowls, garnish each with a mint sprig, and serve.

BELOW: *This Mixed Fruit Salad with Ginger-Honey Dressing makes for a healthful, eye-appealing—and delectable—start to the day's activities.*

ROBERT AND KATIE WAGNER

◆ ◆ ◆ ◆ ◆ ◆ ◆ ◆ ◆ ◆ ◆ ◆

"IT'S BEEN MORE THAN TEN YEARS SINCE I STARTED TRYING TO STRESS HEALTHFUL EATING.
AS A RULE WE AVOID RED MEAT AND CONCENTRATE ON MOSTLY PASTAS, VEGETABLES, AND SHELLFISH."
—ROBERT WAGNER

When you look at them, you see a handsome couple who clearly are fond of each other. You might think this is some sort of May-December relationship—the younger woman, the older man—until you start to realize that these two people resemble each other—especially around the nose, the mouth, the eyes. Is it any wonder? She's his daughter, Katie Wagner, and he is one of this country's favorite actors, Robert (R.J.) Wagner, better known to many of us as Jonathan Hart from "Hart to Hart."

It's lunchtime and we're at R.J.'s house, situated on two acres in the Brentwood section of Los Angeles. Mr. Wagner is purposefully "working" the large country kitchen that he shares with wife, actress and cookbook author Jill St. John. "He really likes to cook," says Katie, watching her dad deftly move between the huge commercial range, the spacious and powerful broiler (known as a salamander to chefs), the refrigerator, the sink, and the spacious butcher-block work island. "He's into simple things, pastas and such; when it comes to major meals, Jill is the cook in that situation." Watching him, one can see that he's enjoying himself, and why not? He's preparing lunch for his first-born child, Katie.

On the other side of the large windows, flowers and shrubs are blooming and the day is warm enough for eating outdoors. Katie gazes around, smiling at what she sees. "I

THE MENU

◆ ◆ ◆ ◆ ◆ ◆ ◆ ◆

for two

PENNE WITH QUICK PLUM TOMATO SAUCE

MARINATED VEGETABLES

GRILLED EGGPLANT

Robert Wagner loves to cook in his huge kitchen in Brentwood; here he prepares a nifty, healthful father-daughter lunch for his eldest, Katie Wagner.

---

love this house—I grew up in this house. Well, not exactly. I mean, I didn't spend my childhood here, just my young adult years—until I went out on my own. I have wonderful memories of this place and that time of my life."

A graduate of Beverly Hills High, Katie attended the University of California at Santa Barbara and then left to pursue the world. She has worked in various aspects of the entertainment field but is firm and very convincing when she says, "I'm not interested in acting at all." Instead, she has established herself as an on-camera street-side reporter, working as Robin Leach's "Lifestyles" co-host, as well as on projects for Disney and Ted Turner's TBS. "My career is moving exactly the way I'd hoped," she reports. "I'm going to continue with "Lifestyles" and that pleases me—it's great to contribute to a successful team."

Meanwhile, Chef R.J. announces that luncheon is served, and they head outdoors to have a bite. Two topics come to the fore: Mr. Wagner's consuming passion for golf—he has just finished narrating *Heroes of the Game*, a video that highlights the world's foremost golfers and golf courses, and a detailed update for Katie's benefit on the twenty-one horses he stables at his nearby ranch. One of them, Madonna Oaks, is a National Champion cutting horse.

The palette of ingredients that turned into the Wagners' impromptu lunch.

incredible, but I also do yoga and attend some of the slower step classes, and lately I've been stopping by a new class called Heat—it's sort of like cross training on a treadmill." Dad sits by her, beaming with parental pride—she obviously has a plan for her future, but her feet seem firmly planted. She turns to her dad and says, "We both just enjoy life, don't we?" And the proud papa nods and smiles.

······································

PENNE WITH QUICK PLUM TOMATO SAUCE

Here's a quick pasta sauce that cooks in the time it takes to boil the pasta—just perfect for an informal meal. Serve with a green salad.

For 4

3 tablespoons olive oil
1 teaspoon anchovy paste (optional)
3 garlic cloves, minced
8 to 10 ripe plum tomatoes, peeled and cut into chunks
3 whole scallions, trimmed and minced
½ cup chicken stock or broth
Dried red pepper flakes
Salt and freshly milled black pepper
1 pound penne
¼ cup chopped fresh basil leaves

1. Bring a large pot of salted water to a boil over high heat.
2. Meanwhile, pour the oil into a large nonreactive sauté pan and set over moderate heat. When the oil starts to shimmer, add the anchovy paste and garlic and sauté for 1 minute. Add the tomatoes and scallions and toss to coat with the oil. Pour in the stock and bring the mixture to a boil. Reduce the heat to low, partially cover the pan, and simmer for 10 minutes. Season the sauce with dried red pepper flakes and salt and pepper to taste.
3. Meanwhile, add the penne to the boiling water and stir until the water returns to a boil. Cook until the pasta is al dente, tender but still firm to the bite. Drain well.
4. Transfer the penne to a large serving dish and pour the sauce over it. Sprinkle on the basil and toss to coat well. Serve at once.

······································

Watching these two talk, you'd think they seldom saw each other, but that, they say, almost in unison, is not the case at all. Mr. Wagner takes the initiative: "We're all so busy, but we try to dine together as often as we can—at least once a week—and it's usually for Italian or Japanese food. Sometimes it's here, at the house, and sometimes we go out to restaurants—it just depends on everyone's schedule at the time. It's been more than ten years since I started trying to stress healthful eating. As a rule we avoid red meat and concentrate on mostly pastas, vegetables, and shellfish."

They look the picture of good health so the choices they make must be effective. Mr. Wagner keeps fit by indulging in golf as well as by working out—alone or with a trainer—at the gym in his house. As for Katie, she admits to not having an established regimen. "Nothing in my life is regimented or routine. My work is erratic, it's always changing, but I do a wide variety of things to stay in shape. If you know this area of California, you know that the opportunities for hiking are

MARINATED VEGETABLES

You can vary the ingredients for this so that it includes your absolute favorite flavors and ingredients.

For 4 to 6

1 large green bell pepper, cut lengthwise into strips
1 large red bell pepper, cut lengthwise into strips
1 large yellow bell pepper, cut lengthwise into strips
2 celery ribs, sliced
4 ounces small white mushrooms, washed and trimmed
1 jar (6 ounces) marinated artichoke hearts, hearts halved or
  quartered, marinade reserved
1 jar (7½ ounces) hearts of palm, drained and sliced
½ cup pimiento-stuffed green olives
2 garlic cloves, minced
½ cup extra-virgin olive oil
2 tablespoons red wine vinegar
2 teaspoons dried oregano
1 teaspoon dried basil
Salt and freshly milled black pepper

1. Combine the bell peppers, celery, mushrooms, artichoke hearts and marinade, hearts of palm, olives, and garlic in a large bowl.

2. In a jar, combine all of the remaining ingredients, and season with salt and pepper to taste. Cover and shake very well. Pour the dressing over the vegetables and toss very well.

3. Cover and set aside at room temperature for at least 1 hour, or refrigerate for up to 2 days. Serve cool or at room temperature.

••••••••••••••••••••••••••••••••

RIGHT: *Use Robert Wagner's mixture of Marinated Vegetables at room temperature to make a terrific topping for fresh-cooked pasta. Just sprinkle on a bit of freshly grated Parmesan or some toasted pine nuts and you're set. You might want to cut some of the Grilled Eggplant into squares and include it, too.*

GRILLED EGGPLANT

You may want to double this easy dish because it's so useful—delicious just as it is, stacked on a sandwich, or cut into strips and scattered over pizza or pasta.

For 4

2 large eggplants, trimmed and cut lengthwise into thin slices
Salt
Olive oil
Balsamic vinegar
Freshly milled black pepper

1. Layer the eggplant slices in a colander, sprinkle with salt, and set aside to drain for about 1 hour. Rinse the eggplant slices well and pat completely dry.

2. Meanwhile, preheat a barbecue or stovetop grill until very hot. Lightly brush each slice of eggplant with oil. Grill, turning after a minute or so, until touched with gold on both sides. As they are cooked, layer the slices on a plate; douse each layer with a few drops of the vinegar and sprinkle with salt and pepper to taste.

3. Cover the eggplant and set aside at room temperature until needed. If making well ahead of time, cover and refrigerate. Let come to room temperature before serving.

••••••••••••••••••••••••••••••••

MAURY AND SUSAN POVICH

• • • • • • • • • • • •

"SUSAN HELPS KEEP ME ON TRACK.
I JUST HAD A LUNCH FROM HER RESTAURANT—WHITE BEAN AND TURNIP SOUP AND
A TURKEY SANDWICH ON SEVEN- OR NINE-GRAIN BREAD. SHE KNOWS WHAT I'D CHOOSE IF SHE LEFT
IT UP TO ME—I JUST CAN'T RESIST RED MEAT AND FRENCH FRIES."
MAURY POVICH

The easy camaraderie between Maury Povich and Susan Povich, the elder of his two daughters, is evidence enough of their close, casual relationship. There's no charading between this dad and daughter. "Susan's a straight-shooter. She tells me what she thinks," says Povich, with more than a hint of fatherly pride. "She can be feisty—I think that comes from being a minority—she was a woman at Harvard Law, and then she was a minority at Paul Weiss [a major Wall Street law firm]. I think she got it from her dad—we march to a different drummer."

Maury Povich admits that he can't always eat what he wants. "I'm eating fish for the first time in my life. Left to my own devices, I'd live on steaks, burgers, and major french fries. But the old cholesterol climbed up the scale a bit, so I have to take steps to keep it down. I eat red meat about once a week now—I can't think of giving it up completely." He is good, though, about exercising. "I submit myself to a personal trainer," he claims. "We work out behind the set of my television show. Two or three times a week, he comes and crunches me and works me out for a couple of hours. There's a TV back there, so I like to watch trials or news shows while I'm dutifully working out. And I love to play golf too." Though Povich mentions this as though it's no big deal, he's said to have a scratch handicap.

---

*A Provençal Lunch at The Cake Bar & Cafe,
New York City*

for 4

PISSALADIÈRE

COD PROVENÇAL

INDIVIDUAL CHOLESTEROL-FREE BERRY PIES

Daughter and Dad: Susan and Maury Povich on a lunch "date" at Susan's Greenwich Village restaurant. The Cholesterol-Free Berry Pie was chosen especially for Dad.

Like her dad, when Susan Povich sets out to do something, she does it. She marched away from a career in corporate law and straight into professional cooking school. With all sorts of new knowledge under her belt and typical determination, she found a partner in Jude Quintiere and opened The Cake Bar & Cafe in New York's Greenwich Village. It's located very near New York University's law school, so you're apt to find groups of law students, their texts and notebooks spread over tables in the large, open upstairs dining room or curled up in the comfortable wing chairs, drinking cappuccinos and lattes and munching on the amazing array of muffins, breads, and other fresh-baked goodies before heading off to class.

"Working out?" asks Susan. "That's something I used to do. Right now I'm working seventy-hour weeks and I just don't have time." All things considered, Susan appears to be in excellent shape—if a bit overworked. "I cook—and eat—healthful, sane foods that are made with great ingredients and without any junk added, the same foods we serve to our customers. The whole idea was to offer good-tasting, well-made food at a fair price in a casual atmosphere, and I think we've managed that beautifully." The recipes that follow are proof positive that Susan is marching to her own tasty and healthful tune.

A Provençal lunch starts with Pissaladière, the luscious French-style caramelized onion and anchovy tart.

PISSALADIÈRE
For 4

DOUGH:

½ cup lukewarm (105°–115°) water
½ teaspoon honey
1 teaspoon active dry yeast
1 to 1¼ cups unbleached all-purpose flour
½ teaspoon salt

2 tablespoons olive oil
1½ large onions, thinly sliced
2 garlic cloves, crushed
1½ large ripe tomatoes, peeled, seeded, and chopped, or 1 small can
    (16 ounces) Italian plum tomatoes, drained, seeded, and coarsely
    chopped
1 tablespoon sugar
Leaves of 3 thyme sprigs
1 bay leaf
Salt and freshly milled pepper
8 anchovy fillets
10 Nyons or Niçoise olives, pitted and halved

1. Make the dough: In a large bowl, combine the warm water, honey, and yeast; stir to dissolve the yeast. Set aside until frothy, 5 to 10 minutes.

2. Stir in 1 cup of the flour and the salt; blend well. Turn out the dough onto a lightly floured surface and knead, adding more flour as needed, until the dough is elastic and smooth, 5 to 10 minutes.

3. Place the dough in an oiled bowl and turn to coat with the oil; cover the bowl with plastic wrap and/or a towel. Set aside in a warm, draft-free place until doubled in bulk, about 1 hour.

4. Meanwhile, heat the oil in a nonreactive large sauté pan or saucepan over moderate heat. When the oil starts to shimmer, reduce the heat to low and add the onions and garlic. Sauté until translucent, 5 to 7 minutes.

5. Stir in the tomatoes, sugar, thyme, bay leaf, and ¼ cup tap water; season with salt and pepper to taste. Bring the mixture to a boil. Reduce the heat to moderately low, and simmer until the flavors are well combined, 10 to 15 minutes. Remove from the heat; remove and discard the bay leaf.

6. Preheat the oven to 350°F. Sprinkle 2 baking sheets or a pizza stone with cornmeal or flour.

7. Punch down the dough; divide into 4 equal parts. Roll out each piece of dough, or oil your hands and stretch out by hand into an 8-inch round; transfer to the prepared baking pans or stone. Lightly brush the top of each round with olive oil; divide the tomato mixture among the rounds. Crisscross 2 anchovies in the center of each pissaladière; dot the top of each with 5 olive halves.

8. Bake until the crust is crisp, about 15 minutes. Serve at once.

COD PROVENÇAL

For 4

4 cod fillets (each about 6 ounces)
Salt and freshly milled black pepper
2 tablespoons plus 1 teaspoon olive oil
2 shallots, finely diced
3 garlic cloves, minced
20 Nyons or kalamata olives, pitted and chopped
2 tablespoons drained capers
½ teaspoon ground cumin
2 large tomatoes, peeled, seeded, and diced, or 1 small can
    (16 ounces) Italian plum tomatoes, drained, seeded, and
    chopped
1 tablespoon chopped parsley
1 teaspoon chopped thyme leaves
½ cup dry white wine
1 pound Swiss chard or spinach, stems and ribs discarded, leaves
    washed (but not dried) and roughly chopped

1. Preheat the oven to 350°F. Sprinkle both sides of each piece of fish with salt and pepper; set aside.

2. Choose a nonreactive large sauté pan that can be placed in the oven (the handle is usually the only vulnerable spot). Pour 2 tablespoons of the oil into the pan and set over moderate heat. When the oil starts to shimmer, add the shallots, 2 cloves of the garlic, and the olives; sauté until softened, 2 to 3 minutes. Add the capers and cumin and sauté for 1 minute. Stir in the tomatoes, parsley, thyme, and wine; simmer for 2 minutes. Scrape the mixture to the sides of the pan and arrange the fillets in the center. Cover the pan with foil.

3. Transfer the pan to the hot oven and bake until the fish is just cooked through, 15 to 20 minutes.

4. Meanwhile, pour the remaining 1 teaspoon oil into a nonreactive large sauté pan or skillet and set over moderate heat. Add the remaining clove of garlic and sauté for 1 minute. Add the chopped chard leaves and toss. Cover the pan and cook until the leaves wilt and become tender, 2 to 3 minutes.

5. Divide the chard among 4 warmed dinner plates, mounding it in the center. Place a fish fillet on top, and spoon some of the sauce over and around the fish. Serve at once.

Cod Provençal—Susan and Maury's main course.

INDIVIDUAL CHOLESTEROL-FREE BERRY PIES
For 4

PIECRUST:

3 cups unbleached all-purpose flour
½ cup sugar
½ teaspoon salt
½ teaspoon ground cinnamon
10 tablespoons (1¼ sticks) cold margarine, cut into bits
7 tablespoons cold vegetable shortening, cut into bits
¼ cup plus 1 tablespoon cold fresh orange juice

FILLING:

2½ cups fresh or quick-frozen raspberries
2½ cups fresh or quick-frozen blueberries
½ cup sugar
¼ cup unbleached all-purpose flour
½ teaspoon ground cardamom
½ teaspoon ground cinnamon

1 egg white, beaten with 1 tablespoon cold water, for egg wash

Picture perfect and absolutely fabulous—The Cake Bar & Cafe's Individual Cholesterol-Free Berry Pie.

1. Make the piecrust: Combine the flour, sugar, salt, and cinnamon in a food processor and pulse to mix. Scatter the margarine and shortening on top and pulse until the mixture resembles coarse meal. Add the orange juice and mix until the dough gathers together in a mass. Divide the dough into 8 equal pieces; pat each into a disk. Wrap each with plastic wrap and refrigerate for 2 hours.

2. Meanwhile, combine all of the filling ingredients in a bowl. Toss together and set aside until needed.

3. Preheat the oven to 350°F. Spray or lightly coat 4 individual-size (usually about 5 inches in diameter) pie pans with oil.

4. On a lightly floured surface, roll out one piece of the dough into a 6- to 7-inch round. Fit the dough into one of the prepared pans and let the dough overhang the edges. Roll out 3 more pieces of dough and line 3 more pans. Chill the filled pans until needed.

5. Roll out each of the remaining 4 pieces of dough into 6-inch rounds, no more than ¼ inch thick. Divide the filling among the pans. Set a round of dough on top of the fruit; decoratively crimp the edges. Brush the tops of the pies with some of the egg wash; cut 3 slits in the top of each pie.

6. Set the pies on baking sheets. Bake for 10 minutes.

7. Reduce the oven temperature to 325°. Continue baking the pies until the crust is browned and the juices bubble, about 20 minutes more.

8. Let the pies cool on a wire rack. Be careful when removing the cooled pies from the pans.

LEFT: *Stairs leading to the upstairs dining room at Susan's Cake Bar & Cafe.*

BELOW: *Jelly-roll pans create a new-style "tin" ceiling in The Cake Bar & Cafe's dining room.*

ABOVE: *Continuing on the cooking equipment theme, Susan uses French molds as wall sconces in the upstairs dining room.*

JACKIE COLLINS

◆ ◆ ◆ ◆ ◆ ◆ ◆ ◆ ◆ ◆ ◆

"Do whatever you want as long as it doesn't hurt anybody.
And *love* what you do."

Is there a soul in the world who wouldn't like to be Jackie Collins' best friend? Wouldn't everybody love to know who or what inspired certain of her characters or plot lines? Is there a single person who has a better line on what goes on in Hollywood?

Jackie Collins smiles as she says, "I have a very active imagination. I keep my eyes and ears open and observe the action. Sure, I like to capture the glamour of Hollywood, but I also try to create situations to show that the unglamorous side is there too. Everything inspires me—especially music—*especially* soul."

Ms. Collins is blessed—she doesn't have to struggle with her weight. Perhaps that's why her favorite food is "spareribs with a great salad to counteract!" As she moves around her huge, curvy, white-on-white kitchen—two sets of double ovens; two cooktops, one with an indoor grill; long, gorgeous stretches of marble countertop dotted here and there with bowls of perfect fresh fruit; and the giant-size refrigerator loaded with juices, fresh fruits

The woman who creates her own Lucky, Jackie Collins as seen by photographer Brian Aris.

and vegetables, and all of the condiments you'll find in the kitchen of a born cook—you know you're in a special domain, a space she planned with care. Her casual dinner parties are a hit with friends—especially when time allows Ms. Collins to prepare her special Shepherd's Pie or indulge her weakness for lobster and shrimp.

But time, as they say, is of the essence, and nowhere more than in Jackie Collins' life. She always has several projects cooking all at once—new books (she's currently working on *Vendetta—Lucky's Revenge*; and just how will the wild, savvy, and beautiful Lucky Santangelo settle the score this time?), a screenplay for the miniseries version of her book *Hollywood Kids,* which she will also produce, plus her regular schedule of swimming and jogging—as both workout and relaxation. Jackie's philosophy on what makes for a healthy and happy life is simple and to the point: "Do whatever you want as long as it doesn't hurt anybody. And *love* what you do."

NICK ANGEL CAKE

Nick Angel is a character from Jackie Collins' novel *American Star*—he's tall, dark, and delicious, just like this cake. Angel food cake has become a hot commodity among people who want a no-fat dessert. But, sometimes, you just need some chocolate. And that's when Nick Angel can be your salvation. The cake requires ⅓ cup of cocoa powder—that's about 1 ounce, which contains 3 grams of fat. Therefore, the whole cake contains just 3 grams of the bad stuff—or less than ½ gram per serving. It's a good way to have your cake and chocolate too.

For 8

1¼ cups egg whites (from about 10 large eggs), at room
    temperature
¼ teaspoon salt
1 teaspoon cream of tartar
1⅓ cups sugar
1 teaspoon vanilla extract
½ cup sifted cake flour
½ cup sifted Dutch-process cocoa powder
Fresh raspberries and mint sprigs, for garnish (optional)

1. Preheat the oven to 375°F. Wash and dry a 10-inch tube pan; do not grease the pan.

2. In a deep mixing bowl, use an electric mixer to beat the egg whites with the salt until frothy. Add the cream of tartar and 2 tablespoons of the sugar and beat until soft peaks form. Gently fold in the remaining sugar, ¼ cup at a time, beating well after each addition. Continue beating the whites until stiff peaks form. Fold in the vanilla.

3. On a sheet of waxed paper, sift together the flour and cocoa powder. Sift the two together 2 more times. Sprinkle about ¼ cup of the mixture over the beaten whites and fold in. Continue adding the sifted ingredients, ¼ cup at a time, and folding in gently but thoroughly. Do not overmix.

4. Scrape the batter into the tube pan; run a knife through the batter to eliminate any air pockets. Bake until the cake is tall, lightly golden, and springs back when lightly pressed, 35 to 40 minutes.

Nick Angel Cake—tall, dark, and delicious.

5. If your tube pan has legs, invert it and let cool completely, upside down. If it doesn't have legs, hang the cake upside down over the narrow neck of a tall bottle. Let the cake cool completely in the pan.

6. Carefully loosen the cake from the sides and tube of the pan and unmold it. Garnish with the berries and mint sprigs, if desired.

SPENCER CHRISTIAN AND CHEF MICHAEL LOMONACO AT "21"

◆ ◆ ◆ ◆ ◆ ◆ ◆ ◆ ◆ ◆ ◆

*"WHAT STANDS OUT IN MY MIND ABOUT THIS MEAL IS
THE EXCELLENCE OF THE PAIRINGS—HOW CAREFULLY THE WINES AND FOODS
WERE CHOSEN TO GO TOGETHER AND HOW WELL THEY COMPLEMENTED EACH OTHER.
THAT'S NO EASY TASK. I LEFT WITH MY TASTE BUDS SINGING."*

Spencer Christian, for nine years now a permanent fixture on ABC-TV's "Good Morning America," is one of the most affable people you could ever hope to meet. He's quick to smile, a great listener, and very well versed on any number of topics, and he simply loves good food and distinguished red wines. Indeed, cable viewers might well have tuned in to his weekly show, "Spencer Christian's Wine Cellar" on the Home & Garden Network (HGTV).

Mr. Christian is a modest man who says, "I love good food, but I try to be careful and eat enough to keep me healthy and going strong without overdoing anything. It isn't easy, but I think it's the only way to go. And I must admit that I do tend to choose foods that lend themselves to red wines, because they're my passion."

How wine became his passion makes a charming tale. It was 1977 and Spencer and his wife, Diane, returned to Baltimore, where Spencer had been a newscaster for two years.

THE MENU

Wine-Tasting Dinner

LEEK RAVIOLI WITH WILD MUSHROOM BROTH

WINE: BISCI 1991 VERDICCHIO DI MATELICA

GRILLED WISCONSIN WHITEFISH SALAD WITH TOMATOES AND TARRAGON VINAIGRETTE

WINE: JOSEPH PHELPS 1991 NAPA VALLEY VIN DU MISTRAL

SEA BASS ON CURRIED LENTILS

WINE: LUCIEN CROCHET 1990 SANCERRE ROUGE—CUVÉE PRESTIGE

VENISON CHOPS WITH OVEN-POACHED PEARS

WINE: CHÂTEAU DE BEAUCASTEL 1991 CHÂTEAUNEUF-DU-PAPE

MIXED BERRY NAPOLEON

WINE: LA SPINETTA 1993 BRICCO QUAGLIA MOSCATO D'ASTI

A private meal in the wine cellar at "21," where there's room for only one table. The ceiling is low and unfinished, the lighting relatively subdued. Spencer Christian and Executive Chef Michael Lomonaco consult on the evening's menu.

The occasion was to celebrate the engagement of two friends. "I wanted to do something a little special," he says, smiling, "and I thought I had little knowledge or great interest in wine. I thought ordering what I knew to be a great wine would be a fitting gesture. When I looked at the wine list, one name popped out—Château Lafite-Rothschild—so that's what I ordered." (It's worth remembering that this was in 1977, and the bottle he'd just ordered was the excellent 1966 vintage, and since it was by then eleven years old, this fine Bordeaux was well on its way to greatness.)

Mr. Christian continues, his voice full of wonder, "From the minute the sommelier pulled the cork, that distinctive Lafite bouquet filled the whole area around our table. We couldn't believe it. I knew enough to swirl the wine a bit, and smell it before tasting, but when I had a sip, and let it linger in my mouth for a few seconds, the taste sensations simply took my breath away.

LEFT: *Spencer Christian explores the shelves in the wine cellar, which includes remarkable stores of some of the rarest classic vintages—1945, 1947, 1949, 1959, 1961—and a slew of the magnificent 1970 and 1975 Bordeaux, as well as an enviable stock of several of the very best 1961, 1969, 1971, and 1976 red Burgundies.*

OPPOSITE, TOP: *The jockeys stand guard outside the famous "21" Club, located at 21 West 52nd Street in New York City. The restaurant was a speakeasy during Prohibition.*

OPPOSITE, BOTTOM: *Walter Weiss, a mainstay at "21" for decades, relaxes for a minute in one of the parlor's comfortable leather wing chairs.*

I was completely and utterly seduced by that taste experience and that bottle of wine. . . . Need I add that we had a second bottle too?"

After returning to New York, Spencer went to the bookstore and bought eight or ten wine books, and his love affair with wine began. "I was on the local WABC news at the time, and I would sit up until two or three in the morning absolutely devouring everything I could about the wines, the grapes, the history. I started searching out the best wine stores and buying wines; in just two months I had accumulated 200 bottles. I kept going, built a real wine cellar in a corner of my basement, and kept buying more fine wines with every extra dollar I could devote to them. By 1979 I had a collection of 1,500 bottles.

These days, he says, "I keep my collection at around 1,000 bottles. My purpose isn't to acquire madly or hoard it for the future; I like to drink fine wines and share them with others who love and appreciate them." A healthy outlook from any angle.

Getting to the wine cellar at New York's legendary "21" is a journey in itself. Entering through the trademark wrought-iron front doors of 21 West 52nd Street, you pass through the foyer and the famed Barroom, go into the kitchen, descend a set of winding stairs, and arrive at a massive door that looks as though it leads to a huge bank vault. You step into the liquor and "everyday" wines bin room, where a surprisingly large stock of bottles stand or are stacked tidily on shelves. Immediately ahead is an archway that's really not very big. When Spencer Christian approaches it, he's forced to bend his lanky frame almost in half to step up and over through the hole into the fine wine cellar. All of the walls of the, say, twenty-by-ten-foot room are lined with shelves or bins. Most of the rest of its area is covered with freestanding shelves, and everywhere you look, all you see is wine. The one clear space in the room is no more than six or seven feet square—just room enough for a table for four—no more. In an instant, Mr. Christian's attention goes to the nearest bottles. The vintages include stores of some of the rarest classics—1945, 1947, 1949, 1959, 1961—and a slew of the magnificent 1970 and 1975 Bordeaux, as well as an enviable stock of several of the very best 1961, 1969, 1971, and 1976 red Burgundies. Many of the bottles wear red labels that identify their owners, many of whom have recognizable names and many whose taste is a personal, not public, fact. Spencer looks like the proverbial kid in the candy store as, eyes literally glowing, he explores the room. From time to time you'll hear a gasp, a chuckle, or a heartrending sigh. Though Christian maintains a personal cellar collection of around 1,000 red wines, clearly "21" has a few he'd love to sample. Most amazing is the vastness and richness of its stock: Literally dozens and dozens of bottles of the world's very, very best wines—many undoubtedly now past their prime—are being perfectly maintained and seem to be, outwardly at least, in pristine condition. Scattered here and there are pre-Prohibition whiskey, gin, scotch, and liqueur bottles—some familiar, most not. Some have handwritten or obviously hand-printed labels and some are merely marked with words describing their contents. It's possible that some of what's here has survived since Prohibition, when "21" was a popular speakeasy; indeed, some of these bottlings could well be the only extant bottles of their kind.

· ·

LEEK RAVIOLI WITH WILD MUSHROOM BROTH

For 4 to 6

RAVIOLI:

1 tablespoon canola oil

1 cup finely chopped, well-washed leeks (the white and light green
    parts only)

¼ cup minced cilantro leaves

2 points of star anise

¼ teaspoon finely chopped or grated fresh ginger

¼ teaspoon salt

¼ teaspoon freshly milled pepper

1 package (usually 25 to 30) round Chinese wonton skins

MUSHROOM BROTH:

1 cup vegetable stock or low-sodium canned vegetable broth

1 cup thinly sliced, cleaned mushrooms (preferably a mixture of
    wild and/or exotic types)

2 tablespoons minced shallots

1 teaspoon minced garlic

1 whole dried hot chile pepper

1. Make the ravioli: Warm the oil in a small nonstick skillet set over low heat. Add the leeks and sauté until thoroughly wilted and soft, 8 to 10 minutes.

2. Stir in the cilantro, star anise, ginger, salt, and pepper; cook for 1 minute. Remove from the heat and allow to cool completely before assembling the ravioli. Remove and discard the star anise points.

3. Keep the stack of wonton skins covered with a damp paper towel to prevent their drying out. Spoon 2 teaspoons of the leek filling into the center of each round. Lightly brush the exposed dough with water; fold into a half-moon shape.

Press outward from the filling to avoid air pockets, and pinch to seal the edges all around. Set aside on a sheet of waxed paper. Continue filling and forming the ravioli; you will have 2 to 3 dozen delicate dumplings. (You'll need 3 or 4 for each serving, but don't panic; the remainder will freeze beautifully and can be cooked while still frozen.)

4. Bring a large pot of water to a boil over high heat. Meanwhile, make the mushroom broth: Pour the vegetable stock into a large saucepan, and bring to a boil over moderately high heat. Add all the remaining broth ingredients. Reduce the heat to moderately low and simmer for 15 minutes.

5. Meanwhile, add 1 teaspoon of salt to the pot of boiling water. Add the ravioli and cook until they rise to the surface, 2 to 3 minutes. Scoop out and drain well.

6. Divide the ravioli among 4 shallow soup plates. Ladle some of the mushroom broth over them, making sure each portion gets some of the mushrooms. When you see it, discard the chile. Serve at once with Bisci 1991 Verdicchio di Matelica.

···

GRILLED WISCONSIN WHITEFISH SALAD WITH TOMATOES AND TARRAGON VINAIGRETTE

The keys to this dish are to use only the freshest ingredients and to serve the salad the minute the fish fillets come off the grill. Then you will achieve the sweet flavor of perfectly cooked fish (crispy outside, moist inside), the ripest tomatoes, just-picked seasonal herbs, and the highest-quality oil and vinegar that finish the dish. You can substitute striped bass or red snapper for the whitefish.

For 6

2 cups mesclun salad leaves, washed and dried

1 pint red or yellow pear tomatoes, currant tomatoes, cherry
    tomatoes, or a mixture, washed, stemmed, and halved

1 ripe avocado, peeled, pitted, cut into ¼-inch dice, and tossed with
    1 teaspoon fresh lime juice

2 tablespoons fresh-picked tarragon leaves

2 tablespoons extra-virgin olive oil

3 tablespoons good-quality balsamic vinegar

Salt and freshly milled pepper

6 fillets (each 4 to 6 ounces) fresh Great Lake Superior whitefish,
    skin on, all bones removed

Canola oil, for brushing the fish

Chive spikes, for garnish

1. If using an outdoor grill, preheat it. If using a stovetop grill, preheat until very hot. If using the broiler, preheat a broiling pan.

2. Meanwhile, divide the salad greens among 4 salad plates. Combine the tomatoes, avocado, tarragon, olive oil, and vinegar in a bowl. Toss gently to combine; season with salt and pepper to taste.

3. Lightly brush each fish fillet with some of the canola oil; season with salt and pepper. Place the fillets, flesh side down, on the hot grill or pan, and cook for 5 minutes. Turn the fillets and cook, skin sides down, until crisp, 4 to 6 minutes more.

4. Transfer a fillet to each plate of greens so that the heat of the fish can warm the greens. Drizzle some of the vinaigrette over the fish and greens, spoon some of the tomato-avocado mixture over each serving, and garnish with the chives. Serve immediately, with the Joseph Phelps 1991 Napa Valley Vin du Mistral.

Another perfect pairing: Grilled Wisconsin Whitefish Salad with Tomatoes and Tarragon Vinaigrette and the 1991 Joseph Phelps Napa Valley Vin du Mistral.

SEA BASS ON CURRIED LENTILS

If sea bass isn't available, both halibut and cod make excellent substitutions.

For 4 to 6

CURRIED LENTILS:

2 tablespoons canola oil

1 onion, finely diced

3 tablespoons curry powder

1 pound dried red (sometimes called yellow) lentils, picked over and
 rinsed

Salt and freshly milled black pepper

SEA BASS:

2 tablespoons canola oil

1 large Spanish onion, thinly sliced (about 1 cup)

1 sweet red bell pepper, cut into fine julienne (about 1 cup)

¼ teaspoon ground cardamom

½ teaspoon ground cumin

1 cinnamon stick

1 vanilla bean, split lengthwise, seeds scraped out and reserved

1 pound skinless sea bass, halibut, or cod steak, bones removed, fish
 cut into 4 portions

¼ cup dry white wine

1 cup vegetable stock

½ cup shelled whole almonds, toasted, for garnish (optional)

1. Make the lentils: Heat the oil in a large saucepan set over moderate heat. Add the diced onion and sauté until translucent, 3 to 5 minutes. Stir in the curry powder and toast it, stirring, until fragrant, about 1 minute. Stir in the lentils. Pour in 2 cups of water and season with salt and pepper to taste; bring to a boil. Reduce the heat to low and simmer until the lentils are tender, about 40 minutes.

2. Meanwhile, make the sea bass: Warm the oil in a dutch oven or casserole set over moderate heat. Reduce the heat to low and add the sliced onion and red pepper. Gently sauté until the onions are translucent, about 10 minutes.

3. Stir in the cardamom, cumin, cinnamon stick, vanilla bean, and vanilla seeds; stir to coat with the oil. Toast, stirring, until fragrant, about 1 minute. Take care not to burn the spices.

4. Add the wine and stock to the spiced onion mixture and bring to a boil. Reduce the heat to low and arrange the pieces of fish on top of the vegetables. Cover and cook until the fish is just cooked through, 10 to 12 minutes.

5. To serve, spoon a bed of lentils over each dinner plate. Set a piece of fish on top. Remove the cinnamon stick and vanilla bean, and season with salt and pepper to taste. Spoon some of the spiced vegetables and broth around the fish. Garnish with the toasted almonds, if desired. Serve with Lucien Crochet 1990 Sancerre Rouge—Cuvée Prestige.

VENISON CHOPS WITH OVEN-POACHED PEARS

A venison rack is somewhat similar to a rack of lamb; there are usually 8 to 9 chops per rack. One rack is sure to yield enough to serve four people, two chops apiece.

For 4

PEARS:

¾ cup maple syrup
¾ cup hot water
1 tablespoon ground cinnamon
4 large, ripe pears (1 to 1½ pounds), peeled, quartered, and cored

VENISON:

2 tablespoons olive oil
2 tablespoons chili powder
2 teaspoons ground cumin
1 rack farm-raised venison, cut into chops
Salt and freshly milled black pepper
Whole or minced sage leaves, for garnish (optional)

1. Preheat the oven to 375° F.
2. Prepare the pears ahead of time: In a bowl, stir together the maple syrup, hot water, and cinnamon until well blended. Arrange the pear quarters close together in a small baking dish. Pour on the maple syrup mixture; turn the pears to coat all over. Oven-poach the pears until the syrup caramelizes and the pears are golden brown and tender to the tip of a knife, 15 to 18 minutes. Check the poaching liquid from time to time, adding hot water to keep the dish moist if necessary.
3. Remove the pears from the baking dish and let cool on a sheet of baking parchment or waxed paper. If any caramelized maple sugar remains, spoon it over the pears.
4. Prepare the venison: Combine 1 tablespoon of the olive oil with the chili powder and cumin. Coat the venison chops with the mixture; season with salt and pepper.
5. Heat the remaining 1 tablespoon olive oil in a large, heavy skillet over moderate heat until the oil shimmers. Add the chops to the pan in a single layer, and cook for 4 minutes. Turn and cook the other side until medium-rare, about 4 minutes. Watch carefully, since the venison will cook quickly because of its naturally lean texture.
6. Transfer 2 chops to each dinner plate; arrange 4 pear quarters alongside. Serve at once, with any seasonal vegetables. If desired, garnish with whole or minced fresh sage. Serve with Château de Beaucastel 1991 Châteauneuf-du-Pape.

....

MIXED BERRY NAPOLEON
For 4 to 6

NAPOLEONS:

¼ cup honey
½ pound (½ package) frozen phyllo pastry sheets, defrosted

BERRIES:

¼ cup dry white wine
¼ cup firmly packed light brown sugar
2 pints ripe berries (any mixture or combination available)
1 cinnamon stick, cracked

Confectioners' sugar, for serving (optional)
Fruit sorbet, for serving (optional)

Spencer looks like the proverbial kid in the candy store as, eyes glowing, he prepares to attack the amazingly delicious Venison Chops with Oven-Poached Pears that goes perfectly with the rich Château de Beaucastel 1991 Châteauneuf-du-Pape.

1. Preheat the oven to 375°F. Line a baking sheet with baking parchment or waxed paper.

2. Combine the honey with ¼ cup water in a nonstick saucepan over low heat. Stir together until mixed and warmed through, usually 2 to 3 minutes; remove from the heat.

3. Keep the phyllo sheets covered with a damp towel to prevent their drying out. Place 1 sheet on a work surface and brush with a very light coating of the honey mixture. Layer another sheet of phyllo on top, and brush with the honey mixture. Continue layering and brushing until all of the phyllo is stacked.

4. With a long edge of the pastry in front of you, halve the pastry widthwise into two 4¼-x-12-inch strips. Cut each strip crosswise into thirds, making a total of six 4-x-4-inch squares. Transfer the squares to the prepared baking sheet, spacing them about 1 inch apart. Brush the tops with a light coating of the honey mixture.

5. Bake the phyllo squares for 12 to 14 minutes, or until crisp and golden brown. Remove from the pans and cool on a wire rack. (The phyllo Napoleon tops can be made in advance. Cool completely and then store in an airtight container for up to a day or two.)

6. Make the berry filling: In a nonreactive small saucepan, combine the wine, brown sugar, and cinnamon stick; bring to a boil over moderate heat. Reduce the heat to very low and add half of the fruit. Cook at a very low simmer until the fruit is just warmed through and has barely begun to soften, 2 to 3 minutes. Do not overcook the berries; if necessary, reduce the cooking time to preserve the integrity of the fruit. Remove and discard the cinnamon stick. Let the berries cool to lukewarm, or chill and serve cold.

7. To assemble, spoon some of the cooked berries onto a plate, and top with a phyllo square. Scatter some of the uncooked berries around the Napoleon. Sift confectioners' sugar around the edges of the plate, if desired. For an even more refreshing dessert, serve the cooked and uncooked berries with small scoops of fresh fruit sorbet.

....

TOP: *Mixed Berry Napoleon with a demitasse of rich espresso.*

RIGHT: *Michael Lomonaco takes a breather with the jockeys outside his domain, the "21" Club.*

SUSAN POWTER

◆ ◆ ◆ ◆ ◆ ◆ ◆ ◆ ◆ ◆ ◆ ◆

"DIETS STINK—THEY SET YOU UP TO FAIL."

She's a hurricane of energy, she's a cyclone of activity, she's a tidal wave of intensity, but this woman is *not* a natural disaster. Nope, she's more of a natural wonder, and she's called Susan Powter. Granted, she took the country by storm when she shouted her message to anyone who'd listen to her "Stop the Insanity!" infomercial. But as storm troopers go, Ms. Powter is deserving of an honorary green beret (and it would help keep her buzz-cut, platinum-blonde head warm) for fighting the good fight on the health and fitness front. Face to face, Susan Powter is no screamer, she speaks calmly but adamantly in normal tones; there's no hard sell, no bluffing; this woman is remarkably compelling. She gathers you into her energy and you're off—on a Powter trip that's truly extraordinary.

We're at Susan's home in Pacific Palisades, California. It's morning and Susan is raring to cook. She seems to be everywhere all at once. Is she hyper? "Noooo," she exclaims. "I'm passionate—I've always been passionate—don't know where it comes from, but even the nuns at the Dominican convent where I went to school couldn't slap it out of me with their rulers." Has she had breakfast? "Sure, I eat all of the time—not just three squares a day, not at all. I take in an enormous amount of food—I just don't eat a lot of fat. I was fat, and I don't like being fat, so I found a way of accommodating eating a lot of food without getting fat. It's not a diet—diets stink—they set you up to fail. The only

THE RECIPE

◆ ◆ ◆ ◆ ◆ ◆ ◆

CHOCOLATE MOUSSE BARS

Susan Powter says of manager and best friend Rusty Robertson: "We are two parts of the same soul."

way I've found to get lean—and, hey, skinny's out, skinny stinks, skinny is gaunt—the only way I've found to get lean and strong and healthy is this: You have to eat; you have to move—a little bit and within your fitness level—and you've got to get oxygen into your body, because oxygen feeds every cell and every muscle. At some point we've all got to realize that our health is all we have. You have to deal with that and start to take care of yourself."

And with that Susan becomes a flurry of activity: She's pulling bowls from under the counters of her gorgeous kitchen. Then she has a bit of difficulty with fitting beaters into a hand mixer. Here comes the flour, the cocoa powder, hey, look out for that egg. Perhaps her greatest talent is her enthusiasm—her passion. She's The Enabler, The Empowerer (The Empowterer?)—she makes you believe that you can do what she tells you you can do.

You believe her when she offers up her dictum: "Eat high-volume, low-fat food. It's very simple—think of the car and the gasoline: If the car stays in the garage all day, it doesn't need to have much gas in it. But if you're running around in it, moving it all of the time, driving all over the place, it needs gasoline. People are like cars: How much fuel you need depends on how much you do—your activity level—that's all."

But does she never break her own rules? Her answer couldn't have been more straightforward: "Sure, some days I do overeat," she tells you. But then she slyly adds, "I think about it when I'm on the treadmill." She's grinning because, in fact, she isn't breaking any rules—just following on through, driving around a bit to use up some of that gas. Would that we all could be so disciplined.

"But you *can*," she says. Is she a mind reader too? "We *all* can. We—all of us—can make informed decisions. We have choices; it's all about choices. We can decide to put a bunch of high-fat food in our mouths and we can be fat. I did it—I ate until four o'clock in the morning! But we can change too, by making the right choices. I did, and I'm a happier person for it." And so begins Susan Powter's personal cooking lesson for us—she's smiling and playing, the picture of mental and physical health.

....

ABOVE AND RIGHT: *Robin and Susan taping a "Lifestyles" segment in the dining room of Adrienne, the restaurant at New York's Peninsula Hotel.*

CHOCOLATE MOUSSE BARS
Makes 16 bars

6 extra-large egg whites
1¼ cups sugar
1 tablespoon canola oil
1½ ounces (1½ squares) unsweetened baking chocolate, melted
⅔ cup unbleached all-purpose flour
⅓ cup unsweetened cocoa powder
¾ cup unsweetened applesauce
½ cup nonfat plain yogurt
1 teaspoon vanilla extract

1. Preheat the oven to 350°F. Spray or very lightly coat an 8-inch-square baking pan with oil or use a nonstick pan.

2. In a large mixing bowl, whisk the egg whites until frothy. Gradually add the sugar and beat until fluffy.

3. Meanwhile, stir the oil into the melted chocolate. Add this mixture to the egg whites and blend in. With the mixer on lowest speed, sift on the flour and cocoa powder and fold together. Beat until very fluffy. Add the applesauce, yogurt, and vanilla; beat until uniformly combined.

4. Scrape the batter into the prepared pan and smooth the top. Bake until the batter in the center of the pan feels firm to the touch but a toothpick still comes out coated with batter, 30 to 35 minutes.

5. Remove the pan to a wire rack to cool to room temperature.

6. Cover with plastic wrap and chill until firm, at least 1 hour. Cut into 16 bars and serve cold.

....

*Clowning in the kitchen—who says cooking is no fun? Susan Powter is
as energetic at home as she is on television or the pages of her books. She's
a major fan of these Chocolate Mousse Bars and admits that "sometimes
I even eat them for breakfast."*

VANNA WHITE

◆ ◆ ◆ ◆ ◆ ◆ ◆ ◆ ◆ ◆ ◆ ◆

"What's a healthy lifestyle?
To me, it's good sleep, good food, good exercise."

She's the apple of America's eye, the epitome of the sweet, all-American girl next door, and she's seen—worldwide—by more than 100 million people every week. No wonder Vanna White keeps smiling. Looking glamorous, applauding enthusiastically, and turning those letters for 260 segments of "Wheel of Fortune" a year isn't the whole story. Vanna White also oversees a business empire that includes her own line of clothing, pearls, shoes, and dolls, and she acts as an infomercial spokesperson for the Perfect Smile Tooth Whitening System. Now, that's a busy schedule.

But despite all that work, Vanna White considers herself the luckiest woman on earth. One reason is her husband, George SantoPietro, a Los Angeles restaurateur; another is their son, Nicholas, born in June 1994. Their life is a good one; when she's too tired or not in the mood to cook, well, hey, these three won't starve—since George is a full-grown Italian-born man, his expertise in the kitchen is considerable. They share cooking chores at home, and Vanna says

Vanna White and her handsome husband, restaurateur George SantoPietro.

that since Nicholas was born, "We do cook more at home. Nicholas gets all freshly cooked foods, veggies, fruits, meats, pastas. Our kitchen is large, and George does *most* of the cooking."

Eating healthfully is a habit for the SantoPietro family. You might say that George has a natural affinity for the Mediterranean diet, and once you taste Vanna's Pasta alla Puttanesca, you'll see she learned her lessons well. If she has a downfall, it's sweets. As she tells it, "I think everyone has a weakness for something! I love sweets but try to stay away from them; I do enjoy them occasionally, though. And when I do, I try to eat only half of a serving instead of the whole thing!"

Vanna also schedules regular workout sessions with her personal trainer. "She inspires me," Vanna says. "Without her, I probably wouldn't work out as much." They put emphasis on toning and stretching, rather than heavy lifting, and by the looks of it, they've done an excellent job of keeping our Ms. White in perfect shape.

PASTA ALLA PUTTANESCA

Since the name of this sauce shares its origin with the Italian word for streetwalker, it's no wonder that the flavors are full, earthy, and rich. And just so you know ahead of time, chances are that even those who claim they don't like anchovies will take to this sauce—the anchovies meld into the other strong-flavored ingredients and become a part of the whole.

For 4

¼ cup olive oil
12 garlic cloves, smashed
6 anchovy fillets
½ yellow onion, thinly sliced
12 ripe tomatoes, peeled, seeded, and chopped
⅓ cup drained capers
12 oil-cured black olives, pitted and torn up by hand
1 pound spaghetti

1. Heat the oil in a large nonreactive saucepan or sauté pan over moderately high heat. When the surface of the oil begins to shimmer, add the garlic and sauté until golden, 3 to 4 minutes. Add the anchovies and cook, stirring, until they break apart and dissolve. Stir in the onion and sauté for 4 minutes, or until softened and wilted.

2. Stir in the tomatoes and bring the mixture to a boil. Reduce the heat to moderately low and cook, stirring occasionally, for 15 minutes.

3. Meanwhile, bring a large pot of salted water to a boil over high heat.

4. When the tomatoes are tender, stir in the capers and olives. Reduce the heat to low, partially cover, and simmer while you cook the pasta.

5. Plunge the pasta into the boiling water and stir until the water returns to a boil. Reduce the heat to moderate and cook until al dente; the timing will vary by brand.

6. Drain the pasta and mound on a serving dish. Pour on the sauce and serve while the pasta's hot.

ABOVE: *Vanna White's Pasta alla Puttanesca is a no-holds barred, full-flavored, main-course dish.*

LEFT: *On the set of "Wheel of Fortune," the "silent" Vanna White has been with the show for twelve years. Her autobiography is titled* Vanna Speaks.

ROXANNE PULITZER

• • • • • • • • • • • •

"I TAUGHT HIGH-IMPACT AEROBICS FOR EIGHT YEARS, AND
I HAVE A BAD HIP TO PROVE IT. . . . NOW IT'S LOW-IMPACT AND
ONLY LOW-IMPACT AEROBICS FOR ME."

"I can't cook," Roxanne Pulitzer confesses from Aspen, Colorado, where she's on a late-winter skiing holiday. "I much prefer to order in or go out to eat. Oh, I can make a salad, easy stuff like that, but I've just never enjoyed cooking. The way I eat here is different from how I eat at home." Roxanne is in the Rockies for a month; her identical twin sons, Mac and Zac (short for Maclean and Zachary), will be joining her at the end of the week so they, too, can indulge their love of wintertime sports. Roxanne speaks from experience when she claims: "It's the best skiing in the West—I've been coming here every year for twenty years, and I think it's absolutely the best. But cold weather really changes me. In Palm Beach I almost never eat soup; we like light, fresh foods—salads, seafood, Chinese, and Thai. Here, the cold weather and vigorous exercise make me want soups, stews, and heavier foods. But I don't worry, I'm working off the extra carbs on the slopes. I don't feel guilty at all."

Ms. Pulitzer's slope schedule differs considerably from life back home in Palm Beach. There, she says, "a typical day in my life isn't very exciting. I try to write from around nine in the morning until fourish every weekday. I don't eat breakfast—though occasionally I might have a glass of juice, nothing more. If I eat lunch, I tend to have something small—just enough to keep me going. Then at dinner, I have pretty much anything I want. I virtually never snack at home—I just don't keep that stuff in the house. When I want something good to eat, I head for Jean-Pierre. The menu has so many good dishes, there's always something that appeals to me. I know this type of diet doesn't sit well with those who are in the know on nutrition, but it works very well for me."

"I have a real six-days-a-week exercise schedule, and usually I take Sundays off. You need that rest time, your body needs it. I work out with a trainer at a studio three days a week, and the other three days I work out on the treadmill in my living room. I taught high-impact aerobics for eight years, and I have a bad hip to prove it. So, I don't run on the treadmill, I walk—one hour total, including a warm-up, peak-time race walking at a fifteen-degree incline, and then a leisurely cool-down. Other than that, now it's low-impact and only low-impact aerobics for me."

THE MENU

• • • • • • •

*Lunch at Jean-Pierre in Palm Beach
Restaurant owned by Jean-Pierre and Nicole Leverrier;
recipes from Chef Jean-Pierre Blouin*

**BEEF CARPACCIO AND ARUGULA SALAD WITH
HONEY-MUSTARD SAUCE**

**GRILLED FRESH SWORDFISH WITH
PINEAPPLE–BELL PEPPER CHUTNEY**

BLACKBERRY AND LEMON SORBETS IN MERINGUES

Roxanne Pulitzer getting ready to tuck into Grilled Fresh Swordfish with Pineapple Bell Pepper Chutney at Jean-Pierre, a bistro in Palm Beach, Florida.

BEEF CARPACCIO AND ARUGULA SALAD WITH HONEY–MUSTARD SAUCE

For 4

8 ounces trimmed beef tenderloin
⅓ cup mayonnaise
1½ tablespoons honey mustard
Juice of ½ lemon
Salt and freshly milled pepper
1 bunch arugula, washed and dried, large stems removed
2 tablespoons drained capers

1. To cut the beef into paper-thin slices, first wrap it in plastic wrap and place in the freezer until at least partially frozen. Using an electric slicer on the thinnest setting or a very sharp slicing knife, cut the beef lengthwise into paper-thin slices. As they are cut, arrange the slices side by side over 4 chilled serving plates. Cover with plastic wrap pressed directly onto the beef; refrigerate until needed.

2. In a small bowl, stir together the mayonnaise, honey mustard, lemon juice, and salt and pepper to make a thinnish, tart-sweet sauce. If desired, spoon some of the sauce into a plastic squeeze bottle so you can make decorative squiggles on the plate.

3. Toss the arugula with about 2 tablespoons of the sauce, using just enough to very lightly coat the greens. Mound one-fourth of the greens over the beef on each plate. Spoon or squeeze some of the sauce over the beef. Scatter some of the capers over each portion. Serve very cold.

•••••••••••••••••••••••••••••••••••••

PINEAPPLE–BELL PEPPER CHUTNEY

This "refrigerator chutney" is easy to make, keeps well in the refrigerator, and is a welcome addition to swordfish or any kind of fish, whether it's grilled, poached, or sautéed. Try it over chicken too, or as an accompaniment to beef or chicken fajitas, or spoon some alongside a bowl of breakfast fruit.

Makes 5 to 6 cups

3 ripe pineapples, trimmed, peeled, and finely diced
3 green bell peppers, cored, seeded, and finely diced
3 yellow bell peppers, cored, seeded, and finely diced
4 cups Champagne vinegar or white wine vinegar
2 cups sugar
1 cinnamon stick, cracked
6 whole cloves

1. Combine all of the ingredients in a nonreactive large saucepan over moderate heat. Slowly bring to a boil, stirring to dissolve the sugar. Boil, stirring occasionally, for 5 minutes.

2. Strain the mixture through a large sieve. Return the liquid to the saucepan and bring to a boil. Boil the syrup until reduced by half, 8 to 10 minutes.

3. Meanwhile, spoon the pineapple mixture into clean jars that have tight-fitting lids. Divide the hot liquid among the jars. Let cool to room temperature. Cover tightly and refrigerate for up to 2 weeks. Serve the chutney cold or at room temperature.

•••••••••••••••••••••••••••••••••••••

LEFT: *Roxanne's favorite—the Beef Carpaccio and Arugula Salad.*

OPPOSITE: *Grilled Swordfish topped with Pineapple–Bell Pepper Chutney with a triangle of chive spikes.*

BLACKBERRY AND LEMON SORBETS IN MERINGUES

At Jean-Pierre, fruit sorbets are made fresh daily in a variety of deep, rich flavors. Many diners want to taste a scoop of this and a scoop of that, and that sort of presentation is made easier when meringues are used as serving cups. And remember, meringues contain absolutely no fat or cholesterol.

Makes about 1½ dozen

4 large egg whites, at room temperature
Pinch of salt
1 cup sugar
1 pint store-bought blackberry sorbet
1 pint store-bought lemon sorbet

1. Preheat the oven to 250°F. Line 2 baking sheets with baking parchment.

2. In a deep bowl, use an electric mixer to beat the egg whites and salt until foamy. Gradually add the sugar, by tablespoonfuls, and continue beating until soft peaks form. Continue beating until the meringue forms stiff, glossy peaks.

3. Spoon or pipe the meringue into 2½-inch rounds, spacing them about 2 inches apart on the baking sheets. Bake the meringues until dry and light, about 1½ hours. Turn off the oven and leave the meringues inside until cooled to room temperature.

4. Store the remaining meringues in an airtight container for up to several days. To serve, place a scoop of each sorbet on a meringue.

TOP LEFT: *Roxanne Pulitzer shares a giggle with owners Jean-Pierre and Nicole Leverrier at Jean-Pierre; her dessert of Blackberry and Lemon Sorbets in Meringues awaits her undivided attention.*

TOP RIGHT: *The exterior of Jean-Pierre on a sunny Palm Beach day.*

LEFT: *Merriment ensued when Roxanne put in a guest appearance on Robin Leach's "Talking Food" on the Television Food Network; she has Kate Connelly and Robin in stitches.*

DAISY FUENTES

◆ ◆ ◆ ◆ ◆ ◆ ◆ ◆ ◆ ◆ ◆ ◆

"LATINA CHIC? IT'S BEING CHIC WITHOUT DENYING YOU'RE LATIN."

What a life! What a schedule! Does Daisy Fuentes stay busy enough? This twenty-eight-year-old Cuban-born woman is more than multitalented: She's an MTV veejay, she's an outspoken advocate for fusing the Spanish- and English-speaking communities, she's a Revlon spokesmodel who travels constantly, and she's co-owner of ¡Dish!, a casual-chic year-old restaurant on Manhattan's Upper West Side. She wanted to create a place where "you don't have to be some pretentious, stylish thing. Come in, let your guard down, have some fun. It really doesn't matter if you're a superstar or a housewife."

The menu at ¡Dish! is studded with healthful food that's *not* health food per se, and the selection offers something for every mood and taste: Lightened and updated versions of many of Daisy's Cuban grandmother's home-cooked classics (try the paella, rice and beans, or bread pudding) creative Mediterranean-influenced dishes, and some purely American favorites (pizza and grilled chicken salad) just for fun. Many of the dishes at ¡Dish! are vegetarian, dressings are served on the side without your having to ask, no-fat dressings are available,

> ## THE RECIPES
>
> ◆ ◆ ◆ ◆ ◆ ◆ ◆
>
> *from ¡DISH! restaurant*
> *recipes from Chef David C. McKenty*
>
> ### GRILLED PORTOBELLOS WITH PESTO SAUCE
>
> ### GRILLED MARINATED MEDITERRANEAN VEGETABLES
>
> ### HEALTHY ¡DISH! BLACK SESAME–CRUST PIZZA
>
> ### PEPPER-CRUSTED TUNA WITH ROASTED RED BELL PEPPER SAUCE

Daisy Fuentes, model, television personality, and outspoken advocate for young people everywhere, pauses for a quick glass of bubbly at ¡Dish!, the restaurant she co-owns in New York City.

the pizzas can be ordered with or without cheese—just ask.

In addition, Daisy is interested in spreading the word about good health and fitness. Special seminars, such as "A Day Just for Women" are scheduled with presentations from the experts at Plus One Nutrition. Over a whole morning, lunch, and afternoon women get the opportunity to ask questions and seek counsel on health, cooking, exercise, and nutrition. Neither Daisy nor ¡Dish! takes the conventional route.

Daisy Fuentes's awareness of what people want is evident everywhere you look. The restaurant is decorated in a sort of nineties-Deco-warehouse style—dining tables dot several different levels; light and fabric sculptures fit into the overall, golden-hued scheme; the exposed brick walls display a changing exhibit of art by up-and-coming young artists, and massive, funnel-shaped columns are wrapped in a warm, light wood veneer, striped at intervals with metallic bands.

These recipes from ¡Dish!'s large and ever-changing menu are some of Daisy's favorites—you'll love them. And as Daisy says, "¡*Ciaocito*, baby!"

PESTO (MAKES 1½ TO 2 CUPS):

½ *cup (2 ounces) pine nuts, lightly toasted*
6 garlic cloves, peeled
1 cup extra-virgin olive oil
4 cups loosely packed basil leaves
½ *cup freshly grated Parmesan cheese*
¼ *cup freshly grated Romano cheese*
Salt and freshly milled black pepper

1 to 2 bunches arugula, washed, dried, and stemmed
3 ripe plum tomatoes, seeded and diced
Thinly shaved Parmesan cheese, for garnish (optional)

1. Marinate the mushrooms: In a nonreactive bowl, combine the vinegar, oil, and garlic; season with salt and pepper to taste. Whisk until well combined. Add the mushroom caps, upside down, and submerge them. Set aside to marinate for at least 30 minutes.

2. Make the pesto: In a blender or food processor, combine the pine nuts, garlic, and oil; puree until smooth. Add the basil and puree again until smooth. Add the cheeses and puree for 5 seconds. Season with salt and pepper to taste.

3. Scrape the sauce into a container and seal airtight. (If you like, spread a thin film of oil over the top to keep the pesto from darkening.) Refrigerate until needed. You will have plenty of leftover pesto; plan to use it within a few days or freeze it for future use.)

4. Preheat a barbecue grill, stovetop grill, or grill pan. Remove the mushroom caps from the marinade and place them, gill side up, on the hot grill. Grill for 3 minutes. Turn and grill the undersides until tender, about 4 minutes more; do not char the mushrooms. Remove from the heat; cut the caps into thick slices. (See NOTE.)

5. To serve, divide the arugula among 6 large plates. Sprinkle with the diced tomatoes; fan out a sliced mushroom cap on top. Drizzle each serving with about 1 tablespoon of the pesto. Decorate with a few shavings of Parmesan, if desired.

NOTE: The mushrooms can be served hot, warm, or at room temperature. They also can be prepared ahead of time, refrigerated, and then rewarmed in a microwave oven just before serving with no loss of flavor or texture.

GRILLED PORTOBELLO MUSHROOMS WITH PESTO SAUCE

Portobello mushrooms have become a favorite of chefs and cooks for several reasons: They're incredibly flavorful; they're sturdy, not delicate, so they can take some abuse; and they're huge. Marinated and grilled as they are here, they are easily mistaken for slices of good steak. Also note that every part of this recipe can be prepared well in advance for easy entertaining.

For 6

BALSAMIC MARINADE AND MUSHROOMS:
¾ *cup balsamic vinegar*
¼ *cup virgin olive oil*
2 garlic cloves, minced
Salt and freshly milled black pepper
6 medium-large portobello mushrooms, stems removed, caps cleaned

GRILLED MARINATED MEDITERRANEAN VEGETABLES

These grilled vegetables can be served as a main course, as a whole meal, or as a side dish to just about anything. The biggest challenge here is in the shopping—seek out the vegetables that make you and yours happiest; any combination will do.

For 6

MARINADE:

½ cup olive oil
2 garlic cloves, minced
2 tablespoons balsamic vinegar
1 to 2 Thai chile peppers or jalapeño chiles, minced, or 1 teaspoon dried red pepper flakes
Salt and freshly milled pepper

VEGETABLES:

5 to 6 cups cut-up mixed vegetables, such as eggplant, zucchini, yellow squash, red onions or sweet onions, mushrooms, leeks, tomatoes, bell peppers, and/or scallions (pineapple makes a terrific addition too)

1. In a large bowl, whisk together all of the marinade ingredients. Add the vegetables and toss to coat well. Let marinate for 20 to 30 minutes.

2. Preheat a barbecue grill or a stovetop grill until very hot.

3. Remove the vegetables from the marinade and grill, turning as necessary and brushing with some of the marinade, if desired, until just tender; the timing will vary with the ingredient. Note: If you plan to use some of the vegetables on the Healthy ¡Dish! Black Sesame–Crust Pizza (recipe follows), undercook them—they'll be cooking more on top of the pizza.

4. Serve the vegetables hot, warm, or at room temperature.

HEALTHY ¡DISH! BLACK SESAME–CRUST PIZZA

This dough makes a toothsome pizza crust, but you might want to use it (or some of it) to make a loaf of bread, focaccia, dinner rolls, or even breadsticks.

BLACK SESAME SEED PIZZA DOUGH (MAKES ENOUGH FOR 2 LARGE OR 4 SMALL PIZZAS):

1 envelope or 2¼ teaspoons active dry yeast
2 teaspoons sugar
2 cups plus 2 tablespoons lukewarm (105°–115°) water
¼ cup olive oil
1 tablespoon black sesame seeds
1 teaspoon minced fresh sage leaves
2 teaspoons salt
4 cups bread flour
2 cups unbleached all-purpose flour

TOPPINGS:

Grilled Marinated Mediterranean Vegetables (see previous recipe)
Pesto (see page 128)
2 to 8 ounces fresh low-fat goat cheese, thinly sliced or crumbled
Chopped fresh herbs, such as basil, thyme, rosemary, or cilantro, for sprinkling (optional)

1. Make the pizza dough: In a large mixing bowl, combine the yeast, the sugar, and ½ cup of the warm water. Stir to dissolve the sugar and yeast; set aside until foamy, 5 to 10 minutes.

2. Add the remaining 1½ cups plus 2 tablespoons warm water, the oil, sesame seeds, sage, salt, and bread flour to the yeast mixture. Stir by hand or beat until very well combined, 2 to 3 minutes.

3. Begin adding the 2 cups all-purpose flour, just ¼ cup at a time. *If you are working by hand:* When the dough becomes too stiff to stir, turn it out onto a lightly floured surface and knead in the remaining flour until the dough is smooth, elastic, and only slightly sticky to the touch, 10 to 15 minutes. *If you are using a heavy-duty mixer:* Scrape the dough off the beater, and switch to the dough hook. Slowly add the flour, stirring on low speed so the flour doesn't fly around, until incorporated. Knead at medium speed until the dough is homogenous and pulls away from the sides of the bowl. Stop the mixer and feel the dough; it should be very elastic and smooth, yet spongy. If it isn't, continue kneading. Turn out the dough onto a lightly floured surface and knead for a minute or two by hand.

4. Lightly oil a large bowl. Put the dough into it and turn to coat the top with oil. Cover the bowl with plastic wrap and/or a clean towel. Set aside in a warm, draft-free place until the dough doubles in bulk, 1 to 1½ hours.

5. About 30 minutes before the dough is ready, preheat the oven to 500°F. Lightly sprinkle pizza pans or baking sheets with cornmeal or flour.

6. Punch down the dough; turn out onto a lightly floured surface; and divide into 2 or 4 balls. Roll out the dough, or oil your hands and stretch it by hand, into the desired shapes. Transfer each pizza crust to one of the prepared pans.

7. Lightly brush the tops of the pizzas with olive oil. Bake for 5 minutes. Remove from the oven.

8. Arrange the grilled vegetables and pesto over the pizzas. Scatter the cheese on top. Bake for 7 to 10 minutes, or until the vegetables are heated through and the cheese melts. Sprinkle with the chopped fresh herbs, if desired, and serve.

. . . .

The menu has something for every taste or eating style, among them, Pepper-Crusted Tuna with Roasted Red Bell Pepper Sauce (at right), and Grilled Marinated Mediterranean Vegetables (foreground, above) with the Healthy ¡Dish! Black Sesame–Crust Pizza behind it.

PEPPER-CRUSTED TUNA WITH ROASTED RED BELL PEPPER SAUCE

If you're having a food fling, go ahead and serve this super-tasty tuna with basil mashed potatoes and some fried leeks. If not, it's great just on its own.

For 6

RED BELL PEPPER SAUCE:
¼ cup plus 2 tablespoons honey
½ teaspoon cayenne pepper
3 tablespoons dry sherry
1 cup chicken stock or broth
12 red bell peppers, roasted, skinned, seeded, and torn apart
Salt

6 loin-cut tuna steaks (each about 6 ounces), bones removed
3 tablespoons coarse (kosher) salt
3 tablespoons coarsely cracked black peppercorns
Olive oil

1. Make the red bell pepper sauce: In a nonstick or nonreactive saucepan, warm the honey over moderately low heat just until it begins to caramelize and darken in color, 30 to 60 seconds. Stir in the cayenne and cook for 30 seconds. Carefully and slowly add the sherry—be careful, the mixture will bubble up—and stir until well combined. Add the chicken stock and roasted peppers. Reduce the heat to low and simmer until the flavors are concentrated, about 10 minutes.

2. Pour the pepper mixture into a blender or food processor and puree until smooth. Pass through a wire-mesh sieve; discard any solids. Season with salt to taste. Cover and keep warm.

3. Set 1 or 2 large skillets over high heat until very hot. Meanwhile, liberally coat the tuna steaks with the salt and cracked pepper. When the pan is very hot, add just enough oil to coat the bottom lightly; heat until smoking. Add the tuna steaks and sear on one side until crisp and golden brown. Turn and cook the other side to the desired degree of doneness. (If you want the fish well done, you might want to sear it on the stovetop and then transfer the fish to a rack in a roasting pan and finish it in a preheated 400°F oven. Timing in the oven will be about 5 minutes for medium and 10 minutes for well done.)

4. Pour about ¼ cup of the roasted red pepper sauce over each dinner plate. Place a tuna steak in the center and serve at once.

. . . .

THE THRILL OF VICTORY

MARY LOU RETTON

• • • • • • • • • • •

"For a tasty low-fat snack, I usually choose sourdough or hard pretzels. They really satisfy the urge to munch."

You could say she's into "heavy medal," considering that she worked hard for and won five big, beautiful ribbons of them at the 1984 Summer Olympic Games in Los Angeles. And after her retirement from competitive gymnastics in 1986, she didn't fade away—not at all. In fact, Mary Lou Retton was appointed Special Advisor to the President's Council on Physical Fitness in 1992, was voted the "Most Popular Athlete in America" by an Associated Press National Survey in 1993, and in 1994 was counted among the "Twenty-five Fittest People in the World" by *Fitness* magazine.

Still reigning as America's Olympic sweetheart, Mary Lou Retton caught our attention in 1984 and has held it ever since. The current focus of her considerable energy is on her family and living a healthy, happy lifestyle.

sion program with my husband." He's Shannon Kelley, once a quarterback for the University of Texas.

"I love to cook," she announces, "and do it every day when I'm not on the road working. To me, all cooking is fun! I get a lot of joy out of making nice meals for my husband. But there's no doubt about it, 'you *are* what you eat!' I'm 4´9´´, and at my height, a few pounds looks like a lot. So, I need to be very careful about what I choose to eat. I follow a low-fat diet consisting primarily of fruits, vegetables, chicken, turkey, fish, bread, and pasta. I avoid butter, oil, and high-fat sauces."

This is a woman who didn't drop the ball when she switched careers: "Sometimes," she admits, "I miss the thrill of competing, but I *never* miss the eight-hour workouts! Actually, I couldn't be happier with what I'm doing now. I'm very busy with several different projects and activities—as a motivational speaker and a spokesperson for some great companies, and I'm currently working on a children's televi-

But that's not enough for Mary Lou Retton. She wisely observes, "The mistake a lot of people make is relying totally on a healthful diet to keep them in shape. There's no denying that diet is very important, but without exercise, you'll never achieve a truly healthy lifestyle. Low-fat eating and exercise go hand in hand." And with that, the Kelleys walk off for a workout—and, you got it, they're holding hands.

GLAZED CHICKEN FROM THE MICROWAVE

Mary Lou chooses Tyson Holly Farms brand of chicken because she learned this recipe while on tour for them. We tried it two ways: It's great as is for dinner, or use the glaze to coat slices of bread and make a chicken sandwich out of it.

For 4

4 skinless, boneless chicken breast halves
1 teaspoon paprika
8 thin slices lemon
⅓ cup honey
⅓ cup spicy brown mustard
1 tablespoon minced fresh onion, or 1 teaspoon dried onion
½ teaspoon fresh lemon juice
½ teaspoon curry powder

1. Sprinkle both sides of each breast half with paprika. Arrange the pieces, thicker areas toward the outside, in a large, round, microwave-safe dish; a glass pie plate is excellent. Place 2 lemon slices on each breast half. Cover loosely with waxed paper.

2. Microwave on HIGH power for 10 minutes. (If you don't have a turntable in your oven, turn the dish after 5 minutes.)

3. Meanwhile, make the sauce in a small microwave-safe bowl. Stir together the honey, mustard, onion, lemon juice, and curry powder until well mixed.

4. When the chicken has cooked for 10 minutes, remove the dish and pour off any accumulated liquid. Be careful; the dish will be hot. Set the chicken aside while you microwave the sauce on HIGH power for 2 minutes.

5. Spoon the hot sauce over the chicken breast halves, and return the dish to the oven. Cook on MEDIUM (50%) heat until the glaze is hot and the chicken is tender, about 2 minutes. Serve with a big mound of yellow rice.

AHMAD RASHAD

◆ ◆ ◆ ◆ ◆ ◆ ◆ ◆ ◆ ◆

"WHAT'S YOUR FAVORITE FOOD, AHMAD?"
"I LOVE POPSICLES."

In person, he's a charmer, this guy, this Ahmad Rashad, and a feisty charmer at that. The energy and brains that made him a leading receiver for the Minnesota Vikings, put him on the NFL's Pro-Bowl team four times, and eventually took him to broadcasting are right there, written plainly across his face. But on the day we caught up with him, it was his impish side that ruled.

Okay, it was midafternoon, he'd been taping his NBC-TV show, "NFL Live," all day long, and the poor thing hadn't had his lunch yet, so, he was just a tad cranky. We can forgive that.

And yes, he was in a hurry; he still had to go home, change clothes, drive into the city, and meet his wife and some friends for a pre-theater dinner before rushing off to see Vanessa Williams in *Kiss of the Spider Woman* on Broadway, so he was a bit fritzed. We can forgive him for that too.

But what we *cannot* forgive is a grown man who plays with his food, as Mr. Rashad insisted on doing that day. He simply couldn't keep his hands off the crate of clementines we'd brought him. Very kindly, very gently, we said, "Now, Ahmad, put the clementines down so we can chat while you eat your lunch." Did he? No.

But he wouldn't eat—not yet. "Ahmad, aren't you hungry? You know you are. Wouldn't you like to start on your

---

WORKDAY LUNCH
Recipes serve two

GRILLED CHICKEN "CLUB" (NO BACON) SANDWICH

TWO AND EIGHT VEGETABLE SALAD

Plus

**"THE SUPER PLATE CHALLENGE":
THE WORLD'S BEST, MOST HEALTHFUL BANANA PANCAKES—EVEN BETTER THAN AHMAD'S**

Ahmad Rashad—all-around sportsman and brat. Will he rise to The Super Plate Challenge?

---

sandwich now? How about some salad? Or some cranberry juice? You must be very, very thirsty after such a hard day." But still, the rascal played on.

Indeed, he got even worse: He started to juggle the clementines. Honestly, he's much like a great, big, oversized eight-year-old—but much smarter. So, we kept trying: "Ahmad, what do you eat and what don't you eat?"

"Well, I eat chicken. When I played football, I was a strict vegetarian, but now I eat chicken," he replied. "Our seven-year-old daughter is a strict vegetarian, so there's no meat in our house; we eat lots of rice and beans."

He wasn't making this any easier, so we asked something that everyone has an opinion on: What's your favorite food?

He hesitated, but after considerable thought, he proclaimed, "I love Popsicles."

Oh, great, Ahmad, that's wonderful, we thought, not that Popsicles are bad for you, but then he added to his list: "I think banana pancakes are my favorite food. They're the only meal that my family begs me to cook—banana pancakes."

Now, that's something: it seemed perfectly natural to ask, "What's your recipe?"

His reply: "Oh, that's a secret. I can't tell."

At this point we were getting aggravated: "Aw, come on,

Ahmad, how secret can a banana pancake recipe be?"

"Very secret—I can't tell" was his answer, one that, by now, we had somehow expected.

And thus, we decided to dig: "Are there bananas in the pancakes? Pureed into the batter? Or just on top?" Something had to get this guy talking.

"Well . . . both," he said, hedging. "You come to my house some Saturday morning, and I'll be making pancakes, and you can try them, and you'll see; they're the best banana pancakes in the world."

Okay, we've got him going now, he's a sportsman, a competitor, we'll go in for the kill: "Okay, we will. But we bet we can make banana pancakes just as good as yours—even better, probably."

"No, you can't," he insisted.

"Yes, we can," we persisted, seeking to give him a dose of his own medicine.

"No, you can't," he calmly replied.

"Yes, we can," we countered, and the refrain repeated on and on. Obviously, he never revealed his secret, but we stepped up to his challenge. Now we wait to hear what Ahmad says . . . we're very confident that ours will be the taste of victory!

Finally, Ahmad began to eat. This is the man, don't forget, whom many of us consider "The Most Romantic Man in America"—or at least "the Sweetest." It was on Thanksgiving Day, 1985, while he was a commentator at the Detroit Lions vs. the New York Jets game, that Ahmad Rashad—live nationwide on NBC-TV—proposed marriage to Phylicia Ayers Allen. The rest is history.

We had one last question: "Ahmad, what's your greatest weakness?"

This time he was quick. "My wife," he said.

We told you he was smart.

....

In the press box at Giants Stadium, Ahmad Rashad demonstrates his juggling expertise with clementines.

GRILLED CHICKEN "CLUB" (NO BACON) SANDWICH

2 skinless, boneless chicken breast halves
Salt and freshly milled pepper
3 to 4 tablespoons honey mustard
6 slices whole wheat bread, toasted
6 to 12 thin tomato slices
4 large lettuce leaves
6 to 12 slices sweet onion, such as Vidalia or a red variety
Dill pickle spears, for serving

1. Place each chicken breast half between 2 sheets of plastic wrap or waxed paper. Gently pound until uniformly ¼ inch thick; they should spread out considerably. (You can buy boneless chicken breasts in quantity and prep lots of these at once. Wrap them individually, stack, and freeze, so they're always close at hand. Pounded thin like this, they won't require defrosting; just cook them "as is," straight from the freezer.) Sprinkle with salt and pepper to taste.

2. Spread some of the honey mustard on 1 side of each slice of bread. Arrange the tomato slices, lettuce, and onion slices on each layer.

3. Preheat a stovetop grill, or spray a large nonstick skillet with oil; set over moderate heat until hot. Add the pounded chicken breast halves and cook for 2 minutes. Turn and cook the other side until just cooked through and tender, 1 to 2 minutes more; do not overcook.

4. Remove the chicken to a cutting board; if desired, cut each breast horizontally into 2 portions (so you can have chicken on both layers of the sandwich). Place a piece of chicken on 2 or 4 layers of the sandwich and stack to make triple-deckers. Cut each into 4 triangles; set on a plate and garnish with a pickle spear.

Food on the fifty-yard-line: Ahmad Rashad's Two and Eight Vegetable Salad and Grilled Chicken "Club" (No Bacon) Sandwich.

TWO AND EIGHT VEGETABLE SALAD

Ahmad couldn't decide between a sesame seed salad dressing and a ginger-scallion version, so he had both—two dressings and eight vegetables. This salad is a lot like crudités; you can pour the dressing over or dip some of the ingredients as you work your way through it and then dress the greens on the bottom.

For 2

Sesame Seed Salad Dressing (recipe follows)
Ginger-Scallion Vinaigrette (recipe follows)
½ small head soft leaf lettuce, washed and dried
½ small head crisp lettuce, washed and dried
8 to 10 mushrooms, washed, trimmed, and quartered or sliced
8 to 12 small broccoli florets
8 to 10 ripe cherry tomatoes
8 to 10 carrot sticks
½ large red onion, thinly sliced, slices separated into rings
1 yellow bell pepper, cut lengthwise into ½-inch strips
Chow mein noodles, for garnish (optional)

1. Make the dressings. Pour each into a small bowl, and serve alongside the salad.

2. Toss the lettuces together; divide between 2 large salad plates. Arrange all of the remaining ingredients in bunches on top.

....

SESAME SEED SALAD DRESSING

If you're watching calories from fat, it makes sense to use an oil that's big in flavor. Asian sesame seed oil is just that. This dressing is great on a Chinese-style chicken salad too.

Makes ½ cup

1 tablespoon tahini or peanut butter
1 tablespoon sesame seeds, toasted
1 tablespoon rice vinegar or white wine vinegar
1 tablespoon cold water
1 teaspoon soy sauce
1 teaspoon sugar
¼ teaspoon freshly milled black pepper
¼ cup dark Asian sesame oil

1. Combine all of the ingredients in a jar, cover tightly, and shake very well—you want to allow time for the seeds to act as little stirrers so they can break up the tahini or peanut butter and you want the sugar to dissolve. Set aside for at least 10 minutes.

2. Shake again; taste and correct the seasonings.

....

GINGER-SCALLION VINAIGRETTE

If you have some pickled ginger in the refrigerator, mince it and use 1 tablespoon or so of its liquid instead of the freshly grated ginger.

Makes ½ cup

4 tablespoons grated fresh ginger (reserve any juices produced in the grating process)
1 whole scallion, trimmed and very thinly sliced into rounds
1 tablespoon white wine vinegar
¼ cup canola or safflower oil
Salt and freshly milled black pepper

1. Spoon 2 tablespoons of the ginger into a small jar. Wrap the remaining ginger in a small square of dampened cheesecloth. Squeeze the ginger over the jar to extract as much juice as you possibly can.

2. Add all of the remaining ingredients. Cover tightly and shake until very well mixed. Set aside for at least 10 minutes. Taste and correct the seasonings.

....

"THE SUPER PLATE CHALLENGE":
THE WORLD'S BEST, MOST HEALTHFUL BANANA PANCAKES—EVEN BETTER THAN AHMAD'S

These flapjacks will knock your socks off—tall, light, and incredibly fluffy, they just have to be better than you-know-who's. Plus, when we asked Ahmad what size his pancakes were, his answer was: "All sizes." So ours are too (but 4-inchers seem to be just about right).

If you think this recipe seems wordy, you're right. We're shooting for perfection here.

Makes 10 pancakes

1 cup buttermilk, or 1 cup milk plus 1 tablespoon lemon juice or
    vinegar (see Step 1)
½ cup whole wheat or buckwheat flour (don't sift it)
½ cup unbleached all-purpose flour, sifted
2 tablespoons firmly packed soft brown sugar
1½ teaspoons baking powder
1¼ teaspoons baking soda
½ teaspoon salt
½ teaspoon ground cinnamon
1 banana (ideally, it should be overripe)
1 large egg
½ teaspoon vanilla extract
2 tablespoons vegetable oil
About 1 tablespoon unsalted butter, for the griddle or pan
Sliced bananas and maple syrup, for serving

1. If you don't keep buttermilk on hand, you can sour the milk yourself with lemon juice or vinegar—just be sure to mix them together before you begin the recipe to give them 5 to 10 minutes to get started. (Also keep in mind that buttermilk is naturally low in fat, whereas this combo will have whatever fat the milk contains.)

2. Measure the whole wheat flour onto a large sheet of waxed paper. Measure the white flour and place in a sifter or strainer and sift over the whole wheat flour. Measure and add the sugar, baking powder, baking soda, salt, and cinnamon to the mound of dry ingredients. Take care that all of these ingredients stay dry. Stir together to mix.

3. Break the ripe banana into chunks and place in a large measuring cup or in a blender. Mash with a fork until thick and gluey; smallish lumps are okay. Add the buttermilk or soured milk, egg, and vanilla; blend until very well mixed.

4. Set a dry stovetop griddle or nonstick skillet over moderately low heat. Preheat it until you can feel the heat coming off it when you hold your hand about 1 inch above the surface, usually about 2 minutes.

5. Meanwhile, add all of the dry ingredients to the wet ingredients and mix just until blended; the mixture will be lumpy. (If using a blender, whirl for 15 to 20 seconds, stir with a spatula to break up the "bubble" of dry ingredients that didn't mix in, and whirl again.) Add the oil and quickly incorporate into the batter.

6. Add a thin slice of butter—probably about ¼ teaspoon if you mushed it into a teaspoon—to the griddle or skillet and let it melt. Use a paper towel to spread it over the bottom and sides of the pan in a thin film. Toss a drop of water onto the hot surface: if it skittles around and evaporates, it's time to make the pancakes.

7. Increase the heat to moderate. Pour in pools of batter in the desired sizes and shapes and cook for 1½ to 2 minutes; you can't wait until the surface is covered with bubbles as you can with other pancakes—you'll have to lift one edge and peek underneath. When the underside is brown and utterly beautiful, flip the pancakes and cook the other side until it, too, is gorgeous and cooked through, 1 to 2 minutes more.

8. Transfer the pancakes to a warm plate, top with sliced bananas and maple syrup, and let someone start eating at once. (For our money, the idea of keeping pancakes warm in a low oven is bunk; they must be eaten as soon as they leave the griddle.) Add another thin sliver of butter to the pan, rub around with the paper towel, and continue making more pancakes, as before.

· ·

LEFT: *"The Super Plate Challenge": The World's Best, Most Healthful Banana Pancakes—Even Better than Ahmad's, served with lots of sliced bananas and a bit of maple syrup.*

GABRIELA SABATINI

◆ ◆ ◆ ◆ ◆ ◆ ◆ ◆ ◆ ◆ ◆

"PASTA IS ONE OF THE BEST THINGS EVER INVENTED."

She's arguably the prettiest professional woman tennis player out there, inarguably one of the sweetest, and unquestionably one of the best. And Argentina-born Gabriela Sabatini, at twenty-five, continues to display her prowess on clay and grass alike. "Gaby" started playing the game at age seven, trailing after her big brother Osvaldo, Jr., when he went to play tennis with friends at courts in Buenos Aires. (Sort of reminds you of a story from *A Chorus Line*, doesn't it?) Suffice it to say, little Gabriela showed promise, and by the time she was fourteen, she had advanced to the third round of the U.S. Open, cementing her ranking as the top Junior player in the world.

Just six years later, at age twenty, Ms. Sabatini permanently carved her name among the all-time best when she defeated Steffi Graf in the finals of the U.S. Open to become the 1990 Women's Champion. And she's still at it—winning the Virginia Slims Championship just last year.

Outside the game, Gaby has taken some bold steps. Introduced in 1989, her first perfume, "Gabriela Sabatini," became a best-seller in Europe. The second in the line, "Magnetic," followed with huge success. Most recently, a third scent, "Cascaya," was introduced, featuring a light, herbal bouquet with hints of grass and the slightest musky note. (Could it be a grass/clay combination?) Other accolades include *People* magazine's naming Gaby among its "Fifty Most Beautiful People" in 1992, and you could argue that, if anything, she's now looking better than ever.

Maintaining good health, good form, and good looks are top priorities for Gabriela. Tennis practice and workouts for strength and aerobic conditioning are a part of her daily routine, of course, and must fit into a travel schedule that would make a less healthy person crawl back into bed. She is very conscious of what and when she eats. By and large, Gaby doesn't drink alcohol, choosing instead to base her food and beverage intake on chicken and pasta main courses and plenty of liquids for hydration. "I avoid fried foods and red meats," she admits. "My ideal meal is very simple—I like to start with a big mixed salad lightly dressed with a basic vinaigrette, follow that with a main course of, say, spinach-stuffed ravioli in a simple tomato sauce, and then finish off with fresh fruits for dessert." What does Gaby drink with this meal? Well, as the first female athlete ever to endorse Pepsi, could it be anything else?

Here's a favorite pasta recipe that's sure to become one of your favorites.

PASTA WITH BROCCOLI

This dish is easy, quick, and addictive. You'll like its clean yet complex flavors enough to make it a regular weeknight meal.

For 4

1 can (2 ounces) flat anchovy fillets packed in olive oil

2 teaspoons extra-virgin olive oil

3 large garlic cloves, minced

¼ to ½ teaspoon dried red pepper flakes

1¾ cups degreased chicken stock or canned low-sodium chicken broth

4 ounces white mushrooms, washed, trimmed, and sliced

3 whole scallions, minced

1 pound store-bought dried linguine (if using fresh, adjust the timing)

1 large bunch broccoli, cut into florets

⅓ cup pine nuts, toasted in a dry skillet until lightly toasted (optional)

1. Bring a large pot of water to a boil over high heat.

2. Meanwhile, in a nonreactive large, deep sauté pan, combine the anchovies and their oil, the olive oil, garlic, and dried red pepper flakes over moderate heat. Cook, shaking the pan from time to time, until the anchovies melt and the garlic is golden, about 5 minutes.

3. Stir in the stock, mushrooms, and scallions and bring the mixture to a boil over moderately high heat. Adjust the heat to maintain a simmer and let the stock reduce while the pasta cooks.

4. Meanwhile, add the linguine to the boiling water and cook until just al dente, usually 9 to 10 minutes.

5. At the same time, rinse the broccoli florets and steam in the water that clings to them in a microwave oven on HIGH for 3 minutes, until just crisp-tender. Drain off the water and keep the broccoli covered until ready to use.

6. When the pasta is al dente, drain it and add to the reduced stock. Toss to coat. Add the broccoli and toss to moisten. Divide the pasta and sauce among 4 shallow bowls. Sprinkle some of the pine nuts over each portion.

Pasta with Broccoli—a great quick dish that is ready to serve in the time it takes to cook the pasta.

KEITH HERNANDEZ

◆ ◆ ◆ ◆ ◆ ◆ ◆ ◆ ◆ ◆ ◆

"HEY, WHEN YOU RUN, YOU CAN EAT.
THE KEY IS WORKING OUT—YOU DO ENOUGH OF THAT AND
YOU CAN EAT *ANYTHING*."

How many little kids will tell you, "When I grow up, I want to be a baseball player?" Lots and lots, thousands probably. However, relatively few make it into the "big time." But just ask Keith Hernandez when he knew his future, and he'll tell you, "When I was seven. I come from a baseball family. My dad played minor league ball and my brothers played ball—we were all into the game in a big way." So, when he was signed by the St. Louis Cardinals in 1971, Keith Hernandez had, indeed, arrived—at the start of a major league career.

In his eight and a half years with the Cardinals, 1979 was a standout year. Hernandez made his mark as National League Batting Champion (.344) and National League Co–Most Valuable Player (shared with Willie Stargell), and he won the first of his eleven consecutive Gold Glove Awards, presented for excellence in the player's position. Three years later the Cards won the 1982 World Series in a seven-game, fight-to-the-finish string against the Milwaukee Brewers.

In June of 1983 Hernandez was traded to the New York Mets and moved to Manhattan the next year. As one of the 1986 Mets team, he again was part of the World Championship when the Mets beat the Boston Red Sox in seven nerve-shattering games. He retired from the Mets in 1991.

He and his significant other, Lisa Arning, spend consider-

THE MENU
◆ ◆ ◆ ◆ ◆ ◆ ◆

for 4 to 6

ROAST CHICKEN WITH LEMON, GARLIC, AND
FRESH HERBS

STEAMED VEGETABLES WITH NO-FAT SAUCE

NO-BAKE CHOCOLATE CHEESECAKE

The gentleman farmer tending his herbs high above Midtown Manhattan.

able time staying fit. "She's an avid runner—a marathon runner—and we run for thirty to sixty minutes, five days a week. In addition, I work out with weights and do cardiovascular work on my Lifecycle at home," he says. He also tends his terrace garden. "It's mostly herbs—lots and lots of basil, rosemary, thyme, sage." Though Keith and Lisa eat in restaurants fairly frequently, he says, "I do most of the cooking, and I try to stay aware of fats. I also try to focus on healthier foods—I pull the skin off chicken, and I eat sushi and lots of vegetables, but I do indulge, sometimes, in desserts. I like chocolate. But, hey, when you run, you can eat. The key is working out—you do enough of that and you can eat *anything*."

When he's not making hilarious cameo appearances on "Seinfeld," or "hanging out" with buddies from the sports world, Hernandez ardently pursues additions to his burgeoning wine collection. He has two temperature-controlled *caves* (wine storage units) in his apartment and a larger storage space in New Jersey. "I got into wine several years ago and started buying, reading, tasting, and just generally learning all I could about it. When Rusty Staub and I get together, it's always a main topic of conversation. And you know what the latest studies say, a glass of good red wine can contribute to good health. I'm all for it."

ROAST CHICKEN WITH LEMON, GARLIC, AND FRESH HERBS

Here are great, old-fashioned roast chickens that are guaranteed to fill your house with their tempting fragrance throughout their roasting time. Though the recipe calls for two small, tender "broiler-fryers," you can substitute one larger "roaster" if you like—the lemon, garlic, and herbs merely come on stronger in the smaller-size birds.

For 4 to 6

2 chickens (each 3 to 3½ pounds), rinsed and patted dry
Salt and freshly milled pepper
2 lemons, washed, dried, and halved
2 heads of garlic, separated into cloves, cloves peeled
1 to 1½ cups loosely packed fresh herb leaves, such as basil, rosemary, and/or sage

1. Preheat the oven to 375°F.

2. Pull off and discard any loose bits of fat from the chickens. Sprinkle the cavities with just a bit of salt and pepper. Place a lemon half in the cavity of each chicken, along with half of the garlic and half of the herbs. Finally, add a remaining lemon half to each. Truss the chickens with kitchen twine, if desired. Place the chickens on a rack in one large roasting pan or two smaller pans.

3. Roast the birds for 1 to 1½ hours, or until the internal temperature registers 190°F on an instant-reading thermometer; the chickens should be golden brown, the thigh juices should run clear, and a leg should move easily in its socket.

4. Remove the chickens and tent with foil to keep warm. Let rest for about 10 minutes.

5. Untruss the birds if necessary, and remove the garlic cloves, if desired (see NOTE). Cut the chickens into serving pieces and serve at once.

NOTE: These lemony roasted garlic cloves offer all sorts of possibilities: Mash them with a fork and spread them over hot bread—no butter necessary; sprinkle them whole over the vegetables, or save them for the next day and use in place of mayonnaise on leftover chicken sandwiches.

ABOVE: *Keith Hernandez describes his last triple to Robin Leach, Kate Connelly, and Emeril Lagasse on the set of "Talking Food" at TVFN.*

LEFT: *Roast Chicken with Lemon, Garlic, and Fresh Herbs surrounded by Steamed Vegetables with Special Sauce.*

STEAMED VEGETABLES WITH NO-FAT SAUCE

Don't say, "Ho-hum, more steamed vegetables" about this recipe. It takes the best fresh vegetables you can find—go with whatever looks tastiest—and sparks them up just beautifully.

For 4 to 6

SAUCE:

2 cups degreased chicken stock or broth
½ cup dry white wine or dry vermouth
1½ tablespoons balsamic vinegar
Large pinch of sugar
Salt and freshly milled pepper

VEGETABLES:

3 celery ribs, cut into 1-inch lengths
1 red bell pepper, cut lengthwise into strips
1 yellow bell pepper, cut lengthwise into strips
1 large portobello or shiitake mushroom, trimmed and sliced
12 ounces white mushrooms, sliced or quartered
12 pearl onions, peeled, or 2 sweet onions, such as Vidalias or Mauis, cut into wedges
3 small yellow squash or zucchinis, trimmed and cut into ½-inch-thick rounds
Fresh herbs, such as rosemary, for serving (optional, but tasty)

1. Make the sauce: Combine the stock, wine, 1 tablespoon of the vinegar, and the sugar in a nonreactive saucepan. Bring to a boil over high heat. Reduce the heat slightly but continue to boil until the mixture reduces to ⅔ cup, 18 to 20 minutes.

2. Remove from the heat and stir in the remaining ½ tablespoon vinegar. Taste and add salt and pepper, if needed. (The sauce can be prepared ahead of time and reheated just before serving.)

3. Combine all of the vegetables and steam until they are just crisp-tender, about 5 minutes.

4. Remove the vegetables to a large bowl and pour the sauce over them. Toss to coat well, and serve at once. Garnish with the herb sprigs or leaves, if desired.

ABOVE: *The former New York Met relaxes in his New York City apartment.*

RIGHT: *The plaque Keith received to commemorate his National League MVP award in 1979. (Willie Stargell was the co-recipient that year.)*

No-Bake Chocolate Cheesecake.

NO-BAKE CHOCOLATE CHEESECAKE

You'll need the oven just to set the crust of this tasty cheese-cake. After that, it's all up to you and your refrigerator.

For 12

CRUST:

1½ cups chocolate wafer crumbs

2 to 3 tablespoons sugar

4 tablespoons (½ stick) unsalted butter, melted

FILLING:

½ cup milk

4 teaspoons (1⅓ envelopes) unflavored gelatin

8 ounces semisweet chocolate, finely chopped

½ teaspoon grated orange or tangerine zest

1½ pounds regular or low-fat cream cheese, at room temperature

1 cup regular or low-fat sour cream or low-fat plain yogurt

⅔ cup sugar

1½ teaspoons vanilla extract

Fresh fruit and mint sprigs, for garnish (optional)

1. Preheat the oven to 350°F. Butter the bottom and sides of a 9- to 10-inch springform pan.

2. Make the crust: Combine all of the crust ingredients in a bowl and toss with a fork to moisten the crumbs with the butter. Press the crumbs over the bottom and up the sides of the springform pan. Bake in the middle of the oven for 10 minutes. Transfer the pan to a rack to cool; turn off the oven.

LEFT: *Keith is "Talking Food" with Robin Leach.*

RIGHT: *Symbols of just a part of Keith Hernandez's baseball career amid the books of his library.*

3. Make the filling: Pour the milk into a small saucepan. Sprinkle on the gelatin; set aside to soften for 5 minutes.

4. Place the pan over moderately low heat and cook, stirring, until the gelatin completely dissolves, 2 to 3 minutes. Add the chocolate and stir just until melted and smooth. Stir in the orange zest. Set aside to cool to room temperature.

5. Using an electric mixer or a large food processor, beat together the cream cheese, sour cream, sugar, and vanilla until smooth. Add the cooled chocolate mixture and beat until the filling is uniform. Spoon the filling into the crust and smooth the top. Cover the top of the pan with plastic wrap, refrigerate for at least 4 hours or overnight.

6. Remove the sides of the pan. Garnish the cheesecake with fresh fruit and mint sprigs, if desired.

CLOCKWISE FROM TOP LEFT: *Giants Stadium at rest—before the fans arrive and the game begins.*

LEFT: *The serious business of football—a practice session the day before a crucial game.*

THE NEW YORK GIANTS

· · · · · · · · · · · ·

"MY MAIN CONCERN IS NUTRITION—AND HOW IT AFFECTS PERFORMANCE."
—HEIDI SKOLNIK, SPORTS NUTRITIONIST TO
THE NEW YORK GIANTS FOOTBALL TEAM

"These guys are big, they eat a lot, are you sure you want to feed a hundred people?" asked Pat Hanlon, public relations director for the New York Giants. He was sounding a bit panicky that his guys would go hungry. "Are you sure you can manage this? You see, these fifty-eight giant guys will come off the practice field and they will be—I guarantee you—*hungry*. Some of these guys are 6´4´´ and weigh three hundred pounds—they have big appetites, they eat a lot. Last week we had sixty orders of barbecued ribs and sixty of chicken and it wasn't enough—we still ran out of food. We can't run out of food." Well, we promised, we won't run out of food, and we'll go a step further: We'll do a Giants lunch that'll be healthful and nutritious and delicious.

That's where team nutritionist Heidi Skolnik entered the fray. After considerable time in the huddle, we came up with a healthful but flavorful lunch menu that she thought would appeal to the players, coaches, and staff: lots of complex carbohydrates (rice, black beans, and potatoes), some familiar regional American dishes (fajitas, gumbo), a moderate amount of protein (chicken, smoked turkey sausage, and seafood), bountiful vegetables (potatoes, cabbage, onions, tomatoes, okra), and whole wheat carrot cake made with canola oil (no butter at all) for dessert.

Ms. Skolnik works with Head Trainer Ronnie Barnes and

> **THE MENU:**
>
> · · · · · · ·
>
> JUMBO (ELLIOTT) GUMBO WITH TEXMATI RICE
>
> CHICKEN FAJITAS (SEE PAGE 78) WITH REFRIED BLACK BEANS AND GRILLED ONIONS AND BELL PEPPERS
>
> MEXICAN POTATO SALAD
>
> CAJUN COLESLAW
>
> WHOLE WHEAT CARROT CAKE
>
> GIANT CUTOUT SUGAR COOKIES

Strength and Conditioning Coach Al Miller to see that each Giant realizes his maximum potential. Together, their concern encompasses virtually every aspect of the players' lives. They know who is in super-fine form and work as a team to determine how and why so they have a better idea of what works for each individual. They know the requirements of each position's physical needs and work to optimize performance, strength, and overall well-being.

"You know, these guys aren't 'big, dumb jocks' like some people think. They're smart, they're well educated, and this is their work; they're *professional* football players. It's part of their job to work out, enhance their health and stamina, eat a reasonable diet, and build a winning frame of mind, and they take it *very* seriously. And whether it's a strained muscle, a food allergy, or their body fat composition, they're very eager to ask for guidance that will help them become stronger and more capable athletes. People seem to think that nutritionists spend all of their time laboring over diets for weight loss. That's really inaccurate; we *can* do that, but I'm much more challenged when I'm trying to make someone stronger and better fit for his sport. There's a big bonus, too; every one of the Giants is a nice guy. They want to learn more, and they want advice. We have a good relationship; they don't hesitate to ask for help."

LEFT: *Keeping trade secrets under wraps at a Giants workout.*

BELOW: *Coach Dan Reeves in the team lunchroom after a satisfying practice session.*

Team nutritionist Heidi Skolnik has a master's degree in exercise physiology as well. Here, she listens to Coleman Rudolph and considers the best route to enhancing his performance.

JUMBO (ELLIOTT) GUMBO

You can vary this gumbo to serve your needs. Some will want to make it with shrimp only, others might want chicken gumbo, and still others might want to forgo all of the seafood and meat to make a completely vegetarian version.

For 12

⅓ cup plus 3 tablespoons vegetable oil

6 garlic cloves, minced

3 large Spanish onions, chopped

3 large green bell peppers, cored, seeded, and chopped

⅓ cup unbleached all-purpose flour

4 to 5 cups chicken or vegetable stock or broth, heated

2 packages (each 10 ounces) frozen sliced okra

2 bay leaves

3 tablespoons filé powder (ground sassafras leaves, sometimes called gumbo filé)

1 tablespoon cayenne pepper

1 tablespoon salt

1 tablespoon freshly milled pepper

1 pound andouille or low-fat smoked turkey kielbasa sausage, cut into bite-size pieces

2 pounds peeled baby shrimp (they won't require deveining)

8 ounces blue crab claws (cocktail size)

2 cups shredded cooked chicken

6 cups cooked Texmati rice, for serving

1 bunch whole scallions, trimmed and thinly sliced, for garnish

1. Pour 3 tablespoons of the oil into a nonreactive large stockpot or soup pot set over moderately high heat. Add the garlic and sauté until lightly browned, 3 to 5 minutes. Add the onions and bell peppers and sauté until softened and lightly browned at the edges, about 5 minutes. Leaving as much of the oil in the pan as possible, scoop out the garlic and vegetables and set aside.

2. Pour the remaining ⅓ cup oil into the pan. Sprinkle on the flour and cook, stirring constantly, until the mixture turns into a golden brown roux, 4 to 7 minutes.

3. Pour in the 3 cups of the stock and stir until the roux dissolves into it. Stir in the reserved garlic-onion-pepper mixture, the okra, bay leaves, filé powder, cayenne, salt, and pepper, and bring the mixture to a boil. Stir in the sausage; add the remaining 1 cup stock if the mixture seems dry. Reduce the heat to moderately low, cover, and simmer until the sausage is cooked through, 15 to 25 minutes, depending on whether the sausage is precooked or raw.

4. Stir the shrimp, crab, and chicken into the gumbo. Cook until the shrimp and crab are opaque and the chicken is heated through, about 5 minutes. Remove and discard the bay leaves. Serve the gumbo at once, over a scoop of hot rice. Scatter some of the scallions over each serving.

MEXICAN POTATO SALAD
For 12

4 pounds new red potatoes (such as Red Bliss), scrubbed
⅓ cup yellow mustard
⅓ cup cider vinegar
⅓ cup canola oil
1 tablespoon ground cumin
1½ teaspoons chili powder
1 teaspoon sugar
Salt and freshly milled pepper
4 hard-cooked eggs, peeled and sliced or chopped
4 whole scallions, trimmed and thinly sliced
½ cup minced cilantro leaves

1. Place the potatoes in a large pot and add cold water to cover by 2 inches. Bring to a boil over high heat. Reduce the heat to moderate and cook the potatoes until fork-tender, 15 to 20 minutes.

2. Meanwhile, in a large mixing bowl, whisk together the mustard, vinegar, oil, cumin, chili powder, and sugar. Taste the dressing and add salt and pepper as needed.

3. When the potatoes are tender, drain well. As soon as they are cool enough to handle, cut them into bite-size chunks, and drop them into the dressing as they are cut. Sprinkle the eggs and scallions on top. Gently fold the potatoes, eggs, and scallions into the dressing, taking care to coat well.

4. If not serving immediately, cover and set aside to cool to room temperature, or cover and chill, if desired. Just before serving, sprinkle the cilantro on top and fold in. This potato salad is delicious at any temperature.

······································

CAJUN COLESLAW
For 12

½ cup reduced-calorie mayonnaise
¾ cup no-fat plain yogurt
¼ cup Dijon or spicy brown mustard
¼ cup white wine vinegar
1 tablespoon sugar
1 tablespoon milk
3 tablespoons celery seeds
1½ teaspoons dried red pepper flakes
1 teaspoon cayenne pepper
1 teaspoon hot sauce
Salt and freshly milled pepper
2 large heads green cabbage (or 1 head each green and red), cored and shredded
4 carrots, cleaned and shredded
1 green bell pepper, cored, seeded, and finely diced
1 large onion, grated or finely chopped

1. In a large mixing bowl, combine the mayonnaise, yogurt, mustard, vinegar, sugar, milk, celery seeds, red pepper flakes, cayenne, and hot sauce. Mix together until well blended; taste and add salt and pepper as necessary.

2. Add the cabbage, carrots, bell pepper, and onion. Fold the vegetables into the dressing until coated completely. Cover and chill until serving time.

·······································

The Giants Kickers with their cookies: #2 Mike Horan, #18 Dave Treadwell, and #3 Brad Daluiso.

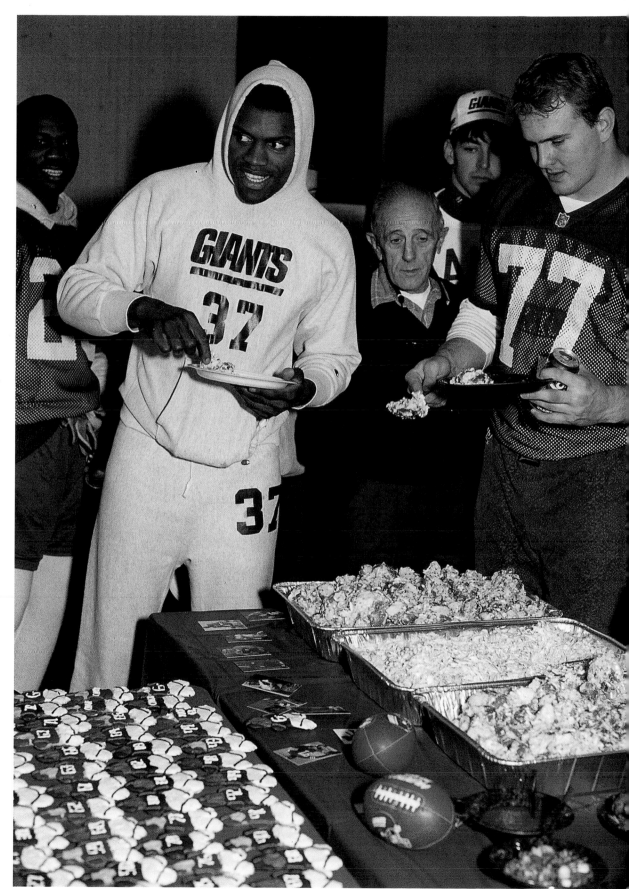

When they said that the Giants really eat, *we took them seriously: 25 gallons of gumbo, 15 pounds of rice, 40 pounds of chicken fajitas, 480 fresh-made flour tortillas, 30 pounds of black beans, 30 pounds of potato salad, 30 pounds of coleslaw, 12 huge carrot cakes, and 100 Giants cookies. Here, #37 defensive back Jesse Campbell and #77 defensive lineman Chad Bratzke take their first turns in line.*

WHOLE WHEAT CARROT CAKE
For 12

2 cups whole wheat flour
2 teaspoons ground cinnamon
1½ teaspoons baking soda
1½ teaspoons baking powder
1 teaspoon salt
½ teaspoon grated nutmeg
½ teaspoon ground allspice
1 cup canola oil
1 cup sugar
4 large eggs, beaten
¾ cup crushed pineapple, with juice (⅔ cup solids plus juice to measure ¾ cup)
2½ cups grated carrots
½ cup chopped walnuts
½ cup golden raisins
Cream Cheese Frosting (recipe follows)

1. Preheat the oven to 325°F. Lightly spray or oil a 13-×-9-inch baking dish.

2. On a sheet of waxed paper, mix together the flour, cinnamon, baking soda, baking powder, salt, nutmeg, and allspice. Set aside.

3. In a mixing bowl, stir together the oil and sugar. Add the beaten eggs and blend well. Stir in the pineapple and juice and the carrots. Gradually add the dry ingredients and mix until combined. Fold in the walnuts and raisins.

4. Pour the batter into the prepared pan and smooth the top. Bake until a toothpick inserted in the center comes out moist but clean, 40 to 45 minutes.

5. Cool the cake in the pan on a wire rack. Frost the cake after it has cooled completely.

CREAM CHEESE FROSTING

This frosting isn't all that sweet—it's more of a tangy, creamy icing that seals the top to keep the carrot cake moist.

8 ounces low-fat cream cheese, at room temperature
1 tablespoon fresh lemon juice
1 teaspoon grated lemon zest
1½ cups confectioners' sugar, sifted

1. In a mixing bowl, beat the cream cheese with the lemon juice and lemon zest until fluffy and light. Gradually add the sugar and beat until creamy and smooth.

2. Spread the frosting over the cooled cake. Cover and chill before serving.

GIANT CUTOUT SUGAR COOKIES
Makes about 4 dozen

8 ounces (2 sticks) unsalted butter, at room temperature
2 cups sugar
2 large eggs
¼ cup sour cream
1½ tablespoons vanilla extract
4 cups unbleached all-purpose flour
2 teaspoons baking powder
1 teaspoon salt
2 ounces (2 squares) semisweet baking chocolate, melted and cooled (optional, for chocolate cookies)

1. In a mixing bowl, use an electric mixer to cream the butter with the sugar until fluffy. Add the eggs, sour cream, and vanilla and beat until light.

2. Meanwhile, stir together the flour, baking powder, and salt. Gradually add the dry ingredients to the butter mixture and beat until the dough is uniform. If making chocolate cookies, beat in the chocolate.

3. Gather the dough into a ball, divide into thirds, and pat each piece into a large disk. Wrap each piece of dough in plastic wrap; refrigerate until chilled, at least 30 minutes.

4. Preheat the oven to 350°F. Have ready 2 nonstick baking sheets, or line 2 baking sheets with baking parchment.

5. Working with 1 piece of the dough at a time, place the dough between 2 sheets of plastic wrap and roll out ¼ inch thick. Cut into shapes with decorative cutters. Transfer the cutouts to the baking sheets, placing them about 1 inch apart. Bake the cookies until just lightly browned around the edges, 8 to 12 minutes, depending on the size of the cutouts (the football players took 10 minutes).

6. Let the cookies set for 1 minute on the baking sheets. Carefully lift the cookies with a spatula and transfer them to wire racks to cool to room temperature. Do not decorate until the cookies are completely cool.

Royal Icing

This sturdy, ornamental icing is ideal for decorations that you want to hold up through thick and thin. Once dried, it's incredibly durable—you can stack the cookies, one atop the other, between layers of waxed paper, without any harm coming to them. If you spread it over a cake, it forms a hard icing that keeps the interior very moist.

Use food colorings to tint the icing; the paste type is best if you want deep, strong colors. And remember to keep the icing covered when you aren't working with it; place plastic wrap directly on the surface to prevent the icing from drying out.

Makes about 3½ cups

3 large egg whites
¼ teaspoon cream of tartar
1 box (1 pound) confectioners' sugar, sifted
Food coloring (optional)

1. In a deep mixing bowl, beat the egg whites and cream of tartar until frothy. Gradually add the sugar, beating until well combined. Continue beating until the mixture is very shiny and stands in stiff peaks when the beaters are lifted.

2. Divide the icing among several smaller bowls—one for each color you plan to use. Stir the food coloring and add to each batch, stirring and adding more until the ideal color is achieved. Spread or pipe the icing over the cooled cookies. Let the icing set completely before stacking.

••

ABOVE: *The whole team in full regalia.*

LEFT: *Linebacker Corey Miller (#57) and safety Jarvis Williams (#26) biting their heads off.*

THE NEW YORK KNICKERBOCKERS

◆ ◆ ◆ ◆ ◆ ◆ ◆ ◆ ◆ ◆ ◆

"WE LIKE TO THINK OF FOOD AS THE 'FUEL SUPPLY,' SO WE STRESS FILLING UP
WITH THE BEST POSSIBLE, HIGH-ENERGY, LOW-FAT SOURCES AVAILABLE."
—GREG BRITTENHAM, THE KNICKS' STRENGTH AND CONDITIONING COACH

Part of the experience of going to a New York Knicks game lies in the crush of heavy-duty fans that mob the awesome Madison Square Garden. You'll see it all—incredibly tall teenagers who look as though they're visiting a shrine; impeccably groomed, Levi-ed and loafer-ed executive types carefully instructing their limo drivers on where to pick them up; moms and dads with kids clad in blue and orange in tow; duos and trios of every stripe and style; determined-looking loners who tote briefcases or personal computers; gangs of towering men who, no doubt, once played the game themselves; and a goodly number of female fans who clearly know just what they're doing and just where they're going. This is a serious group—almost every one of them can spout arcane sports statistics, and virtually every one of them is a tough critic.

New Coach Don Nelson demands the best performance from each of the knavish Knicks. He's been there—as an NBA player and then as a coach, first for Milwaukee and then for Golden State before joining the Knicks—so he's completely aware of what it takes to play good professional basketball. And anyone will tell you, he doesn't suffer fools gladly; indeed, he seems to have no compunction about showing his determined, get-out-there-and-win, passionate side. The best thing is you just never know what's going to

---

THE RECIPES:

◆ ◆ ◆ ◆ ◆ ◆ ◆

COACH KNISHES

GRILLED KNOCKWURST

KNICKERDOODLES

The Knicks' center of attention, Patrick Ewing, demonstrates his commitment to the game of basketball.

---

happen at a Knicks game.

It makes sense that New York's "Hometown Team," the Knicks, have a knack for attracting celebrity fans. Like the Los Angeles Lakers, they just happen to be based where celebrities live or spend a good deal of their time. And celebs, just like the rest of us, can't resist wanting to see real pros make a tough game look so easy. You have to admit: Madison Square Garden is prime celebrity-watcher territory. And, in addition to watching whoever's watching the game, there's watching the game itself. There's always the chance that Patrick Ewing will break another record or outdo himself some other way, somehow; that The Mighty Oak, Charles Oakley, will hurl his 6′9″, 250-pound body into the crowd in pursuit of a loose ball, or that the amazing John Starks will run a streak of six consecutive three-pointers. Then, too, maybe a hard-defense player—Derek Harper, Hubert Davis, or Anthony Mason will steal the ball or sprint the floor. You never can tell.

Everybody seems to go to Knicks games—models Cindy Crawford and Vendela; actors Mandy Patinkin, Danny Aiello, and the Baldwin brothers; director/screenwriters Spike Lee, Woody Allen (with Soon-Yi Previn), and William Goldman; Connie Chung and Maury Povich. Madonna, Tom Brokaw, John McEnroe, Lou Gossett, Michael Douglas, and Bill Murray often can be seen court-

Guard John Starks, a native of Tulsa, Oklahoma, makes a power move in a game against the Pacers.

side, as can Knicks alumni Senator Bill Bradley, Dave De-Busschere, and Walt Frazier. Even Robin Leach is a loyal fan: "Basketball is the only American sport that I understand. I love this game."

Greg Brittenham, the Knicks' strength and conditioning coach, has a big job. "We're trying to build the total athlete," he explained, "so we emphasize athletic characteristics, such as speed, agility, coordination, power, strength, and cardiovascular conditioning. And of course, nutrition is part of that whole. We like to think of food as the 'fuel supply,' so we stress filling up with the best possible, high-energy, low-fat sources available. We urge the players to choose fresh natural ingredients, stressing complex carbohydrate from pasta, whole grains, vegetables, and fruits. We recommend low-cholesterol proteins from meat alternatives, such as beans, nuts, seeds, and legumes. Generally speaking, we emphasize low-fat choices—baked rather than fried, lean meats rather than marbled, low-fat dairy products like skim milk and yogurt. We try to stay away from processed foods, sugars, and white flour."

Knicks' practice sessions are scheduled for every non-game day, and even when they travel, the team often leaves for the airport en masse *after* practice is completed. On average, this baker's dozen of players has only four or five days off each month. And to sustain that kind of intense output, Brittenham has devised a before-the-game and after-the-game eating regimen. "Pregame and prepractice, we like to emphasize lots of complex carbohydrate and keep protein and fat intake low. Carbohydrate will help the players sustain energy during the forty-eight minutes of the game. Postgame and postpractice, we still consume carbohydrate, but I also recommend some extra protein to help rebuild, recharge, and repair the muscle tissue that has been subjected to the rigors of the workout. These guys are burning so many calories during the game, and because of that, we need to keep their caloric intake in the right proportions for optimal energy. That's my definition of a successful diet."

Brittenham "guesstimates" that each Knick consumes a whopping 5,500 to 6,200 calories a day—two to three times what an average adult male needs. (Makes you want to play pro basketball, doesn't it?) But the Knicks aren't average. Brittenham is quick to point out that "Fifty-five hundred calories is a lot of food. To maintain that type of intake, a like number of calories need to be 'burned' *daily*. Ideally, each player's caloric intake will be in balance with his caloric expenditure." Of course, the calories "burned" will vary from player to player, depending on each man's playing time, position, and metabolism. "You'd be surprised," Brittenham adds, "these guys' weights don't vary; they burn what they eat. We monitor their weight and body composition—that is, the percentage of fat—on a regular basis, and they're remarkably consistent week-in, week-out. And though I like them to eat the right foods from the right sources, I don't deny them anything: If they want a cheeseburger, they can have a cheeseburger. They're completely aware that there are better choices for them, and more often than not, they 'do the right thing.' But I don't like to deprive them of an occasional treat. Everything in moderation—I bet you've heard *that* before." You bet we have—from everyone, amateur to expert, who knows what people need to lead a healthful and healthy lifestyle.

COACH KNISHES

Although knishes can have any number of fillings, this is a version of the classic onion-and-potato knish, a knockoff of what's sold at Knicks games at Madison Square Garden.

For 6 to 10

DOUGH:

3 cups unbleached all-purpose flour
1½ teaspoons baking powder
½ teaspoon salt
3 tablespoons melted chicken fat (if you want to be authentic) or canola oil
¼ to ⅓ cup chicken stock or broth
3 large eggs

FILLING:

¼ cup melted chicken fat, or 4 tablespoons (½ stick) unsalted butter
3 to 4 large sweet onions, thinly sliced
Pinch of sugar
3 cups well-seasoned mashed potatoes (leftovers are fine)

1 egg white, beaten with 2 tablespoons cold water, for egg white wash (optional)

1. Make the dough: Combine the flour, baking powder, and salt in a food processor. Pulse to blend the ingredients. Add the fat, ¼ cup of the stock, and the eggs. Process and pulse until the dough forms a ball around the blade. Remove from the processor and knead by hand until the mixture holds together; if necessary, sprinkle on a little additional stock. Divide the dough into 3 equal parts. Pat each into a wide disk; wrap individually in plastic wrap and refrigerate until needed.

2. Make the filling: Pour the melted fat (or melt the butter) in a large sauté pan set over moderate heat. When the fat is hot, add the onions and sauté, tossing, until the onions are limp, about 5 minutes.

3. Sprinkle the sugar over the onions, reduce the heat to moderately low, and cook the onions, stirring from time to time, until they caramelize to golden brown, 20 to 25 minutes. If the onions seem dry, add a bit of water or stock to keep them from sticking; the onions will reduce greatly in volume. Add the mashed potatoes to the caramelized onions and loosely combine. Remove the mixture from the heat.

4. Preheat the oven to 350°F. Line 2 baking sheets with foil or baking parchment.

5. Using 1 piece of the dough at a time and working on a lightly floured surface, roll out the dough into a rough 10-x-5-inch rectangle. Spread one-third of the onion-potato mixture over the dough, leaving a 1-inch border all around. Roll up, jelly-roll-style, and pinch the seam to seal it. Transfer the roll to one of the baking sheets. Roll out, fill, and roll up the remaining knishes. Brush the tops of the rolls with the egg white wash, if desired.

6. Bake the rolls until the dough is golden brown, 30 to 35 minutes. Remove from the pans to a rack. Cut into slices to serve.

GRILLED KNICKS KNOCKWURST

These are knockwurst served with a homemade version of New York's own orange-colored onions.

For 4

2 tablespoons canola oil
2 large onions, thinly sliced
3 tablespoons chili sauce or ketchup
2 teaspoons yellow mustard
1 tablespoon firmly packed brown sugar
2 tablespoons fresh orange juice
¼ to ½ teaspoon cayenne pepper
½ teaspoon salt
4 kosher knockwurst, grilled until the casings split
4 hot dog buns

1. Heat the oil in a nonreactive saucepan over moderately high heat. Add the onions and sauté until translucent, about 5 minutes.

2. Stir in the chili sauce, mustard, sugar, orange juice, cayenne, and salt. Mix very well and cook until the onions are completely limp.

3. Place a knockwurst in a bun and spoon a large quantity—enough to be messy—of the onion mixture on top. Dig in.

KNICKERDOODLES

These soft, chewy cookies make excellent snacks whether you're an ardent Knicks fan or not. Take some to a Knicks game or make a batch to eat while watching the game on television.

Makes 4 to 5 dozen

2½ cups unbleached all-purpose flour

2 teaspoons cream of tartar

1 teaspoon baking soda

¼ teaspoon salt

12 tablespoons (1½ sticks) unsalted butter, at room temperature

1 cup sugar

2 eggs

1½ teaspoons vanilla extract

¼ cup sugar mixed with 1 tablespoon ground cinnamon, for rolling the cookies

1. Preheat the oven to 375°F.

2. Stir together the flour, cream of tartar, baking soda, and salt on a sheet of waxed paper. In a mixing bowl, beat the butter with the sugar until mixed well. Add the eggs and vanilla and beat until worked into the dough. Gradually add the dry ingredients and beat until the dough is uniform.

3. Place the sugar and cinnamon mixture on a plate or in a shallow bowl. Roll the dough into 1-inch balls. Roll each ball in the cinnamon sugar until coated all over. Arrange the balls on ungreased baking sheets, spacing them about 2 inches apart.

4. Bake the Knickerdoodles for 8 to 10 minutes, until spread out and crinkly on top but still soft. Transfer to wire racks to cool. These will go quickly, especially when they're still warm; if you have any left over, store in an airtight container.

RUSTY STAUB

◆ ◆ ◆ ◆ ◆ ◆ ◆ ◆ ◆ ◆ ◆

"WHEN YOU GROW UP IN NEW ORLEANS,
GOOD FOOD IS A BIG PART OF YOUR LIFE—IT'S SORT OF BRED INTO YOU."

How did a New Orleans native named Daniel Joseph Staub come to be called Rusty? Just one look gives the answer; Rusty Staub is a redhead. This same distinctive feature has played a role throughout his twenty-three-year career as a professional baseball player and ever since. He is known to all by his nickname, The Big Orange. He became the only player in the history of major league baseball to have had five hundred hits with four different teams (the Houston Astros, Montreal Expos, Detroit Tigers, and New York Mets), Staub has been a successful restaurateur since 1977. "When you grow up in New Orleans," he says, "good food is a big part of your life—it's sort of bred into you."

In the early days of his baseball career, Staub played off-season in the "instructional league," a group of promising players who were organized to play for a few extra months over the wintertime to increase their skills. The pay was poor—"about $160 a month," says Staub—so it was vital that Staub and his roommates cook meals for themselves; there simply wasn't money for eating in restaurants. That's when The Big Orange struck a deal: "I grew up eating well—my mom was a terrific cook and my dad was great at the barbe-

Rusty Staub, Le Grand Orange, sniffing the bouquet of his Le Grand Orange Cabernet Sauvignon in his Manhattan restaurant.

cue pit. And since my dad was a schoolteacher, he almost always had some extra work, often in the meat business. I'd learned from both of them and decided I could learn to cook too. The deal was, I'd cook if the other guys would do all the cleaning and washing up. It was sweet."

If food has played a major role in Staub's life, so has wine. "It's simply the best accompaniment to food—there's no question about it," he pronounces. His current restaurant, Rusty Staub's on 5th, located in Midtown Manhattan, won *Wine Spectator* magazine's Award of Excellence for three consecutive years. A member of many prestigious wine and food societies, Rusty has his own line of wines (Rusty Staub's Le Grand Orange Chardonnay and Cabernet).

Staub is also an active fundraiser for charitable organizations, helping to raise more than $10 million for a number of local and national causes. How does he find the time? "It's not easy," he admits. "Baseball will always take precedence in my life. Sure, it has enabled me to do all these other things, but my job broadcasting Mets games on the SportsChannel is my first priority. Time is precious, but I can tell you one thing for sure, there's never enough time in life to drink bad wine."

ROASTED RED SNAPPER FILLETS WITH MUSHROOMS AND HERBS

For 2

2 teaspoons balsamic vinegar
2 red snapper fillets (each 6 ounces)
8 tablespoons (1 stick) unsalted butter
6 garlic cloves, minced
2 tablespoons chopped basil leaves
1 teaspoon chopped thyme leaves
8 ounces button mushrooms, washed and thinly sliced
1 teaspoon Worcestershire sauce
½ teaspoon Tabasco sauce
Salt and freshly milled black pepper
Fresh herbs and mixed lettuces, for garnish

1. Preheat the oven to 400°F. Lightly spray or oil a baking dish or use a nonstick dish or pan.

2. Rub 1 teaspoon of the vinegar on each fish fillet; arrange the fillets in the pan. Cut 4 tablespoons of the butter into small bits; scatter the bits over the fillets. Bake the fish until the flesh just flakes when tested with the tines of a fork, about 8 minutes.

3. Meanwhile, melt the remaining 4 tablespoons butter in a large sauté pan over moderately high heat. Add the garlic and sauté until translucent, 2 to 3 minutes. Stir in the basil and thyme. Add the mushrooms and sauté until soft and limp, about 4 minutes. Season the mushrooms and sauce with salt and pepper to taste.

4. Push the mushrooms to the sides of the pan, and transfer the fish fillets to the sauté pan. Spoon the mushrooms and sauce over the top and cook for 2 to 3 minutes to blend the flavors. Divide the fish, mushrooms, and sauce between 2 warmed dinner plates and garnish with fresh herbs and lettuces. Serve at once, with Rusty Staub's Le Grand Orange 1992 Chardonnay or his Le Grand Orange 1991 Cabernet Sauvignon.

Rusty Staub's cooking expertise is evident in his luscious-looking Roasted Red Snapper Fillets with Mushrooms and Herbs. Keeping fit and maintaining good health isn't easy, but as a professional athlete he knows his priorities: "I run most days, and work out in the gym about three days a week," he says, adding, "plus the occasional game of golf."

NOTHING SUCCEEDS
LIKE SUCCESS

IVANA TRUMP

* * * * * * * * * * * *

"THIS IS EXACTLY WHAT I LOVE TO EAT—LOTS OF VEGGIES AND
A BIT OF FISH OR CHICKEN. YOU HAVE TO, YOU KNOW?
YOU HAVE TO STAY AWAY FROM FATS."

It was going to be a very big, very important night. Ivana Trump, world-famous socialite, novelist, business-woman, and humanitarian, was one of the co-chairs for Cooks for Kids II, a benefit in aid of the nonprofit, all-volunteer Children's Friends for Life, a cause very near and dear to her heart. "It's a difficult thing," Ivana said, "to organize an event of this size. Dozens and dozens of people have been working on it for months. There are so many details to attend to." Indeed, the co-chairs had done an amazing job of eliciting commitments from thirty chefs, fifty newscasters, twenty models, and a host of entertainers to cook and serve attendees at the event. If you were lucky, maybe Lucky Vanous would pour you a glass of wine, or maybe the willowy Paulina Porizkova would smile and make your dessert just a little bit sweeter. Since all of the celebrities would be stationed at showrooms scattered over eight floors of the Architects and Designers Building, it's no wonder that Ivana was concerned.

Since the event was scheduled to begin at 6:00 P.M. and wouldn't end until after 9:00, eating a light meal before departing for the festivities was essential. And though Ivana says she enjoys cooking when she has time—"especially

> ## THE RECIPES
>
> ◆ ◆ ◆ ◆ ◆ ◆ ◆
>
> *from Alva Restaurant, New York*
>
> **ALVA'S SALMON AND CRAB DUMPLINGS IN
> VEGETABLE-HERB BROTH**
>
> **ALVA'S VEGETABLE PLATE WITH STEAMED
> COUSCOUS AND GRILLED PORTOBELLOS**

Ivana Trump gathering her energies before heading out to raise money for one of her favorite good causes. "Wish us luck!" she called out, but the event was guaranteed to be a big success.

Czechoslovakian goulash and the other wonderful dishes from my childhood"—this was certainly not the day to dabble in the kitchen.

Dressed in a stunning short black cocktail dress from her own House of Ivana designs and wearing a fabulously intricate, tasseled pendant necklace fashioned from precious gems of every color inset in gold, Ivana looked surprisingly relaxed. Ye food was on this lovely lady's mind. As she entered the kitchen, she crossed immediately to the range to taste the soup and then whirled around to survey the grilled vegetables and couscous. "This is perfect," she said, "exactly the right choices. There's a bit of salmon in the dumplings—no? And the grilled vegetables—the portobellos—I'm thrilled. This is exactly what I love to eat—lots of veggies and a bit of fish or chicken. You have to, you know? You have to stay away from fats."

With that, Ivana Trump sat down at the kitchen counter and nibbled at just enough of the soup and vegetables to satisfy her appetite. And then, with a call to "Wish us luck!" she and her entourage were off into the night. Need we add that the event was a rousing success, raising a whopping $250,000 for children with HIV/AIDS. *Brava,* Ivana!

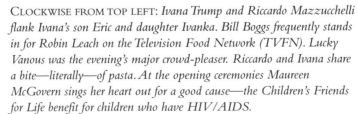

CLOCKWISE FROM TOP LEFT: *Ivana Trump and Riccardo Mazzucchelli flank Ivana's son Eric and daughter Ivanka. Bill Boggs frequently stands in for Robin Leach on the Television Food Network (TVFN). Lucky Vanous was the evening's major crowd-pleaser. Riccardo and Ivana share a bite—literally—of pasta. At the opening ceremonies Maureen McGovern sings her heart out for a good cause—the Children's Friends for Life benefit for children who have HIV/AIDS.*

ALVA'S SALMON AND CRAB DUMPLINGS IN VEGETABLE-HERB BROTH

Every part of this dish is delectable and at the same time light, filling, and soothing. It makes a great light meal all by itself. The broth can be made well ahead of time; cover and refrigerate until needed.

For 4 to 6

VEGETABLE-HERB BROTH (MAKES ABOUT 8 CUPS):
3 fennel ribs or 1 bulb, roughly chopped
2 carrots, roughly chopped
2 to 3 onions, roughly chopped
3 celery ribs with leaves, roughly chopped
1 head of garlic, halved
1 bunch thyme
2 bunches flat-leaf parsley
2 bay leaves
2 tablespoons coriander seeds
1 tablespoon black peppercorns
2 cups tomato juice
Salt and freshly milled pepper

SALMON AND CRAB DUMPLINGS (MAKES ABOUT 2 DOZEN):
1 pound lump crabmeat, picked over and shredded
6 ounces fresh salmon fillet, very finely chopped or ground
2 tablespoons minced shallots
1 tablespoon dried fines herbes, or 1 teaspoon each dried tarragon, chervil, and chives
¼ teaspoon cayenne pepper
2 pinches grated nutmeg
Salt
1 package (usually 25 to 30) square Chinese wonton skins
1 egg, beaten with 1 tablespoon water, for egg wash
Julienne of zucchini, yellow squash, and carrot, to garnish the soup (optional)

1. Make the vegetable broth: Combine all of the vegetables, herbs, and peppercorns in a large stockpot. Add cold tap water to cover the vegetables by 1 inch, and bring to a boil over high heat. Reduce the heat to moderately low and simmer, skimming off any foam that rises to the top, for 2 hours.

2. Stir in the tomato juice. Ladle the broth through a fine-mesh sieve into a clean saucepan; discard the solids. Season with salt and pepper to taste.

3. Make the dumplings: In a bowl, combine the crabmeat, salmon, shallots, *fines herbes,* cayenne, and nutmeg. Gently stir together until well mixed. Season with salt to taste.

4. Keep the stack of wonton skins covered with a damp paper towel to prevent their drying out. To shape the dumplings, place a wonton skin in front of you and rotate it so that a pointed corner is at the top, bottom, right, and left. Spoon about 1 tablespoon of the filling into the center of each skin. Lightly brush the top right and left edges of dough with some of the egg wash. Fold up the bottom point to meet the top point, enclosing the filling and forming a triangle. Press outward from the filling to expel any air captured inside. Brush the left and right points with egg wash. Fold them toward you until they meet; overlap the points a bit and pinch closed. Set aside on a sheet of waxed paper. Continue filling and forming the dumplings; you will have about 2 dozen delicate dumplings. (You'll need 3 for each serving, but don't panic; the extra dumplings will freeze beautifully and can be cooked while still frozen.)

5. Bring a large pot of water to a boil over high heat. Stir in 1 teaspoon salt. Add the dumplings and cook until they rise to the surface, 2 to 3 minutes. Scoop out and drain well.

6. Divide the dumplings among 4 shallow soup plates. Ladle some of the hot vegetable broth over them, and garnish with the julienne. Serve hot.

VEGETABLE PLATE WITH STEAMED COUSCOUS AND GRILLED PORTOBELLOS

This dish alone is enough to fill up Scarlett, Rhett, and anyone else they would choose to invite. It's just the thing to fit into a busy schedule, and it's just as tasty at room temperature as it is hot off the grill.

For 2

COUSCOUS:

1 cup couscous

1 cup chicken stock, broth, or water

1½ tablespoons olive oil

1 garlic clove, crushed

½ cup finely diced zucchini and/or yellow squash

1 bay leaf

½ teaspoon salt

¼ teaspoon freshly milled white pepper

2 large portobello mushrooms, stems removed, cleaned

3 ripe plum tomatoes, halved crosswise

1 yellow squash, trimmed and sliced lengthwise about ½ inch thick

1 zucchini, trimmed and sliced lengthwise about ½ inch thick

1 handful fresh haricots verts (skinny French green beans), topped and tailed

Olive oil

Salt and freshly milled black pepper

Fresh herb sprigs and lemon juice or balsamic vinegar, for serving (optional)

LEFT: *Someone's in the kitchen with Ivana—it's Robin Leach, cutting up.*

ABOVE: *The graceful marble stairway from the foyer to the parlor floor.*

1. Make the couscous: Pour the couscous into a heatproof bowl.

2. In a saucepan, combine the stock, oil, garlic, zucchini, bay leaf, salt, and white pepper. Bring the mixture to a boil over high heat.

3. Pour the mixture over the couscous. Cover with plastic wrap or a lid. Set aside for 1 hour.

4. Preheat a barbecue grill or stovetop grill until very hot. Meanwhile, lightly brush all of the vegetables with a bit of olive oil; season with salt and pepper.

5. Grill the vegetables, turning to cook both sides, until just cooked through and tender but not mushy, usually 3 to 5 minutes (depending on the heat source).

6. Arrange half of the vegetables and a mound of the couscous on each plate. Garnish with sprigs of fresh herbs and sprinkle with lemon juice or balsamic vinegar, if desired.

THE WOLFGANG PUCK AND BARBARA LAZAROFF FAMILY

◆ ◆ ◆ ◆ ◆ ◆ ◆ ◆ ◆ ◆ ◆

"'MODERATION IN ALL THINGS.'
WE ALL HAVE TO MAKE CHOICES."

When the "Wolf" is at the door of the Lazaroff-Puck house in Beverly Hills, it's nothing to worry about at all. Indeed, this Wolf's arrival is joyful; it means "Daddy's home." But with the schedule that Wolfgang Puck keeps, it's surprising that he even sees home any too often.

> ## THE RECIPES
> ◆ ◆ ◆ ◆ ◆ ◆ ◆ ◆
> ### ALMOND TUILES
> ### RASPBERRY SORBET

A portrait of the Puck-Lazaroff family: Cameron, Wolfgang (with Irving on his shoulder), and Barbara holding Byron Jason, then just two months old.

Mrs. Puck, Barbara Lazaroff, however, is frequently at home, since she conducts her Imaginings Interior Design company's business from a home office. Besides, with a "family" of more than twenty-nine—more about that later—to oversee, it's a wonder that she ever gets out at all. But get out she does, as co-owner and co-operator of the Puck restaurant empire. There's mega-successful Spago in West Hollywood, Spago Las Vegas, Spago Tokyo, Spago Mexico City, Chinois on Main in Santa Monica, Granita in Malibu, a partnership in Postrio in San Francisco, and Wolfgang Puck Cafes (several locations and growing). She also participates in other ventures, including the Wolfgang Puck Food Company; an instructional video, *Cooking with Wolfgang Puck*, for which she was writer-designer; and commercial and residential design projects for a host of outside clients.

One thing is clear, however, in the Puck-Lazaroff house, family comes first. Firstborn son, Cameron Lazaroff-Puck, now age six, was joined on October 30, 1994, by Byron Jason. In addition, there are eight birds; two llamas; six in-door cats; five outdoor cats; two dogs; two bunnies; and lots and lots of fish, led by Goldilocks, "the longest-living goldfish in all mankind."

"Our lifestyle is frenetic," Barbara Lazaroff admits, "but that's good—it keeps you slim and young. You have to stay busy, don't you? I do, if only to keep up with Cameron." Cameron, you see, typical of many six-year-olds, is somewhat hyper. "He's curious, he learns more at home than at school, he's a 'night kid' who never seems to wind down. His appetite used to be wonderfully exotic—his favorite foods were caviar and smoked salmon. But now he's in a more particular stage; he's eating more vegetables lately—especially spinach and broccoli."

Cameron has familial high cholesterol, meaning he's genetically predisposed to elevated cholesterol levels. As Barbara, who has degrees in biochemistry and experimental psychology, explains it: "This condition isn't life-threatening in and of itself, and nothing you do can directly or dramatically affect it. The great thing about health today is that you can find out these things early on, and then you can deal with them reasonably by being aware and taking steps not to exacerbate the condition. Do I deny him eggs and saturated fats? Well, no, but I try to limit his intake. I really believe that if I 'outlaw' certain foods, it'll just make him crave them more. So, I don't avoid anything across the board." She sounds like the voice of reason.

Basically, Barbara Lazaroff seems to be a "low-fat person." "I really don't like rich foods. I'll choose olive oil over butter every time. My body can't assimilate rich ingredients, and I tend to eat a well-balanced diet. During my pregnancy last year, I ate a broader spectrum of foods—you have to have more protein. I eat fish, chicken, and legumes, but as a rule I rarely eat red meat. When I do, it's usually lamb. I avoid fake sugars and, well, fake anything. You don't want to fill up on empty calories, but you do want calcium. I've nursed both of our children, and when you're nursing, you must eat and be well hydrated. But drinking milk doesn't make milk—I drink lots of other liquids."

Spago is well known for serving a regular celebrity clientele, and Wolfgang Puck regularly caters to customers' special diets and needs. "As restaurateurs, we'd be idiots not to," says Lazaroff, "you really can't expect people to dine on rich food every night. Look, Terence said it and it still holds true: 'Moderation in all things.' We all have to make choices."

Barbara Lazaroff and Cameron appeared on behalf of the American Heart Association in an effort to make parents aware of testing available to diagnose familial high cholesterol. She says, "I'm really happy to participate in this; we need to make people familiar with this condition, so they can make dealing with it a part of their lifestyle." She continues, ruing the lifestyle of most Americans, "In general, across the U.S., the fat content of people's diets is *too high*. Fast-food restaurants reuse oil until it's broken down to dangerous levels. Hot dogs contain nitrites that have been proved—scientifically—to be carcinogenic. People need to learn to eat fresh foods. I'm not saying they should be fanatics abut it; just that they should make informed choices, and go up the rungs one step in the quality of what they buy and eat. If they have a weakness, they have to stay aware of it and watch what they put in their mouths."

Wolfgang, Barbara, and their parrot, Irving.

ALMOND TUILES

Tuiles, named for the French word for tiles and shaped like the curved tiles used on roofs, are luscious, crisp cookies that are baked flat and then curled over a form while they're still warm. These tuiles are uncharacteristically huge—about six inches in diameter—just the thing when you're limiting yourself to just one.

Makes 8 to 10

1 tablespoon plus 1 teaspoon unsalted butter
¼ cup plus 1 tablespoon sugar
2 tablespoons honey
1 tablespoon nonfat milk
3 egg whites
1 cup sliced almonds
1 teaspoon finely grated orange zest

1. Preheat the oven to 350°F. Have ready several large nonstick baking sheets or baking sheets lined with baking parchment, and several large cylinders for curling the cookies—tall drinking glasses or tomato cans covered with waxed paper are excellent.

2. Combine the butter, sugar, honey, and milk in a small saucepan and stir until melted together. Remove from the heat.

3. In a bowl, whisk the egg whites to break them up, about 30 seconds. Stir in the almonds, orange zest, and the melted mixture; combine well. Set aside to cool to room temperature.

4. Spoon about 2 tablespoons of the tuile batter onto a baking sheet. Use a fork to spread the batter into a large, thin wafer that's 5 to 6 inches in diameter. Continue with the remaining batter.

5. Place the baking sheets in the oven and bake for 5 minutes.

6. Turn the sheets around and bake for 3 to 5 minutes more, until golden brown.

7. Remove the baking sheets and let the cookies set for about 1 minute. Use a large spatula to gently remove each cookie from the baking sheet or parchment. Drape each cookie over the curved sides of the glass or can and let cool completely. Peel the cookies off the waxed paper and serve or store in an airtight container.

TOP: *Cameron in his I'm-an-old-cowhand getup is having a chat with one of the two llamas, Pecas (freckles) and Ffeiffer (pepper).*

BOTTOM: *Profiles of two stars: one from the Alps, the other from the Andes.*

RASPBERRY SORBET

So simple to make—it's remarkable. The balsamic vinegar adds just a hint of sweet-tart goodness that really makes a difference.

Makes about 1 pint

2 pints fresh raspberries, rinsed
¼ cup sugar
1 teaspoon balsamic vinegar
1 teaspoon fresh lemon juice

1. Combine the berries, sugar, vinegar, and lemon juice in a blender or food processor; purée until smooth. Sieve the mixture to remove the seeds.

2. Taste the purée and add more sugar or a touch of honey, if necessary, to achieve the desired sweetness.

3. Freeze the mixture in an ice cream maker according to the manufacturer's directions.

OPPOSITE: *Wolfgang, Cameron, and Barbara having a grand old time just before starting dessert. Wolfgang's collection of grappas awaits sampling if the mood strikes later on.*

NOBU MATSUHISA AND DREW NIEPORENT AT NOBU

◆ ◆ ◆ ◆ ◆ ◆ ◆ ◆ ◆ ◆

"NOBU MATSUHISA, MY FRIEND AND PARTNER, IS ONE OF THE MOST INVENTIVE, EXCITING CHEFS I'VE EVER ENCOUNTERED—ANYWHERE."
—DREW NIEPORENT

Drew Nieporent's Nobu isn't Tokyo or Los Angeles on the Hudson, nor is it typically TriBeCa either. It's more like a flight on the Concorde that starts in Tokyo, stops briefly in L.A., and then zooms off to The Big Apple. But when you go to Nobu, the latest of Drew Nieporent and Robert DeNiro's triumphant restaurant escapades, don't think you'll get airplane food. Instead, chef/co-owner Nobu Matsuhisa will take you on a gustatory flight of his own design that will lift you away to places you've never been before.

Like the food, the atmosphere at Nobu is magical: Huge vaulted windows light the high ceilings; odd treelike structures (or are they sculptures of a sort?) line the pathway to the rear; the onyx-fronted sushi bar fairly vibrates with a citron-chartreuse glow; a curved wall has been constructed from 50,000 black Japanese river stones that look so shiny and smooth that you can barely keep your hands off it, and then, in the rear, a screen of twig "trees" creates a wall of sorts that masks but does not hide an equally mysterious dining room beyond.

James Beard Award winner Drew Nieporent is well on his way to reaching that much-strived-for but infrequently attained status as "a restaurateur's restaurateur." Much of the magic (and publicity) comes from his list of glitterati partners, who number Christopher Walken, Mikhail Baryshnikov,

> ### THE MENU
> ◆ ◆ ◆ ◆ ◆ ◆ ◆
> *For four*
> **MUSHROOM SALAD WITH YUZU DRESSING**
> **GRILLED SHRIMP WITH SPICY LEMON-GARLIC SAUCE**
> **NEW-STYLE SASHIMI**

Nobu sharing a bit of his art and experience with one of his sous chefs. He handles sushi and sashimi as if they were the most fragile Venetian glass.

Sean Penn, Bill Murray, Ed Harris, Francis Ford Coppola, and Robin Williams among them. Then, there's the list of celebs who frequent Nieporent's restaurants—Kenny G., Madonna, Harvey Keitel, Michael Jordan, Demi Moore and Bruce Willis, Ralph and Ricki Lauren, Elle Macpherson, and Vendela were at Nobu during a single typical week.

Most people who know him and his restaurants well credit Nieporent's tendency to overwork for at least a portion of his success. "I know I'm not in great physical shape," he confesses, "and everybody tells me I work too much and should take time off. But I love what I do, and if you love your work, it's therapeutic, it's energizing. Work is my fuel. I have to believe that doing what you love is good for you. I know the food pyramid backwards and forwards—very little fat, moderate protein, and lots of grains and vegetables. When I'm ready, I'll do it." And somehow, you don't doubt it for a minute. Nieporent is gregarious and ebullient, and has the determination of a former New York City marathon runner (which he is—and his time was good). And he is sure to be up-to-date on the latest healthy eating guidelines, because one of his current projects includes running the restaurant facilities at the huge Reebok Sports Club that's due to open uptown. "We're planning menus that focus on high-energy, low-fat foods. It's a really exciting, challenging project."

Mushroom Salad with Yuzu Dressing—the mushroom caps have been turned with the tip of a paring knife to incise them with a decorative pattern.

To tell the truth, the idea of dieting for weight loss when surrounded by the great dishes put out by the chefs at Nieporent's restaurants—Chris Gesualdi at Montrachet, Don Pintabono at Tribeca Grill, Traci Des Jardins at Rubicon, Nobu at Nobu—seems impossible. These talented people are capable of creating some astoundingly delicious foods. "The good thing is that anyone who's looking for a healthful meal will always be able to get one at any restaurant I'm affiliated with. We are here to serve our customers, to make them comfortable, to make them happy. If that's what they want, that's what we're here to give them."

MUSHROOM SALAD WITH YUZU DRESSING

Yuzu juice is a popular ingredient in Chef Matsuhisa's dishes, and there is no U.S. equivalent. However, you can find yuzu juice—bottled—in Japanese specialty-food stores. Yuzu juice looks like orange juice, tastes somewhat like lemon-lime juice (but with its own distinctive flavor), and comes from the Japanese citron.

For 4 to 6

YUZU DRESSING:
½ cup extra-virgin olive oil
¼ cup Japanese sake
3 tablespoons soy sauce
3 tablespoons yuzu juice
1½ teaspoons minced garlic
1½ teaspoons salt
4 pinches freshly milled black pepper

6 ounces trumpet mushrooms, cleaned
6 ounces shiitake mushrooms, cleaned
6 ounces enoki mushrooms, cleaned
6 ounces shimeji (oyster) mushrooms, cleaned
2 ounces fresh matsutake mushrooms (seasonally available), cleaned
4 tablespoons (½ stick) unsalted butter
1 lime, sliced

1. Combine all of the dressing ingredients and whisk together. Set aside until needed.
2. Trim the mushrooms, if necessary. Slice or cut up some of the larger ones; make petal-like cuts in the caps of other ones, if desired.
3. Melt the butter in a nonreactive large sauté pan over moderate heat. Add the mushrooms and sauté, tossing, until heated through and just limp, about 3 minutes. Pour on the yuzu dressing and toss to coat. Divide the mushrooms among 4 to 6 salad plates. Garnish each portion with a lime slice, and serve.

GRILLED SHRIMP WITH SPICY LEMON-GARLIC SAUCE
For 4

8 jumbo shrimp or prawns, butterflied, deveined, rinsed, and dried
2½ tablespoons extra-virgin olive oil
3 tablespoons Japanese sake
2 tablespoons soy sauce
1 teaspoon pureed minced garlic
2 tablespoons fresh lemon juice
1 teaspoon yuzu juice
Pinch of cayenne pepper
Red beet strings or julienne, and lemon slices, for garnish

1. Preheat a stovetop grill or grill pan until very hot. Add the shrimp and cook until just opaque in the thickest part, about 2 minutes. Transfer 2 shrimp to each of 4 plates.
2. Combine the olive oil, sake, soy sauce, and garlic in a nonreactive small saucepan. Bring the mixture to a rolling boil over high heat. Remove the pan from the heat and add the lemon juice, yuzu juice, and cayenne. Swirl the pan to blend together.
3. Drizzle some of the sauce over each serving of shrimp. Garnish with the beets and lemon slices. Serve hot.

LEFT: *The Grilled Shrimp with Spicy Lemon-Garlic Sauce is a study in color, texture, and beautiful presentation.*

RIGHT: *Nobu in all its splendor—as designed by the Rockwell group, the superstar design team headed by David Rockwell. Materials include 50,000 Japanese black river stones, birch tree trunks, quartz, all sorts of fabrics, bamboo, ceramic tiles, and heavily grained wood.*

NEW-STYLE SASHIMI

Nobu has built a reputation on this, his signature dish, an incredible mingling of textures and flavors.

For 4

8 to 12 ounces sashimi-quality halibut or other light, non-oily fish
  fillet (salmon, tuna, fluke, red snapper)
2 teaspoons minced garlic
2 pieces (each about 1½ inches long) fresh ginger, peeled, cut into
  fine julienne
2 whole scallions, trimmed and cut into fine julienne
2 teaspoons white sesame seeds
1½ tablespoons light soy sauce
1½ tablespoons yuzu juice
¾ cup extra-virgin olive oil
¼ cup Asian sesame oil

1. Cut the fish fillet into paper-thin slices. Fan out the slices in a circle over 4 dinner plates. Scatter some of the minced garlic and some of the ginger and scallion julienne over the fish; sprinkle with the sesame seeds. Sprinkle on the soy sauce and yuzu juice.

2. Combine the olive oil and sesame oil in a nonreactive small saucepan. Set over moderately high heat and bring almost to a boil (about 200°F.); the surface will shimmer. Remove from the heat and immediately pour one-fourth of the sauce over each serving of fish. The hot oil will sear the fish as you pour it on. Serve at once.

· ·

LEFT: *New-Style Sashimi, the signature dish at Nobu.*

RIGHT: *Nobuyuki Matsuhisa poses with Robin Leach during a rare quiet moment before the restaurant opens.*

ABOVE: *Each of Nobu's owners is a star in his own right: restaurant mogul Drew Nieporent, megastar Robert DeNiro, and stellar chef Nobu himself. The trio's other partner, Hollywood financier Meir Tepper, missed getting into the picture.*

BELOW, LEFT: *David Rockwell of the Rockwell Group designed these extraordinary "chopstick chairs" for seating at the luminescent sushi bar.*

BELOW, RIGHT: *"X" marks the spot with these wall sconces that appear throughout the restaurant.*

185

CAROLYN FARB

❖ ❖ ❖ ❖ ❖ ❖ ❖ ❖ ❖ ❖ ❖ ❖

"JOHN WESLEY SUMMED UP A PURPOSEFUL LIFE BETTER THAN I EVER COULD:
'DO ALL THE GOOD YOU CAN, BY ALL THE MEANS YOU CAN, IN ALL THE WAYS YOU CAN,
IN ALL THE PLACES YOU CAN, AT ALL THE TIMES YOU CAN, TO ALL THE PEOPLE YOU CAN,
AS LONG AS EVER YOU CAN.'"

Texas born and bred, Carolyn Farb is a woman blessed with a heart of gold, who spends her time getting others to part with some of theirs in aid of some very worthwhile causes. Fundraising is no easy task, but Carolyn Farb is a genius at it. "When you first begin to lend yourself to such efforts, your motives arouse curiosity. You have to persevere until people realize that *this is your calling in life*. It's not an ego trip; you aren't a dilettante."

It should come as no surprise, then, that Carolyn Farb's life and the way she entertains are as structured, stylish, and bountiful as the events she oversees. The backdrop is astounding: her home, Carolina (kair-oh-LEEN-a), built more than fifty years ago by Aspinwall and Simpson, is a grand mansion, located in the River Oaks area of Houston. Her scheme for entertaining closely resembles her schemes for fundraising; her goal is "to create a wonderful environment that is a special treat. The menu that is served, to the paintings on the wall, the music, flowers, table settings—everything matters. It's all in the details."

We were there for a stylish fall dinner party presided over by Ms. Farb, her companion Eckhard Pfeiffer, and Bogie (a

---

MENU FOR EIGHT

❖ ❖ ❖ ❖ ❖ ❖ ❖

Houston Hospitality at Carolina
Recipes by Chef Bruce Molzan; Dessert by Susan Molzan

**POLENTA WITH ROASTED CORN AND CRAB SALSA
ON ROASTED TOMATO COULIS**

WINE: SONOMA-LOEB 1993 CHARDONNAY

**WILD BABY GREENS WITH GRILLED
TAMARIND SHRIMP**

*WINE: SONOMA-LOEB 1993
PRIVATE RESERVE CHARDONNAY*

GRILLED RISOTTO-STUFFED QUAIL

WINE: SONOMA-LOEB 1991 CABERNET SAUVIGNON

INDIVIDUAL CHAMBORD CHEESECAKES

WINE: ROEDERER CRISTAL CHAMPAGNE

*Carolyn Farb, Eckhard Pfeiffer, and Bogie, all dressed up and
waiting for their guests to arrive.*

---

prized Shih-Tzu named after guess who?). Outdoors, by the fishpond, the atmosphere is Zenlike and massive oaks dot the lawn; indoors, the ambience is magical, a mingling of sensual stimuli. The tuberoses, hyacinths, and hydrangeas lightly scent the air here and there; the candlelight flatters everyone and everything, the music is lovely yet not at all intrusive, and just scanning the menu gets the juices going.

When serving a number of guests a formal meal, Ms. Farb doesn't hesitate to get help, this time in the form of Bruce and Susan Molzan, chef and pastry chef at Ruggles, a highly rated Houston restaurant. And though Carolyn helps with the pre-dinner preparation, as dinnertime nears, she devotes herself to her duties as hostess. "We're all moving so fast these days," she says, "that sometimes we don't take good care of ourselves. I try to provide my guests with a healthful, beautiful, and delicious dinner. I like to delight them with something unexpected and special." And whether it's hors d'oeuvres in the foyer or Champagne in the music room, just one thing is essential: nuts for Bogie—"He has a passion for them."

POLENTA WITH ROASTED CORN AND CRAB SALSA ON ROASTED TOMATO COULIS

All three parts of this recipe are terrific in and of themselves. Put them all together and—well, you'll see. Several of the ingredients require roasting, which you can do well ahead of time—on the barbecue grill or in the oven—so that when it's time to cook, you're ready to go. You might want to use this recipe as the main course for a light lunch or brunch.

For 8

POLENTA:

4½ cups chicken stock or broth
1 tablespoon minced jalapeño chile
1 tablespoon minced roasted garlic
1 tablespoon minced onion
2 tablespoons minced cilantro leaves
2 cups yellow cornmeal
1 cup shredded cheddar cheese (low-fat or no-fat can be used)
Salt and freshly milled pepper

ROASTED CORN AND CRAB SALSA:

4 ears sweet corn, silk removed, roasted in the husks until tender
1 pound lump crabmeat, picked over and shredded or chunked
1 to 2 jalapeño chiles, seeds and ribs removed, flesh minced
1 cup crushed tomatoes
½ cup extra-virgin olive oil
¼ cup fresh lime or lemon juice
½ bunch cilantro, leaves minced
Salt and freshly milled pepper

ROASTED TOMATO COULIS:

8 roasted Roma tomatoes, coarsely chopped
½ roasted onion, coarsely chopped
3 roasted garlic cloves, peeled
¼ cup olive oil
8 basil leaves
Salt and freshly milled pepper

1. Make the polenta: Preheat the oven to 325°F. Spray or coat a 15-×-10-inch jelly-roll pan with vegetable oil.

2. Combine the stock, jalapeño, garlic, onion, and cilantro in a heavy saucepan and bring to a boil over moderate heat. Slowly add the cornmeal and whisk continuously to prevent lumps from forming. Cook, stirring, for 10 minutes.

TOP: *Texas-style bounty à la Carolyn Farb.*

ABOVE: *Carolyn gets a lesson in stuffing the tiny Texas quail from chef Bruce Molzan.*

OPPOSITE: *Polenta with Roasted Corn and Crab Salsa on Roasted Tomato Coulis makes an excellent prelude to a gala dinner at Carolina.*

3. Remove the pan from the heat and stir in the cheese; season with salt and pepper to taste. Spread the polenta in an even layer over the prepared pan. Bake for 15 to 20 minutes, until firm and lightly browned. Remove to a rack and let set.

4. Meanwhile, make the salsa: Cut the corn off the cobs and place the kernels in a large bowl. Add all of the remaining salsa ingredients; season with salt and pepper to taste. Mix well; set aside.

5. Make the coulis: Combine all of the coulis ingredients in a blender or food processor. Puree until smooth. Transfer the mixture to a nonreactive saucepan; set aside until needed.

6. To assemble, cook the coulis over moderate heat just until heated through; keep warm. Use a 2½-inch round cutter to cut out 16 rounds of polenta. Place one polenta round on a plate, top with a layer of the salsa, and set another round on top. If desired, spoon a dollop of salsa on top. Continue until all 8 servings are completed. Spoon some of the warm coulis around the base of each portion. Serve at once, with the Sonoma–Loeb 1993 Chardonnay.

Carolyn Farb's mega-successful fundraising efforts have benefited dozens of good causes; she was the first woman to raise $1 million in a single evening, on behalf of Houston's Stehlin Foundation for Cancer Research. Whether you're a volunteer, amateur fundraiser, or professional, you'd do well to read Ms. Farb's book, How to Raise Millions Helping Others, Having a Ball! *(Eakin Press). In it, she generously shares her experiences, along with dozens of dos and don'ts and several "case studies" that are an education in themselves.*

WILD BABY GREENS WITH GRILLED TAMARIND SHRIMP

Tamarind is an addictive flavor that's both sweet and sour at the same time. You'll see big chunks of its seedy pulp in ethnic food stores, or you can buy the concentrated, strained pulp in small jars or packages.

For 8

TAMARIND MARINADE:
⅓ *cup tamarind concentrate*
2 cups chicken stock or broth
5 ancho chiles, stemmed, seeded, and cut up
1 cup ketchup
1 onion, chopped
1 jalapeño chile, seeded and chopped
½ *bunch cilantro, chopped*
½ *cup firmly packed brown sugar*
¼ *cup red wine vinegar*
2 tablespoons Worcestershire sauce
1 teaspoon fennel seeds

16 large or jumbo fresh shrimp in their shells
1 pound (5 to 6 loosely packed cups) wild baby salad greens, washed and dried
2 tablespoons dry sherry
2 tablespoons red wine vinegar
1½ teaspoons minced fresh tarragon leaves
1½ teaspoons minced opal basil
½ *cup safflower oil*
Salt and freshly milled pepper

1. Make the marinade: Combine all of the marinade ingredients in a nonreactive saucepan. Bring to a boil over moderate heat, stirring to dissolve the tamarind and sugar. Reduce the heat to low and simmer until the sauce thickens and is very flavorful, about 30 minutes. Remove from the heat and let cool to room temperature. (The marinade can be prepared up to 3 days in advance; cover and refrigerate.)

2. Submerge the shrimp in the marinade. Set aside at room temperature for at least 1 hour, or cover and refrigerate for up to 1 full day.

Houston hospitality at Carolina—Carolyn Farb's sumptuous meals for friends are designed to be a treat, to excite them and their taste buds and guarantee a good time.

3. Prepare a barbecue grill or stovetop grill, or preheat the broiler.

4. Place the salad greens in a large bowl. In a jar, combine the sherry, vinegar, tarragon, basil, and oil. Cover tightly and shake until emulsified. Taste and season as necessary. Pour about half of the vinaigrette over the greens and toss to coat lightly; add more, if necessary, until coated but not too wet. Reserve any remaining vinaigrette for another use. Divide the greens among 8 salad plates.

5. Remove the shrimp from the marinade. Grill until opaque and/or just cooked through, about 1 minute on each side. Place 2 shrimp alongside each mound of greens. Serve at once, with the Sonoma-Loeb 1993 Private Reserve Chardonnay.

GRILLED RISOTTO-STUFFED QUAIL

You'll use some of this risotto to stuff the quail and the remainder can be piled high in a pretty bowl for serving at table. If truffles aren't available in your specialty store or to your pocketbook, just omit them.

For 8

VEGETABLE AND TRUFFLE RISOTTO:
2 tablespoons olive oil
¼ cup minced carrot
¼ cup minced celery
¼ cup minced red bell pepper
¼ cup minced yellow bell pepper
3 tablespoons minced shallots
2 tablespoons minced roasted garlic
2 tablespoons minced jalapeño chile
2 cups arborio rice
6 to 8 cups rich chicken stock, heated
½ teaspoon dried thyme
¼ teaspoon dried sage
Salt and freshly milled pepper
1 black truffle, thinly shaved or finely diced

QUAIL:
16 fresh quail, cleaned
Olive oil
Salt and freshly milled pepper

1. Make the risotto: Warm the oil in a large, heavy sauté pan or saucepan over moderately high heat. Add the carrot, celery, bell peppers, shallots, garlic, and jalapeños; sauté until softened, 3 to 5 minutes.

2. Stir in the rice and cook, stirring, for 1 minute. Stir in 1 cup of the stock, reduce the heat to moderate, and cook, stirring, until the rice absorbs the stock. Add 1 cup more stock, and cook, stirring, until absorbed. Continue adding the stock, 1 cup at a time, and stirring until absorbed and the rice is al dente; the total cooking time will be 20 to 30 minutes. Remove from the heat.

3. Stir in the thyme, sage, and salt and pepper to taste. Set aside about one-third of the risotto for stuffing the quail; sprinkle about one-third of the truffle over this portion. Cover and keep the remaining risotto warm. (If making well ahead of time, spread the risotto into a layer in a baking pan or jelly-roll pan; sprinkle lightly with stock. Cover the pan with foil. Reheat in a 350°F oven before serving.)

4. Stuff the quail with the truffle-spiked risotto. Rub the quail with olive oil; sprinkle with salt and pepper.

5. Prepare a barbecue grill, or preheat the oven to 400°F.

6. If using a grill, cook the quail until done, about 8 minutes. If cooking in the oven, arrange the quail on a rack in 1 or 2 roasting pans, and roast until cooked through, about 12 minutes.

7. Arrange the quail on a platter along with the seasonal vegetables. Add the remaining truffles to the warm risotto and mound in a serving bowl. Serve at once, with Sonoma-Loeb 1991 Cabernet Sauvignon..

....

INDIVIDUAL CHAMBORD CHEESECAKES

For 8

1 cup graham cracker crumbs
4 tablespoons (½ stick) unsalted butter, melted
2 pounds low-fat cream cheese, at room temperature
1 cup sugar
2 tablespoons Chambord (raspberry liqueur)
4 eggs
1 pint fresh raspberries
¼ cup chopped almonds, toasted, for garnish
¼ cup shredded coconut, toasted, for garnish
Mint sprigs, for garnish

1. Preheat the oven to 275°F. You will need eight 6- to 8-ounce ramekins or custard cups.

2. Combine the graham cracker crumbs and melted butter; toss until evenly moistened. Evenly divide the crumbs among the ramekins and press in to cover the bottoms only.

3. Using an electric mixer, beat together the cream cheese, sugar, and Chambord until smooth. Add the eggs one at a time, beating well after each addition. Continue beating until the filling is smooth.

4. Divide the filling in half. Using one-half of it and dividing evenly, spoon some of the filling into the ramekins, filling no more than halfway. Arrange several raspberries on top. Divide the remaining filling among the ramekins, covering the berries completely. Smooth the tops. Set the cheesecakes on a jelly-roll pan.

5. Bake the cheesecakes for 30 to 40 minutes, or until they don't wiggle when shaken and the edges are very lightly browned. Transfer the ramekins to a wire rack to cool to room temperature.

6. These cheesecakes are best served at room temperature, though they can be chilled and served cold. Just before serving, garnish each cheesecake with some of the remaining raspberries, the almonds, coconut, and mint. Serve with Champagne.

JEREMIAH TOWER AT STARS OAKVILLE CAFE

◆ ◆ ◆ ◆ ◆ ◆ ◆ ◆ ◆ ◆ ◆

"I REALLY BELIEVE THERE ARE NO UNHEALTHFUL FOODS;
BUTTER AND CHOCOLATE AREN'T BAD—IT'S HOW YOU USE THEM."

You could say that Jeremiah Tower, American chef-restaurateur *extraordinaire*, almost always has Stars on his mind. There's Stars, his hugely successful eleven-year-old restaurant in San Francisco; Stars Cafe, a more casual bistro just around the corner from Stars; StarBake and Coffee, his drop-in or take-out store that sells Executive Pastry Chef Emily Luchetti's luscious baked goods and desserts; StarTeam, his group of talented chefs and managers; and Twinkle, Inc., his corporate entity; and then there's Stars Oakville Cafe, his wine-country outpost that's located on Highway 29, smack-dab in the middle of California's Napa Valley.

"I don't work out," he says, without a hint of guilt or remorse. "I do swim, though. I have an indoor pool and there are speakers so that music can be piped in. I like to put on opera, or lately, Placido Domingo singing Mexican music, and swim with my two Yorkshire terriers. One of them dives. Yes, head first. Other than that, I garden. I know it's not a sport, but it is good exercise." And indeed, that's true—all that bending, pulling, toting, and hoeing isn't too very different from many upper-body workout routines.

WINE COUNTRY DINNER FOR FOUR

◆ ◆ ◆ ◆ ◆ ◆ ◆

JEREMIAH'S PEAR AND GORGONZOLA SALAD
KUENTZ-BAS RIESLING, RÉSERVE PERSONNELLE 1991

MONTEREY PRAWNS WITH HALIBUT, TOMATOES, AND OLIVES
JOSEPH PHELPS 1993 VIN DU MISTRAL VIOGNIER

STARS OAKVILLE CAFE'S WOOD-OVEN-ROASTED VENISON WITH GARDEN VEGETABLES
FAR NIENTE 1990 CABERNET SAUVIGNON

STARS CAFE PINEAPPLE WITH BERRIES AND SPUN SUGAR
CHAMPAGNE KIR ROYALE MADE WITH DOMAINE CARNEROS 1990 BRUT

Vegetable lessons from the boss—Jeremiah Tower consults with members of his Stars Oakville Cafe staff.

But all that happens at Tower's home, cleverly situated halfway between San Francisco and the Napa Valley. Behind the simple building that houses Stars Cafe Oakville is an awning-covered patio for dining outdoors in good weather. Nearby is an enclosed area where lemon trees, olive trees, and lavender flourish. Beyond that is the garden, where Tower and company grow some of the produce for the restaurant. "We get two seasons," he says, sounding like a proud father. "The early one of lettuces, herbs, arugula, mâche, edible flowers, zucchini, corn, and tomatoes, and then a later one that gives pumpkins, squashes, cabbages, and potatoes." At the very back, the property edges the famed Robert Mondavi–Château Rothschild Opus One vineyard. Several weeks after the primary grape harvest in late September, Jeremiah, Chef Mark Franz, and staff have permission to pick some of the Cabernet Sauvignon grapes that remain on the vines. These grapes, too unripe to harvest earlier, develop sweetness as they remain on the vines during the sunny days and cool fall nights. And once they are sweet, that's when the Opus One Cabernet Sorbet hits the menu for a brief time.

Do many of Tower's patrons ask for specially prepared dishes to suit their diets? "Oh, yes," he claims, "and we do everything we can to make them happy—everything from straight Pritikin to some unusual, rather quirky requests. Most people look forward to my pulling out the stops for them—but in a healthful way. I really believe there are no unhealthful foods; butter and chocolate aren't bad—it's how you use them. A good cook knows to choose high quality and serve less. You can use butter and chocolate and still produce a healthful meal—if the cook knows what he or she is doing. Generally, I'd say it's improper cooking practices and poor planning that make you feel unwell after an unhealthful meal. Do it right and you can eat anything."

LEFT: *Jeremiah Tower choosing perfectly ripened tomatoes from the vegetable patch that's just behind Stars Oakville Cafe in California's Napa Valley.*

RIGHT: *Not your average backyard barbecue chef, Jeremiah works out his way at Stars Oakville Cafe.*

JEREMIAH'S PEAR AND GORGONZOLA SALAD

The photograph shows Seckel pears, but because they can be hard to find in some areas, substitute Comice or whatever sweet, ripe pears you can find. Two of the toast fingers in the photograph are spread with a mild olive puree and the other two with red bell pepper puree.

For 4

2 ripe pears, preferably Seckel or Comice
Juice of 1 lemon
¼ cup extra-virgin olive oil
1 tablespoon walnut oil
Salt and freshly milled black pepper
1 bunch watercress or other soft greens, washed and dried
½ cup walnut halves
4 ounces Gorgonzola or other blue cheese, sliced
4 small clusters Champagne grapes
Edible flowers, for garnish (optional)

1. Preheat the oven to 200°F. Line a baking sheet with baking parchment.

2. Cut the pears lengthwise in half. Place them, cut sides down, on the parchment-lined pan. Bake for 1 hour.

3. Allow the pears to cool enough to be handled. Peel, core, and slice the pears; set aside.

4. In a bowl, whisk together the lemon juice, both oils, and salt and pepper to taste until well blended. Pour about half of the dressing over the greens and toss to coat lightly.

5. Arrange the greens over a serving plate; scatter the walnuts on top. Arrange the pear slices, cheese, and grape clusters in a pleasing pattern over the greens. Spoon the remaining dressing over the pears and cheese. Garnish with edible flowers, if desired. Serve with a glass of the 1991 Kuentz-Bas Riesling, Réserve Personnelle.

Jeremiah's Pear and Gorgonzola Salad, garnished with toast fingers spread with olive and red bell pepper purees.

Monterey Prawns with Halibut, Tomatoes, and Olives—rich flavors in a light setting.

MONTEREY PRAWNS WITH HALIBUT, TOMATOES, AND OLIVES

Jeremiah Tower has found that both Monterey prawns from California and Spot prawns from Louisiana benefit from a bit of special handling to ensure that their flesh remains firm. Accordingly, he likes to deep-fry them in their shells or shock them in boiling salted water and dip them in ice water before sautéing.

For 4

12 fresh prawns
1 lemon, chopped
2 thyme sprigs
6 garlic cloves, crushed
1 cup olive oil
Salt and freshly milled pepper
2 cups fish stock
4 pieces of halibut fillet (each about 4 ounces)
1 cup peeled, seeded, and chopped tomatoes
½ cup cured black olives, pitted and chopped

1. Bring a pot of water to a boil. Add salt. Add the prawns and cook for 30 seconds. Scoop out and shock in ice water for 10 seconds; drain and pat dry.

2. In a bowl, combine the lemon, thyme, garlic, ½ cup of the oil, and salt and pepper to taste. Add the prawns and toss gently to coat well. Cover the bowl and refrigerate for 1 hour.

3. Remove the prawns from the marinade; reserve the marinade. Sauté, grill, or broil the prawns at high heat for 1 minute per side, turning once. Set aside.

4. In a nonreactive sauté pan, combine the remaining ½ cup oil, the fish stock, and salt to taste. Bring to a simmer over moderate heat. Add the pieces of fish, reduce the heat to low, cover the pan, and poach the fish for 5 minutes. Transfer the fish to 4 heated dinner plates.

5. Strain the reserved marinade into a nonreactive small saucepan. Add the tomatoes and olives and bring to a boil. Taste and correct the seasonings, if necessary. Pour the sauce over the fish. Stand 3 prawns in the center of each plate, and serve at once, with the Joseph Phelps 1993 Vin du Mistral Viognier.

STARS OAKVILLE CAFE'S WOOD-OVEN-ROASTED VENISON WITH GARDEN VEGETABLES

The photograph shows this dish garnished with oyster mushrooms, which have been steamed in a little butter and chicken stock. They make a wonderful, if not essential, addition—as does any wild mushroom.

For 4

2 bay leaves
2 fresh thyme sprigs
4 juniper berries
1 loin of venison (about 3 pounds), bones or trimmings reserved
¼ cup olive oil
Salt and freshly milled pepper
4 cups rich chicken stock
2 green figs
2 red figs
8 small boiling onions, trimmed
2 pounds seeded fresh pumpkin, peeled and cut into ½-inch cubes (about 2 cups)
2 tablespoons white truffle oil or extra-virgin olive oil

1. In a mortar, crush together the bay leaves, thyme, and juniper berries. Coat the venison with the olive oil, and then rub in the herb mixture, coating well on all sides. Sprinkle with salt and pepper. Cover and set aside at room temperature for at least 3 hours.

2. Meanwhile, combine the chicken stock with the venison trimmings and bones or, lacking those, some veal trimmings and bones. Bring to a boil over high heat. Reduce the heat to low, cover, and simmer for 2 hours. Strain the stock into a clean saucepan; discard the solids.

3. Preheat the oven to 400°F.

4. Stand the figs in a dry baking pan, and bake for 10 minutes. Remove and leave the oven on. Set the figs aside to cool.

5. Place the venison on a rack in a roasting pan. Roast until medium-rare, about 20 minutes. Remove from the oven, and tent the roast with foil to keep it warm. Set aside until needed.

6. Meanwhile, place the onions in the strained stock. Cover and cook over moderate heat until tender, about 10 minutes. Remove the onions from the stock; cover to keep warm.

ABOVE: *Stars Oakville Cafe's Wood-Oven-Roasted Venison with Garden Vegetables—venison was chosen specifically because of its low fat content.*

7. Add the pumpkin to the hot stock. Cover and cook until fork-tender, 5 to 10 minutes. Remove the cubes to a bowl. Sprinkle on the truffle oil or extra-virgin olive oil and toss gently to coat. Cover and keep warm.

8. Continue to simmer the stock until thickened and reduced by about half. Meanwhile, slice the venison into 4 equal pieces; quarter the figs. Arrange the meat, pumpkin, onions, and figs over warmed dinner plates. Pour some of the stock over each portion. Serve with the Far Niente 1990 Cabernet Sauvignon.

STARS CAFE PINEAPPLE WITH BERRIES AND SPUN SUGAR

Chefs can do all sorts of things that regular mortals can't—that's part of why we admire them so. But even some chefs are "challenged" when it comes to spinning sugar: It requires practice, a fair amount of floor space, a dry—no rain, not humid—day, and a cleanup crew with lots of elbow grease. If you want to try it, do—any general cookbook will give you the formula and technique—but, you might be better off going for a walk or tending your garden.

For 4

1 cup Simple Syrup (recipe follows)
2 fresh rosemary sprigs
2 ripe peaches
1 ripe pineapple
1 cup raspberries, rinsed
1 cup huckleberries or blueberries, rinsed
Spun sugar nests, for garnish (optional)

1. Bring the syrup to a boil in a small, deep saucepan. Add the rosemary and the whole peaches; cook for 1 minute. Remove the pan from the heat; remove the peaches from the syrup and run under cold water. Let the rosemary steep in the syrup for 5 minutes; remove and discard the rosemary.

2. Peel, halve, stone, and slice the peaches; set aside.

3. Peel the pineapple, taking care to cut out all of the eyes. Quarter the pineapple lengthwise, cutting down from the top to the stem end. Slice away the inner core. Cut each quarter lengthwise into 3 long spears.

4. Place all of the pineapple in a dish and pour on half of the rosemary-infused syrup. Set aside for 2 hours at room temperature.

5. Puree half of the remaining syrup with half of the raspberries to make a sauce. Puree the remaining syrup with half of the huckleberries. Strain each sauce and keep separate.

6. To serve, arrange 3 pineapple spears on each plate. Drizzle with a bit of each sauce. Garnish each serving with some of the peach slices, some of the remaining berries, and a nest of spun sugar, if you dared try it. Serve with a Kir Royale.

SIMPLE SYRUP

Makes 3½ cups

2½ cups sugar
2 cups cold water

Combine the sugar and water in a small pot and bring to a boil. Stir to make sure the sugar completely dissolves. Boil for 1 minute. Let the mixture cool, pour into a jar, and store indefinitely in the refrigerator.

• •

OPPOSITE: *A view of a stunningly statuesque dessert—Stars Cafe Pineapple with Berries and Spun Sugar.*

DANIEL BOULUD AT RESTAURANT DANIEL

◆ ◆ ◆ ◆ ◆ ◆ ◆ ◆ ◆ ◆ ◆

"DANIEL BOULUD WAS, FOR SIX YEARS, THE MUCH-ACCLAIMED CHEF AT LE CIRQUE, BUT IN HIS OWN RESTAURANT HE IS WORKING WITH A NEW CONFIDENCE. HE SEEMS TO BE COOKING FOR HIMSELF WITH A MENU THAT OFFERS BOTH HEARTY FRENCH FOOD AND CLASSIC COOKING SO TECHNICALLY PROFICIENT IT TAKES YOUR BREATH AWAY." —RUTH REICHL, IN HER FOUR-STAR REVIEW OF RESTAURANT DANIEL FOR *THE NEW YORK TIMES*, NOVEMBER 11, 1994.

Daniel Boulud, chef-owner of Restaurant Daniel on Manhattan's Upper East Side, has created perfection. As a man, he is somewhat shy, though he is quick to smile and his way with people is pleasing; as a restaurateur, he is accomplished, energetic, and a perfection-demanding genius who knows exactly what he wants. As a chef, Boulud is truly inspired, able to coax every scintilla of flavor out of each ingredient, while somehow making the individual flavors mingle clearly and separately on the plate and palate. How he does this is a mystery, but like all good mysteries, it pulls you in, it makes you want more.

The aura of mystery begins as you enter the restaurant. Immediately in front of you is a short, arched passageway, gorgeously paved with irregular, handmade, eighteenth-century clay tiles, that leads to the small bar area. At the corner of the bar, a cluster of Russian olive branches, complete with berries, is combined with persimmon-color roses, eucalyptus buds and seeds, and of all things, a pineapple. Opposite the bar is an upholstered banquette faced with small tables and short stools. The seats of the bar stools and the throw pillows are covered with needlepoint; the feeling is both intimate and comfortable.

Just to the side is the restaurant's softly lighted, pale green and honey-toned dining room. The ambience of the room

---

THE RECIPES

◆ ◆ ◆ ◆ ◆ ◆ ◆

for 4

ASPARAGUS, ARTICHOKE, AND HERB SALAD WITH LEMON VINAIGRETTE

STEAMED SALMON WITH SAVOY CABBAGE AND ROSEMARY

Taking a quick midafternoon coffee break, Daniel Boulud scans Le Monde *for news of what's happening in his homeland.*

---

is reminiscent of many of the finest restaurants in France, complete with the requisite monumental floral displays that are artfully arranged in several locations. These, however, are more than big, they're stunning, and often amusing, and they change so frequently that it's worth popping your head in to see what's "showing" this week.

In front of an antique gilt-framed mirror sits a massive still life of traveler palm, philodendron, and a small pot of sodded lilies of the valley mingling somehow quite naturally with big, fluffy-looking heads of white cauliflower. A makeshift bamboo trellis of sorts surrounds the display, hung with clumps of tall grass trussed up with the same bear grass that's used to tie the linen napkins into neat cylinders.

In another corner is a sculpture of fishtail broom, bamboo, and banana clusters amid chunks of dried Saguaro cactus that look somewhat like New Age driftwood. Occasionally, nestled together in the bottom of the small glass vase of colorful flowers on each table, you'll spot a half dozen or so tiny cherry or pear tomatoes—just for an extra dash of color. You're beginning to see a trend here: At Daniel, food and flowers seem to combine and mingle almost interchangeably in the most delightful way. (As the meal progresses, though, you'll note that M. Boulud does not often use edible flowers on the plate; he lets the food and the beau-

tiful array of Bernaudaud Limoges china manage impeccably on their own.)

In his kitchen, amid his large staff "family," Daniel Boulud is a demanding taskmaster, yet very much one of the crowd. He works alongside his crew during lunch and dinner service. Quick trips to say hello to diners are just that—you won't find him lingering in the dining room when there's work to be done.

And work he does, at a grueling schedule that offers only Sundays off and a two-week vacation every summer. "I'm afraid," Daniel admits, "that I don't have much time for exercise; I work all of the time." But his work is a workout of sorts—Daniel estimates that he spends "too much time— probably twelve hours a day" on his feet. "And then I'm usu-

ABOVE: *A light fixture at Restaurant Daniel.*

RIGHT: *Just one of the ever-changing floral still-lifes at the restaurant. Somehow, food always enters the picture.*

ally in the office for four hours or so, so I do sit sometimes," he adds. As a rule, staff meals are simple, and if you ever have the opportunity to share in one, you'll have a ham and cheese or BLT sandwich that is beyond description. Suffice to it say, the meal will be sublime.

Daniel says that at home, with his wife of nine years, Micky Boulud Palmer, and their five-year-old daughter, Alix, "We eat simple, healthy foods. Sometimes I cook, or Micky cooks, or we cook together, but it's always simple. Alix doesn't like foods that are too rich or overly spicy—she loves pasta, and that's the kind of thing we eat."

As for diners at Daniel who request dishes that are low in fat or calories or cholesterol, Boulud promises, "That's no problem. We will do everything we can to accommodate special needs; indeed, many of our dishes already suit them. Our staff is very familiar with our menu and can describe what's in each one and how it's prepared; they know which ones are low in cholesterol or fat or sodium and can advise our customers on that. This salmon dish is a perfect example; the only added fat is a touch of the best olive oil, but only just enough for flavor. But I have to admit, most of our customers don't worry too much—at least not while they're here."

And who can blame them? A brilliant meal at Daniel is worth making some "sacrifices" for—before or after. Daniel the man and Daniel the restaurant are a mentally healthful experience—they're both absolutely divine.

LEFT: *The entryway at Restaurant Daniel.*

ABOVE: *A close-up look at an arrangement on the corner of the bar.*

ASPARAGUS, ARTICHOKE, AND HERB SALAD WITH LEMON VINAIGRETTE

If you can find baby artichokes—the imported, goose-egg-size, reddish-pink ones—grab a bunch of them. As a rule, these diminutive vegetables are so tender and young that a choke hasn't even developed yet; virtually the whole thing is edible and delicious. If these mini-miracles aren't available, use the smallest globe artichokes you can find for this recipe. If white asparagus isn't available, double the amount of green.

For 4

HERB SALAD:

8 green and/or purple basil leaves, cut into chiffonade (see page 23)

½ cup loosely packed small chervil sprigs

½ cup loosely packed small dill sprigs

¼ cup loosely packed tarragon leaves

¼ cup loosely packed cilantro leaves

¼ cup loosely packed sliced celery leaves (the inner, tenderest ones)

¼ cup loosely packed flat-leaf parsley leaves

VINAIGRETTE:

1½ tablespoons fresh lemon juice

3½ tablespoons extra-virgin olive oil

Salt and freshly milled black pepper

1 tablespoon finely snipped fresh chives

VEGETABLES:

Salt

4 ounces white asparagus, the bottoms of the spears peeled, cut into 3-inch lengths

4 ounces green asparagus, the bottoms of the spears peeled, cut into 3-inch lengths

1½ teaspoons olive oil

8 ounces baby artichokes, trimmed and steamed until tender, or 2 artichoke hearts, steamed and rubbed with lemon juice

1 large red bell pepper, roasted and peeled, the flesh cut into ¼-inch strips

1 large yellow bell pepper, roasted and peeled, the flesh cut into ¼-inch strips

1. Combine all the herb salad ingredients and toss to mix well. Refrigerate until needed.

2. Bring a large pot of water to a boil.

3. Meanwhile, make the vinaigrette: Combine the lemon juice, olive oil, and a few pinches of salt and pepper in a jar. Cover and shake until emulsified. Taste and adjust the seasonings; add the chives and shake again. Set aside.

4. When the pot of water is boiling, stir in 2 tablespoons salt. Plunge the white asparagus into the boiling water and cook for 3 minutes. Remove with tongs to a bowl of ice water and let chill for 5 minutes. Remove and drain; set aside.

5. While the white asparagus is chilling, add the green asparagus to the pot of boiling water. Cook until tender, 4 to 5 minutes. Remove with tongs and add to the ice water. Remove and drain; set aside.

6. Warm the oil in a nonreactive large sauté pan over moderate heat. Add the asparagus, artichokes (or hearts), and all the roasted peppers. Toss just until warmed through, 3 to 4 minutes. Pour on half of the vinaigrette and toss to coat well.

7. Divide the vegetables among 4 salad plates. Toss the herb salad with the remaining vinaigrette and mound it over the vegetables. Serve while the vegetables are still warm.

••

OPPOSITE: *Daniel's Asparagus, Artichoke, and Herb Salad with Lemon Vinaigrette.*

Daniel Boulud and crew in the kitchens at Restaurant Daniel.

The fruit of his labors: Daniel's Steamed Salmon with Savoy Cabbage and Rosemary—c'est fantastique!

STEAMED SALMON WITH SAVOY CABBAGE AND ROSEMARY

This combination of ingredients will work just as well on other types of fish, but the color and texture of salmon is absolutely ideal. Take care not to overcook the fish; it should remain at least a bit chewy.

For 4

1 small head of savoy cabbage, leaves separated, large stems shaved down or cut away
Salt
2 rosemary sprigs, the leaves of 1 sprig chopped
1 lemon, halved
1 teaspoon pink peppercorns, coarsely crushed
Freshly milled black pepper
4 salmon fillets (each cut about ¾-inch thick and weighing 7 ounces)
4 ounces chanterelles, sliced cap-to-stem (so they resemble fish scales)
2 tablespoons extra-virgin olive oil
4 small rosemary sprigs and 8 thin lemon slices, for garnish

1. Bring a large pot of salted water to a boil over high heat. Add the cabbage leaves and boil until the leaves are flexible and somewhat tender, 6 to 8 minutes. Drain, then run under cold water till cool. Drain again.

2. Pour 4 cups of water into a fish poacher, wok, or other pot large enough to hold a steaming rack or bamboo steamer. Add 1 teaspoon salt, the whole rosemary sprig, and half of the lemon. Bring the water to a boil.

3. Meanwhile, arrange the cabbage leaves over the steaming rack, overlapping as necessary. Sprinkle on half of the chopped rosemary, half of the crushed pink peppercorns, a pinch of salt, and a pinch of pepper. Combine the remaining rosemary, pink peppercorns, and more salt and pepper, and rub the mixture over both sides of the fish fillets. Set the fillets on the cabbage leaves and arrange the chanterelle slices over the top of each so they look like a line of fish scales. Set the steaming rack in place, cover, and steam until the fish is cooked through but not well done, usually 5 to 7 minutes. Remove the rack from the steamer as soon as the fish is cooked.

4. Line 4 warmed dinner plates with the cabbage leaves. Transfer a fillet to each plate. Squeeze the juice of the remaining half lemon over the fillets, and drizzle each serving with ½ tablespoon of the oil. Garnish with rosemary sprigs and lemon slices, and serve at once. Serve with a rich Chardonnay or a lightly chilled dry rosé wine.

GEORGETTE MOSBACHER

◆ ◆ ◆ ◆ ◆ ◆ ◆ ◆ ◆ ◆

"HAVING IT ALL MAY MEAN HAVING A FEW EXTRA POUNDS."
GEORGETTE MOSBACHER'S FEMININE FORCE PRINCIPLE #18,
FROM HER BOOK, *FEMININE FORCE*

"Georgette would like to do a late Sunday afternoon dinner at her new house in Southampton—would that be okay?" asked Lyn Paulsin, Georgette Mosbacher's sister, business associate, and closest confidante. "It's called Waterview and it's really beautiful—with the bay on one side of the property and ocean on the other. How does that sound to you?" Sounds great, and indeed, it *is* great.

Though she is married to Robert Mosbacher, a mega-successful Texas businessman and former Secretary of Commerce under Ronald Reagan, and has homes in Houston and New York City as well, Waterview is Georgette's own personal retreat—designed, built, and furnished by her, for her, and with her own money. Mr. Mosbacher is, of course, welcome there anytime, but the whole idea of Waterview was to give Georgette a "peaceful place away from but near to New York City," where her company, Georgette Mosbacher Enterprises, is based. "Every woman should have a place of her own, where she can get away." Ms. Mosbacher is quick to add, "Mental health is as important as physical health in promoting an overall sense of well being and power."

EARLY SUNDAY SUPPER

◆ ◆ ◆ ◆ ◆ ◆ ◆

for ten

as prepared by Chef Antoine Bouterin of New York City's Le Périgord

SALMON TARTARE WITH SWEET SPICES AND FRESH HERBS

BEEF, CHICKEN, AND VEGETABLE KEBABS "BORD DE MER"

APPLE TART WITH RASPBERRIES, STRAWBERRIES, AND POMEGRANATE SEEDS

Georgette and Adam Mosbacher in Southampton, New York, with the dunes and the Atlantic Ocean in the background.

Although Georgette isn't expecting her guests for several hours, she is intent on making sure that everything is picture-perfect when they arrive. The white-on-white, second-story living room and dining room afford a view that astounds—the grassy dunes that grow like a tall carpet and wend their way to the ocean on one side; on the other are the pool, tennis court, gated entrance, and marina beyond. Here and there small sailboats and Windsurfers ply the waters of the bay, while bunches of neighbors bicycle down the road in quest of a tennis match or on their way to the stables.

Indoors, the action is focused on the massive round dining room table. In the center Georgette is arranging a huge fishbowl, filled with goldfish—a living centerpiece that she outfits with an aerator to keep the water fully oxygenated for her "pets." Next up is deciding which of the ten or so table settings is the one that's just right for tonight's Sunday supper. Out comes a photo album filled with snapshots of the possibilities—several settings of formal, gold-trimmed or hand-painted fine china coupled with equally magnificent linens mix with more casual, colorful, equally well-

Decks off nearly every room offer stunning ocean views.

coordinated choices. Each setting is displayed on two oppos-
ing pages that illustrate the flatware, crystal, linens, serving
pieces, and accessories that combine to make an impressive
display. This is amazing, Georgette! "Oh, I insist on it—being
organized is very important to me. Photos save having to
look in a million cupboards and closets and trying to remember what you have; they really save time."

It is decided that a day this glorious and a menu this varied
deserve a colorful seashore motif, and so the table is set and
readied. With the help of superstar French chef Antoine
Bouterin of New York's Le Périgord, this meal is sure to be
magnificent. "We have something for everyone," says Georgette, "seafood, beef and chicken kebabs, and lots and lots of
grilled vegetables—a personal favorite. Wines will be red,
white, and sparkling—I like everyone to be as comfortable as
possible, to have anything they want right there close at hand.
When everyone's truly comfortable, they relax and the conversation just gets better and better."

But before her guests arrive, Georgette will have to put her
"eating plan" into action. "There's a weight problem on both
sides of my family," she declares, "so I have to be very conscious of what I eat. I enjoy eating, but since so much of our
lifestyle centers around social events and every event seems to
involve food, I've had to develop a system that works for me.
As a rule, I eat several little meals a day—snacks, really. But
before I go out—whether it's to an event or a dinner party, I
eat a meal at home. It's always low in fat—we just don't do
dairy and cheese anymore—but I try to fill up before I leave
the house. For me at least, not being hungry is the key. That
way, I can move food around on my plate, pick at the foods
that are good for me, and I'm not famished."

Then, too, there's walking, Ms. Mosbacher's primary form
of exercise. "I love to walk," she proclaims. "I walk at least

three miles a day. I'm a 'books on tape' junkie! I walk and I listen, and let me tell you, I've probably enhanced my intellectual capacity more than my health, but I love my walking-reading sessions. I walk to and from the office every day, and do you know how many times I've walked right past my apartment building? All of a sudden, I look up and nothing is familiar—I get so carried away. I do a little weights every morning too—just five stretching-toning routines, twenty reps each—but walking is it for me, my favorite basic exercise."

Ms. Mosbacher has a travel schedule that would make a lesser person cringe. "Travel can be difficult," she admits, "but that's where exercise is very important. If my schedule is too busy or my destination isn't conducive to walking, I pack a collapsible step machine and do my walking in the hotel room. But I do love good food, so when I go to France or Italy, I eat whatever I want. I know that when I get home, I'll have to deal with any weight gain, but while I'm there I enjoy it. Frankly, as long as I can get into my clothes, I can't get obsessed with my weight. But when the clothes get a little tight, I become *very* conscientious about taking it off—as soon as possible."

As she relaxes—just momentarily, mind you—in her white-on-white living room at Waterview, her Balmain couture gown fits just right. Surrounded by a baby grand piano, vase after vase of fragrant white roses, books, family photographs, and Adam Mosbacher, Georgette's eight-and-a-half-year-old Cavalier King Charles spaniel, or "dog-child" as Mr. Mosbacher likes to call him, Georgette looks content and happy. And she should be. If she believes in nothing else on earth, Georgette Mosbacher believes in women. Her book, *Feminine Force,* is a first-person primer-style case study designed to help women seize control of their lives, take responsibility for their actions, and build the life they want to live. Georgette Mosbacher has done it. She believes that every person can do it, and that all women have a fund of strengths that must be cultivated and allowed to grow.

Top: *If you're going for a stroll on the beach, just follow the boardwalk.*
Center: *Georgette Mosbacher's house, Waterview—amid the grass and dunes—offers great views of the water from every room.*
Bottom: *Graceful and comfortable courtside shade on Long Island.*

SALMON TARTARE WITH SWEET SPICES AND FRESH HERBS

Here's a "fancy" recipe that's quick and easy to make and is sure to impress everyone who tastes it. The secret is to use all of the fresh herbs called for; it's worth going out of your way to include *all* of them. If you're not serving a formal meal, treat this tartare as a one-dish lunch, or spoon some into a pita pocket for an impromptu snack or picnic.

For 10

2 pounds fresh salmon fillet, cut into 1-inch squares
½ teaspoon curry powder
¼ teaspoon ground cumin
¼ teaspoon ground coriander
1 tablespoon minced shallot
1 tablespoon minced fresh basil
½ teaspoon minced fresh thyme
½ teaspoon minced fresh oregano
2 tablespoons minced flat-leaf parsley
½ teaspoon Tabasco sauce
½ teaspoon red wine vinegar
Salt and freshly milled white pepper
Dill sprigs, for garnish

1. The goal is to cut up the salmon into smaller pieces while maintaining its character and translucence: You can do this by hand with a chef's knife; you can pass the salmon through the large screen of a meat grinder and then pass it through again; or you can pulse the salmon in a food processor, but go easy—5 to 10 pulses should do it. In any case do NOT puree the salmon. Transfer the salmon to a bowl.

2. Sprinkle on the spices, shallots, herbs, Tabasco, and vinegar. Mix very gently—you might want to use chopsticks—taking care not to mash the salmon. Season the mixture with salt and pepper to taste.

3. Lightly oil a 3- to 4-ounce ramekin or decorative mold. Spoon in the tartare and press to shape it. Unmold onto a chilled salad plate and garnish with a dill sprig. Shape the remaining servings. Serve at once; the tartare will be best if served at cool room temperature.

ABOVE: *Georgette and Antoine Bouterin, chef at New York's top-notch Le Périgord, team up to check the heat of the grill before the kebabs go on.*

BELOW: *Salmon Tartare with Sweet Spices and Fresh Herbs. Ms. Mosbacher planned to serve red, white, and sparkling wines to her guests—"So each person can have exactly what suits his or her mood."*

1. In a nonreactive bowl, combine the wine, vinegar, Worcestershire, garlic, chopped onion, peppercorns, and rosemary branches. Add the beef, cover, and refrigerate for at least 40 minutes.

2. Preheat a barbecue grill until very hot, or preheat the broiler.

3. Thread 10 stainless-steel skewers with alternating chunks of the beef, chicken, and vegetables. (If you err here, err on the side of using lots of vegetables.) Reserve the marinade for basting.

4. Grill or broil the kebabs over very high heat, brushing all of the ingredients with some of the marinade and turning to cook evenly, until the chicken and vegetables are tender and the beef is cooked to the desired degree of doneness, usually 6 to 8 minutes. Sprinkle the kebabs with salt and pepper to taste. Serve at once, on or off of the skewers, with additional vegetables or oven-roasted potatoes.

....

BEEF, CHICKEN, AND VEGETABLE KEBABS "BORD DE MER"

There's a place for red meat in a healthful lifestyle; it's all a matter of portion size. And don't forget, a simple marinade and an outdoor grill can make all the difference in the world.

For 10

¾ cup dry red wine

¾ cup top-quality red wine vinegar

3 tablespoons Worcestershire sauce

3 garlic cloves, smashed

1 onion, chopped

1 teaspoon whole black peppercorns

4 rosemary branches

1½ pounds lean beef, such as chuck or sirloin, trimmed of all fat and cut into 1-inch chunks

1½ pounds boneless, skinless chicken breasts, trimmed of all fat and cut into 1-inch chunks

2 pints cherry tomatoes, stems removed, rinsed

2 half pints pearl onions, peeled, or 2 cups cubed larger onions

6 to 8 small zucchinis, trimmed and cut into 1-inch lengths

1½ pounds small button mushrooms, washed and trimmed

2 yellow bell peppers, cut into 1-inch squares

2 red bell peppers, cut into 1-inch squares

2 green bell peppers, cut into 1-inch squares

Salt and freshly milled pepper

ABOVE, LEFT: *Beef, Chicken, and Vegetable Kebabs "Bord de Mer."*

BELOW: *Poolside serenity at Waterview.*

APPLE TART WITH RASPBERRIES, STRAWBERRIES, AND POMEGRANATE SEEDS

Feel free to substitute pears, ripe peaches, or nectarines for the apples in this recipe. Any sweet, fresh fruit will do when it receives this stellar treatment.

Makes one 9- or 10-inch tart

TART DOUGH:

1½ cups unbleached all-purpose flour

Pinch of salt

8 tablespoons (1 stick) cold unsalted butter, cut up

5 tablespoons ice water

FILLING:

3 tablespoons unsweetened applesauce

3 apples, such as Golden Delicious, peeled, cored, quartered, and cut into ¼-inch-thick slices

¼ cup sugar

2 tablespoons unsalted butter, cut into bits (optional)

FINISHING:

¾ to 1 cup strained apricot preserves

10 small strawberries, hulled

12 raspberries

¼ cup pomegranate seeds

1 mint sprig, for garnish

1. Make the tart dough: Combine the flour and salt in a large bowl, or pulse twice in a food processor. Add the butter and cut in with a pastry blender or pulse until the mixture forms coarse crumbs. Sprinkle on the ice water and toss together or pulse for 5 seconds; do not overmix. Gather the dough into a ball, flatten it into a disk, and wrap it in plastic wrap. Refrigerate for at least 20 minutes.

2. Meanwhile, preheat the oven to 350°F. Butter a 9- to 10-inch loose-bottomed tart pan or pie plate.

3. On a lightly floured surface, roll out the dough into a thin, 12-inch round. Fit the dough into the prepared pan. Trim and crimp the edges. Prick the bottom of the dough with a fork. Line the dough with a sheet of foil; weigh down with pie weights, dried rice, or beans. (Or in a pinch, use some well-washed gravel from the driveway, as Chef Bouterin did.) Bake the tart shell for 10 minutes.

Apple Tart with Raspberries, Strawberries, and Pomegranate Seeds.

RIGHT: *The glassed-in, skylit living room at Waterview.*

BELOW, RIGHT: *Casual and colorful place settings surround a huge fishbowl at the table; coordinated placemats, dinnerware, flatware, and glasses add to the fun of a seashore dinner at Waterview.*

4. Remove the weights and foil. Return the tart shell to the oven, and bake for about 10 minutes more, or until lightly browned. Remove to a wire rack.

5. Fill and bake the tart: Spread the applesauce over the bottom of the tart shell. Arrange the apple slices in concentric circles on top. Sprinkle on the sugar, dot with the butter; set the pan on a baking sheet. Bake for 30 minutes, or until the pastry is browned around the edges and the apples are tender.

6. While the tart bakes, heat the preserves in a saucepan or microwave oven until melted. As soon as the tart is done, remove it to a wire rack and brush the top with the melted preserves, coating the fruit and the edges of the pastry. Let cool to room temperature on the rack.

7. Just before serving, sprinkle the pie with the strawberries, raspberries, and pomegranate seeds. Garnish with the mint.

HARRY MARIANI AT BANFI VINTNERS

◆ ◆ ◆ ◆ ◆ ◆ ◆ ◆ ◆ ◆ ◆

"NOT ONLY IS TWO GLASSES OF WINE WITH THE MAIN MEAL OF THE DAY
GOOD FOR YOU—AS COUNTLESS STUDIES HAVE REVEALED—BUT THE WINE ELEVATES THE
FLAVORS OF THE OTHER FOODS. COMBINING WINE WITH FOOD IS THE TRUEST WAY TO MAKE THE
CIVILIZATION OF THE TABLE COMPLETE AND TO LIVE LIFE TO THE FULLEST."

Driving through the massive wrought-iron gates at Banfi Vintners' world headquarters in Old Brookville, Long Island, New York, is an awesome experience. You feel—almost—that you have somehow "become" Robin Leach and are embarking on a real-life "Lifestyles" episode. This magnificent estate, built in 1927, boasts a sixty-room mansion, formal English gardens, and a seventy-five-acre vineyard that's planted to Chardonnay grapes. But to Harry Mariani, president and chief operating officer, and his elder brother, John Mariani, chairman and chief executive officer, this is the office and the showcase where they display their wares and meet with their customers.

Banfi Vintners' merchandise goes beyond the estate-bottled wines they produce at Castello Banfi in Tuscany and the other wines they produce elsewhere in Italy. The com-

---

ITALIAN MENU FOR EIGHT AT BANFI VINTNERS

◆ ◆ ◆ ◆ ◆ ◆ ◆

recipes by Jeffrey Lawton, chef-in-residence

CROSTINI DI TONNO
WINE: CASTELLO BANFI 1992 SERENA SAUVIGNON BLANC (TUSCANY)

SHRIMP AND WHITE BEAN SALAD
WINE: CASTELLO BANFI 1994 SAN ANGELO PINOT GRIGIO

CAPELLINI WITH PROSCIUTTO DI PARMA
WINE: CASTELLO BANFI 1992 CENTINE ROSSO DI MONTALCINO, D.O.C.

SCOTTADITO (GRILLED BABY LAMB CHOPS)
WINE: CASTELLO BANFI 1990 SUMMUS (MONTALCINO)

POACHED PEARS IN SPICED WINE
WINE: "B" MOSCADELLO, D.O.C.

Harry Mariani and family: wife, Anne; daughter Virginia; son, James; and daughter Katherine (Katy). Together with John Mariani they run the Jumby Bay Island resort in Antigua (see p. 24).

pany acts as U.S. distributors of a large number of wines, and produces the Castello Banfi line of six grappas, a vintage-dated extra-virgin olive oil, and Salsa Balsamica Etrusca, a ten-year-old balsamic vinegar.

Harry Mariani clearly expresses the ties among his products: "More than most businesses, the wine trade revolves around the pleasures of the table. Often, our business is conducted at lunch or dinner—occasions that are suitable for the presentation of new products or new vintages of existing products. Primarily, our menus are Mediterranean-influenced, favoring simple but flavorful dishes prepared with fresh ingredients from local markets and farm stands. Low-fat dishes are the standard. We rarely taste wine without the presence of food—the proper food complement can elevate a wine to sainthood."

John Mariani's office was once the manor's library. The room features vaulted ceilings, medieval tapestries, a small choir loft, a seventeenth-century George Brooke grandfather clock, a Queen Anne tallboy, and a magnificent twelfth-century Tuscan table.

THE MATCHING OF WINE AND FOOD: A COMMON-SENSE APPROACH FROM HARRY MARIANI

- Wine is the lifeblood of food. There is no mystique to the art of matching wine and food—and no ironclad rules.

- There is not a single "right" wine for any particular food. A well-made wine, no matter where it comes from, will enhance the appropriate food no matter what its ethnic origin.

- What the person who enjoys food (be it a lowly sandwich, an unsophisticated chicken wing, or a royal roast of beef) seeks is palate enjoyment—a fusion of two different taste experiences that creates a whole that is greater than the sum of its individual parts.

- Wine is a natural, complex, yet easy-to-appreciate beverage. The primary consideration for a proper marriage is that the character of the wine and that of the food do not overwhelm or suffocate each other. Wine and food are not meant to quarrel with each other.

- General rules for harmonizing wine with food date back to the days of ancient Greece and Rome. While rigid, specific rules regarding the serving of appropriate wines and foods were written in the 1500s and were followed for centuries, today's consumer drinks and eats what pleases the palate.

- Red wine with red meats makes gastronomic sense. The tannin in the wine marries with the proteins in the red meat, causing digestion to begin almost immediately. Drunk with certain seafood, however, a tannic red wine can play havoc and might even acquire a certain metallic taste. Fresh salmon, tuna, and swordfish, being rich in natural oils, marry well with light-bodied reds.

- White wine with white meat and seafood is also a good general recommendation. Certain white wines might be overwhelmed by beef or lamb but will rise to gastronomic heights when married with sole, shrimp, lobster, or grilled breast of chicken.

- Salads do not impart any characteristics to wine, but if dressed with vinegar, they inhibit the palate's assessment, rob wine of its liveliness, and make it taste flabby and dull. Lemon juice is preferred, as citric acid blends well with wine's makeup.

- Cheese and wine are an ideal combination—just take care not to serve rich, piquant cheeses with light-bodied wines and vice versa.

- Spicy food can be a problem with wines, but when it is served with a spicy or very fruity wine, the two meet their mates (try Lambrusco from Italy or Shiraz from Australia).

- Chocolate may also upset the taste of wine. Some people claim that an old Cabernet Sauvignon will do the trick. We've found that the Banfi Brachetto d'Acqui makes an excellent, delightful combination with chocolate, especially dark chocolate. The wine has fruitiness, crispness, and the right natural acidity to balance rich chocolate desserts and keep the palate fresh and clean.

RIGHT: *The hallway between the butler's pantry and the formal dining room is used for an informal display of the wines that Banfi Vintners makes and imports. Italian plates and planters decorate the walls.*

DELOW. *The breakfast room in Banfi Vintners' headquarters in Old Brookville, Long Island.*

LEFT: *A view of the estate's seventy-five-acre Chardonnay vineyard, which is overseen by Frederick Frank, grandson of Konstantin Frank, legendary viticulturist.*

Architectural detail and putti keep watch over the formal gardens.

RIGHT: *The classic Elizabethan-style manor house, once a country retreat for members of the Vanderbilt family, in its gloriously restored and renewed state. The property spans 127 acres and includes formal gardens and its own vineyards. The restoration required the talents of fifty artists, artisans, and horticulturists over a period of three years.*

An arched stone walkway leads from the west wing to the east wing of the mansion. The feeling is hushed and serene, the sunshine divine.

CROSTINI DI TONNO

This tuna crostini is a classic hors d'oeuvre that couldn't be simpler to make or devour.

For 8

1 can (6 ounces) water-packed albacore tuna, drained
2 anchovy fillets
1 tablespoon Banfi extra-virgin olive oil
1 tablespoon drained capers
4 to 5 cornichons or other tiny gherkins
1 long loaf Italian bread, thinly sliced on the diagonal
2 garlic cloves, halved lengthwise

1. Combine the tuna, anchovies, oil, capers, and cornichons in a food processor; blend to a thick paste. Scrape the mixture into a bowl, cover, and refrigerate for at least 30 minutes.

2. Toast the bread slices. While still hot, rub one side with a piece of the garlic. Spread the tuna mixture over each toast. Serve at once, with Castello Banfi 1992 Serena Sauvignon Blanc.

SHRIMP AND WHITE BEAN SALAD

You can use fresh or dried cannellini or white beans to make this simple dish that's sure to please any crowd. The quality of the olive oil is key to the end result.

For 8

2 to 3 pounds fresh white or cranberry beans, shelled, or 1 pound dried cannellini or Great Northern beans, soaked overnight
½ cup Banfi extra-virgin olive oil
Salt and freshly milled black pepper
1 pound baby shrimp, cooked and cooled to room temperature
2 celery ribs, diced

1. *If you are using fresh beans,* cover them with cold water and let sit for 20 minutes. Drain, turn into a large pot, add cold water to cover, and bring the water to a boil. Reduce the heat to low, and simmer until the beans are tender but not falling apart, about 30 minutes. *If you are using soaked dried beans,* place the beans in a large pot and add cold water to cover by 2 inches. Set over moderately high heat and bring to a boil. Reduce the heat and simmer until tender but not falling apart, usually 30 to 40 minutes, depending on the beans. Drain well.

2. Transfer the warm beans to a large bowl. Sprinkle on the oil and season with salt and pepper to taste; toss to blend well. Set aside to cool to room temperature.

3. Just before serving, add the shrimp and celery and toss to blend well. Adjust the seasonings with care. Serve at room temperature, accompanied by Castello Banfi's 1994 San Angelo Pinot Grigio.

Both of these dishes were photographed in the heavily paneled wine taster's room. The table and chairs are eighth-century Tuscan.

CAPELLINI WITH PROSCIUTTO DI PARMA

True prosciutto di Parma, the famous cured ham from Parma, is an Italian original that can be copied in style but never duplicated. Once you've had it, nothing less will do.

For 8

1 cup Banfi extra-virgin olive oil
3 garlic cloves, peeled
8 ounces prosciutto di Parma, sliced paper-thin, cut into julienne
6 large sage leaves, minced
2 pounds dried capellini (angel hair) pasta
Salt and freshly milled black pepper
1 cup freshly grated Parmesan cheese

1. Bring a very large pot of water to a boil over high heat.
2. Meanwhile, heat the oil in a large sauté pan over moderate heat until almost smoking. Add the garlic cloves and cook, without burning, until browned, about 3 minutes. Remove and discard the garlic. Add the prosciutto and sauté for 2 minutes. Add the sage and sauté for 1 minute. Remove the pan from the heat.
3. When the water boils, add the pasta and stir until the water returns to a boil. Reduce the heat to moderate and cook until the capellini is just al dente, usually just 3 to 4 minutes. Drain well.
4. Add the pasta to the sauté pan and toss to mix with the prosciutto and coat the capellini with the oil. Season with salt and pepper to taste. Sprinkle on the cheese and toss again. Mound into a large serving bowl and serve at once. Pour glasses of Castello Banfi 1992 Centine Rosso di Montalcino to accompany this dish.

TOP AND BOTTOM, RIGHT: *Chef-in-residence Jeffrey Lawton prepares a typically healthful Mediterranean-influenced meal—including the Capellini with Prosciutto di Parma—that will complement the Banfi wines. The professional kitchen offers all the pleasures of a restaurant along with plenty of natural sunlight and a stunning view of the courtyard.*

SCOTTADITO (GRILLED BABY LAMB CHOPS)

The ultimate finger food, *scottadito* takes its name from the verb *scottare,* meaning to burn your fingers. And indeed, the bones that make eating these so easy do get hot, so be careful. If you don't have a grill, cook them in a skillet.

For 8

16 baby loin lamb chops
½ to ¾ cup Banfi extra-virgin olive oil
1 tablespoon coarsely chopped rosemary leaves
Salt and freshly milled black pepper
Lemon wedges, for garnish

1. Place each chop between 2 pieces of plastic wrap or waxed paper and pound to an even thickness.

2. Stir together the oil and the rosemary in a deep bowl. Submerge the whole chops or at least the meaty ends in the marinade. Set aside to marinate for 1 to 2 hours.

3. If using a grill, preheat it until very hot. If using a skillet, lightly coat with olive oil, and set over moderately high heat until almost smoking. Meanwhile, remove the chops from the marinade; season with salt and pepper to taste. Cook the chops for about 1 minute on each side, until medium-rare. Arrange on a platter and garnish with the lemon wedges. Serve at once, with Castello Banfi 1990 Summus.

POACHED PEARS IN SPICED WINE

This recipe is wonderfully adaptable: You can substitute apples, such as Granny Smiths, for the pears, and you can choose red wine instead of white—whatever suits your mood or purpose.

For 8

1 bottle (750 milliliters) or 4 cups Banfi Asti Spumante (white) or
  Brachetto d'Acqui (red)
9 whole cloves
2 cinnamon sticks
2 tablespoons firmly packed brown sugar
8 ripe pears (preferably Bartletts) with stems attached

1. Preheat the oven to 350°F. Lightly butter a nonreactive shallow baking dish that's just large enough to hold the pears upright.

2. Combine the wine, cloves, cinnamon sticks, brown sugar, and 2 cups water in a nonreactive saucepan over mod-erately high heat. Bring to a boil, stirring from time to time to dissolve the sugar. Reduce the heat to moderately low and simmer the syrup for 10 minutes.

3. Meanwhile, peel the pears, leaving the stems attached. Working from the bottom of each pear, cut out as much of the core as possible (don't worry if you can't get all of it). Stand the pears upright in the prepared baking dish. When the poaching syrup is ready, pour it over the pears into the bottom of the dish.

4. Bake the pears until the tip of a knife enters the thick-est part with ease, about 20 minutes.

5. Remove the pears to a shallow serving dish. Pour the poaching syrup into a nonreactive saucepan and boil over moderately high heat until reduced by half, 3 to 5 minutes. Spoon the syrup over the pears; garnish the serving dish with the cloves and cinnamon sticks, if desired. Serve at room temperature. Sip a glass of Castello Banfi "B" Moscadello alongside.

DONALD AND MARLA MAPLES TRUMP

* * * * * * * * * * * *

"THE MOTTO SHOULD BE 'NOTHING IN EXCESS.'"

It's too bad that Tiffany Ariana Trump can't talk well enough yet to give us the lowdown on her favorite foods, but you can bet that they're healthful and plentiful. While Mom, Marla Maples Trump, and Dad, Donald J. Trump, are doting parents who go to great lengths to keep Tiffany happy, both of them are only too aware of the temptations—and downfalls—of excess.

Mrs. Trump's efforts to live a healthful lifestyle and maintain her shapely figure are all part of her job—as a mother, wife, actress, dancer, entertainer, and all-around personality. As she puts it, "Family's always going to be first for me—that's just the way I was brought up, the way my mother was, the way my grandmother was. That's the number-one thing for me."

A little closer to home, Mrs. Trump has embraced many holistic traditions, seeking overall well-being through a deli-

THE RECIPE

* * * * *

**MARLA MAPLES TRUMP'S
LEMON-CAPER CHICKEN**

Mega-mogul Donald Trump shares some Champagne grapes with his wife, Marla Maples Trump.

cately balanced mind-body relationship. When the hustle-bustle of modern life gets a bit too close, Mrs. Trump has a private getaway close at hand—the roof of Trump Tower. "The roof is my favorite place," she says somewhat wistfully, "because you can be above New York, you can look out—it's so surreal, and you're above all the noise, the congestion, and the anxiety. There's really a peace up there." And clearly, it works for her—just take a look.

The meals the Trumps eat at home are simple, healthful, and well balanced; any not-so-healthful treats can be sampled when they're attending to their hectic schedule of social, charitable, and business events. And by the look of it, Donald Trump counts Champagne grapes among his favorite foods. Indeed, who wouldn't when they're being served up in such a provocative manner and setting by someone so beautiful?

LEFT: *For dinners at home Marla Trump prepares healthful, well-balanced dishes such as her Lemon-Caper Chicken.*

OPPOSITE: *Keeping warm on Colorado's chilly slopes.*

MARLA MAPLES TRUMP'S LEMON-CAPER CHICKEN

Serve this with steamed or boiled brown rice and some perfectly ripe cherry or pear tomatoes.

For 2

2 boneless, skinless chicken breast halves
1 tablespoon unsalted butter
2 tablespoons olive oil
2 shallots, minced
1 garlic clove, minced
¼ cup dry white wine
1½ tablespoons drained capers
Sea salt and freshly milled black pepper
Cayenne pepper
Juice of ½ lemon

1. Place each chicken breast half between 2 sheets of waxed paper or plastic wrap. Pound gently and evenly until ½ inch thick. Set aside until needed.

2. Melt the butter with the oil in a nonreactive large skillet or sauté pan over moderately high heat. Add the shallots and garlic and sauté for 1 minute. Stir in the wine and capers and simmer for 1 minute.

3. Sprinkle the chicken breasts with salt, pepper, and cayenne to taste. Add to the pan, cover, and sauté until just cooked through, 5 to 7 minutes.

4. Uncover the pan and drizzle the chicken with the lemon juice. Transfer to warmed dinner plates and spoon some of the cooking sauce over the top. Serve at once.

SIRIO MACCIONI AT LE CIRQUE

• • • • • • • • • • • •

"MACCIONI IS BOTH BUSINESSMAN AND DIPLOMAT, COURTIER TO THE RICH AND FAMOUS AND FIELD MARSHAL TO A KITCHEN STAFF OF THIRTY-FIVE. HE HAS BEEN DESCRIBED AS A RINGMASTER, ITALY'S ANSWER TO JOHN WAYNE AND AN EAGLE FLYING OVER THE ROOM BECAUSE OF HIS ACUTE AND UNERRING ATTENTION TO DETAIL. ABOVE ALL, HE TIRELESSLY STRUGGLES TO BE THE BEST."—*FOOD ARTS*

Meet Sirio Maccioni just once and you'll become a Maccionimaniac. Is it possible that this Continental gentleman is paying attention to you and yours? Revel in the atmosphere that is Le Cirque, New York City's towering temple of tastefulness for more than twenty years, where the world's elite meet to greet and be coddled by Mr. Maccioni, and then taste the sumptuous fare. Have you ever seen such a wealth of or inhaled the scent of so much finely shaved white truffle? Is it possible he's confusing you with someone else— someone more important than you? You hope not, because you're sold, you've become a Le Cirquist clown of sorts, a total devotee.

Talk to any of Le Cirque's tony clientele—Barbara Walters, Ivana Trump, Beverly Sills, and Robin Leach, among them— and they'll tell you this: Sirio Maccioni is Le Cirque; Le Cirque is Sirio Maccioni. You can't have one without the other.

When you enter into Le Cirque for the first time, you know, Toto, that you're not in Kansas anymore. Indeed, though you're in the heart of New York City, you think that Walt Disney or George Lucas might have contrived—somehow—to transport you elsewhere. If this is a circus, surely it's the most elegant circus in the world.

You are first taken over by the warmth of the room, and then quickly do a double take. This room is relatively small—you'd pictured it much larger. But while you pause to

THE RECIPES

• • • • • • • •

from Executive Chef Silvain Portay

TUNA TARTARE WITH PINK RADISHES AND CURRY DRESSING

BRAISED VEAL SHANKS WITH SWISS CHARD IN PEPPER-VINEGAR SAUCE

Sirio Maccioni, maker and master of Le Cirque's tony universe, with two of his sons, Marco and Mario.

figure it out, you realize that most of the world's best restaurants aren't large, because chefs—no matter how numerous their staff—are limited in the number of first-rate meals that can be prepared and served in a brief period of time. At Le Cirque, about four hundred meals are served every day—an amazing output for food of this quality.

In his "Living Legend" tribute for *NEWS from the Beard House*, Bryan Miller, former *New York Times* restaurant critic, said: "Few restaurants in the United States offer such a range of dishes, such a staggering bounty, as Le Cirque. To pull off just half of the menu items well would be impressive. Sirio, however, believes in 'haute cuisine' of the highest level. The menu must carry something for people of every taste. And with a gastronomic UN in the dining room daily, that takes some fancy footwork in the kitchen." Any customer who asks for unadorned broiled fish or a poached skinless, boneless chicken breast will be accommodated without question; special diets will be catered to, and the presentation—no matter what was ordered—will be glorious. This is a kitchen and team as synchronized and precise as Radio City's famed Rockettes.

"We are here to serve," says Sirio Maccioni. "If I teach my sons nothing else, I want them to understand that the service people receive must always be the very, very best, most impeccable service."

TUNA TARTARE WITH PINK RADISHES AND CURRY DRESSING

Like many of the appetizers in this book, this would make a perfect light lunch or brunch main course.

For 4

2 tablespoons curry powder
1 tablespoon strained fruit chutney, such as Major Grey's
½ teaspoon saffron threads
¼ cup hot water
12 ounces sushi-quality belly of tuna, cut into ¼-inch dice
⅓ cup minced red radishes
⅓ cup minced celery
1½ tablespoons finely snipped fresh chives
Salt and freshly milled pepper
1 tablespoon crème fraîche or sour cream
1½ tablespoons mayonnaise

FOR SERVING:

32 very thin, uniform slices red radish (use a mandoline to get perfect rounds)
4 to 12 short fresh chive spikes, for garnish
4 small celery leaf sprigs, for garnish
Basil vinaigrette (optional)

1. In a small bowl, stir together the curry powder, chutney, saffron, and hot water. Set aside to infuse until cooled to room temperature.

2. Meanwhile, place the diced tuna in a small bowl and add the minced radishes, celery, chives, and salt and pepper to taste. Mix well. Cover and chill until needed.

3. When the dressing is cool, stir in the crème fraîche and mayonnaise and beat together until the mixture is fragrant and the texture is creamy. Spoon about half of the dressing over the tartare and mix well to bind; you don't want the tartare to be too moist.

4. To assemble, divide the tartare into 4 equal portions. Shape each into a flattened mound; transfer each to the center of a chilled salad plate. Arrange the radish slices around the circumference of the tartare and add a few to the top—they'll adhere all by themselves. Insert a few chive spikes and a celery leaf in the top of each serving. Surround with some of the remaining curry dressing or substitute basil vinaigrette to add more color contrast. Serve at once.

••

Executive Chef Silvain Portay's luscious Tuna Tartare with Pink Radishes and Curry Dressing.

LEFT: *Setting up Le Cirque in preparation for the lunchtime crush. How on earth can anyone carry so many glasses at once?*

BELOW, LEFT: *A genius with pastry, Jacques Torres performs his magic with a playful attitude and brilliant technique.*

BELOW, RIGHT: *Moments before service starts, Benito Sevarin, a well-known face at Le Cirque, checks the reservations to see who's on today's roster.*

BRAISED VEAL SHANKS WITH SWISS CHARD IN PEPPER-VINEGAR SAUCE

Le Cirque's veal shanks are picture-perfect, the meat knotted at one end and the bone protruding from the other. If your butcher can't deliver shanks that look like Le Cirque's, never mind—choose meaty cuts of the shank and run home to braise them.

For 4

4 veal shanks or pieces of shank (each about 1 pound)
Salt and freshly milled pepper
Unbleached all-purpose flour, for dredging
2 tablespoons unsalted butter
2 tablespoons vegetable oil
2 carrots, scraped and halved
2 onions, peeled and halved

2 celery ribs, halved
4 cups veal, beef, or chicken stock or broth, OR 2 cups stock and 2 cups dry wine or water
2 thyme sprigs
1 pound Swiss chard, washed, leaves pulled off and reserved, tender ribs cut into 2-inch lengths
2 tomatoes, peeled, seeded, and each cut into 6 wedges
1 teaspoon sherry vinegar

1. Sprinkle each shank with salt and pepper; lightly dredge in flour, shaking off any excess.
2. Preheat the oven to 375°F.
3. In a dutch oven or casserole large enough to hold the shanks in a single layer, melt the butter with the oil over moderately high heat. When the fats begin to shimmer, add the shanks and brown all over, about 5 minutes on each side.

Le Cirque's Braised Veal Shank with Swiss Chard in Pepper-Vinegar Sauce.

4. Remove the shanks, and add the carrots, onions, and celery to the pan. Sauté until lightly browned, about 5 minutes.

5. Pour in the stock, add the thyme, and return the shanks to the pan. Tightly cover, and braise in the oven until the shanks are tender, about 2 hours.

6. About 20 minutes before the shanks are done, remove about 1 cup of the braising liquid. Pour it into a nonreactive sauté pan or skillet set over moderate heat. Add the Swiss chard ribs—not the leaves. Cover the pan and cook until slightly tender, usually 5 to 8 minutes.

7. Reduce the heat to moderately low, and add the tomatoes to the chard ribs. Place the chard leaves on top of the ribs and tomatoes, cover, and cook until all of the vegetables are tender, 5 to 10 minutes more.

8. Using tongs, remove all of the vegetables and arrange over 4 warmed dinner plates. Increase the heat under the vegetable braising liquid, stir in the vinegar, and boil, uncovered, until thick, syrupy, and reduced to about ¼ cup; watch carefully, this can go quickly. Taste and season as needed.

9. Place a veal shank on each plate and spoon a tablespoon of the reduced stock over the top. Serve very hot.

ABOVE: *The seldom-seen Egidiana Maccioni, wife of Sirio and mother of Mauro, Mario, and Marco, holds the key to the clan's next success: Saltimbanca, on Manhattan's West 55th Street.*

LEFT: *An intimate corner table in the restaurant where royalty, presidents, moguls, and celebrities of all stripes go to visit Sirio, eat, see, and be seen.*

NICOLAS FEUILLATTE

◆ ◆ ◆ ◆ ◆ ◆ ◆ ◆ ◆ ◆ ◆

"CHAMPAGNE IS A NOBLE DRINK THAT SHOULD BE DRUNK AS IT IS, WITHOUT ANY GIMMICKS."

Nicolas Feuillatte looks like a French film star in the Belmondo style. He's beautifully clothed, he lives in beautifully appointed surroundings, and he drinks his own beautifully bubbly Champagnes—virtually all of the time. His company, Champagne Nicolas Feuillatte, produces nearly two million bottles of Champagne every year; worldwide exports amount to about 40 percent of that amount. Could there be a better authority on Champagne? We don't think so, thus, here are Nicolas Feuillatte's personal Champagne pointers—how to drink it, serve it, store it, what to eat with it, and more.

1. Champagne should be drunk on an empty stomach, preferably before meals, and must be served very cold. Salmon, bass, and other types of mild white fish are appropriate as a first course and are excellent with Champagne. I do not believe that one should mix wines at lunch or dinner. Serving different bottlings of Champagne, on the other hand, during the course of a meal, and finishing with a rosé, is very appropriate.

2. It is a mistake to mix other liquids, such as cassis or orange juice, with good Champagne. Champagne is a noble drink that should be drunk as it is, without any gimmicks.

3. When I'm entertaining at home and plan to serve Champagne to my guests before meals or with a first course, I put a carafe in the freezer two hours ahead of time. Before serving, the butler pours the Champagne into the iced carafe. It is an elegant and sophisticated way to serve Champagne. This will also make the Champagne less fizzy.

4. The best way to chill Champagne is to put it in an ice bucket and add ice and water. Let chill for thirty minutes. It is not good to leave Champagne in a refrigerator for too long—and it should never be kept in the freezer.

5. The Champagne in my wine cellar is stored lying down and brought up as I use it.

6. It is important to serve Champagne in flutes washed in water only—no soap—and, preferably, to have the flute well chilled before serving.

7. Rosé Champagne is excellent with sweets and as an apéritif, where it takes the place of white wine.

8. You can find a food that will go with every Champagne.

....

"For a Champagne dinner party, serving only my Champagnes, I would start with an apéritif of my Réserve Particulière, Brut Premier Cru. With the first course of Fillet of Sole à la Normande, I would serve the Palmes d'Or 1985, followed by Canard à l'Orange paired with the Cuvée Spéciale 1986. Salad and cheese would follow. Finally, for dessert, a special meringue cake, served with Champagne Nicolas Feuillatte Rosé."

JOHN PAUL AND ELOISE DeJORIA

◆ ◆ ◆ ◆ ◆ ◆ ◆ ◆ ◆ ◆ ◆

"NOTHING IN LIFE IS WORTH DOING UNLESS YOU HAVE FUN DOING IT."
—JOHN PAUL DeJORIA

Believe it or not, they met on a blind date, were engaged a year later, and married the year after that. And since that fateful date, every day of their lives has been something straight out of a fairy tale. They are John Paul and Eloise DeJoria, prince and princess of the worldwide empire built around John Paul Mitchell Systems hair and beauty products. He is generally regarded as the entrepreneurial genius who, in partnership with the late Paul Mitchell took an initial $700 investment and turned it into a multimillion-dollar force in the professional and consumer beauty industry—a force that has been copied but never duplicated. She is his beautiful, savvy, walking, talking, Texas-born personification of what an active, healthy lifestyle can bring to anyone willing to spend the time and effort.

The DeJorias travel constantly throughout their far-flung domain—from home base in Nevada to points all over the United States and Canada, to Europe, South America, Israel, and the Pacific Rim. In addition to appearing in TV and print advertisements, they act as spokespeople for their products and work one-on-one with their network of independent distributors. Somehow, in spite of their hectic schedule, the DeJorias still manage to be benevolent givers of their time, effort, and money in support of good causes; to remain

---

MINI MEALS

recipes from Kevin Adams Stuessi, sous chef at Spago Las Vegas

MANGO-BANANA SMOOTHIE

CITRUS AND FENNEL SALAD

SWEET CORN AND WILD MUSHROOM RISOTTO WITH TRUFFLES

BELUGA BATH WITH BUBBLY

John Paul and Eloise DeJoria are the picture-perfect couple in every sense of the word.

close, loving parents to their five children; and to remain very much, very obviously in love. Indeed, after more than two years of marriage, Eloise DeJoria says, "We're still on our honeymoon—it hasn't stopped for a minute."

The DeJoria's summer house is one of Eloise's favorite places to be: "I love it, I love being outside, looking at the view of the ocean and mountains, feeling the warmth. I'm just a country girl at heart—there's a spiritual lift when I'm outdoors." But don't think you'll find covergirl model Eloise Broady DeJoria languishing by the pool; it's far more likely that she'll be in the pool, dancing in the buoyant water, involved in a spirited volleyball game, or swimming laps underwater so she can enjoy her favorite tunes on the sound system they had installed.

If tennis is in order, that, too, offers an excellent workout. The Kramer Kramer surface, which Eloise describes as "a sort of synthetic grass that is similar to clay—very easy on the knees," was chosen for its friendliness to the body. "It's an excellent surface for running—the very best there is to ease the impact on your joints," Eloise adds. There's also a trampoline for a lighthearted, bouncy workout, horses for riding, and hiking trails in the nearby hills.

This mother of five—her two (Michael Harvey, age

twenty-one, and Justin Harvey, age seventeen) and John Paul's three (John Paul Jr., age twenty-nine; Alexis, age seventeen; and Michaline, age eleven)—has strong opinions about what makes her happy. A large part of that is living a healthy lifestyle. "I stay active because I love it. We have a gym in the house and I do two-hour workouts with my trainer, Ray Kybartas [Madonna's trainer for four years]—he's one of my favorite people. I'd say that, for me at least, good health and overall well-being is John Paul, our kids, and our work."

Eloise and John Paul have a live-in chef/assistant, Jennifer Lewis, who helps keep things on an even keel. "Jennifer knows exactly what I love to eat. I almost never eat a large meal; instead I have a series of small meals all day long—I'm always eating. I'll have a fruit smoothie, a bit of salad—small tastes of healthful, good foods. I'd say the balance for me is 30 percent exercise and 70 percent diet." Jennifer concurs: "Both Eloise and John Paul are constantly moving—they never stop for a minute. I prepare small portions of high-energy foods— lots of carbohydrates and no fat, adequate amounts of vegetables and fruits. Eloise is very strict about what she eats; for John Paul, I'll add a bit of butter or oil or cheese."

Eloise's eating regimen is easy to remember: She eats no fat, no dairy, and nothing after seven o'clock in the evening. "I drink very little alcohol—maybe a glass of wine a day," she adds, "and that's because John Paul picks the best wines, and I just have to have a taste of them. I eat no desserts—never. One of my favorite things is to hard-boil some eggs—throw the egg yolk away—and chop up the egg whites along with nonfat mayonnaise and tuna fish. It's a great snack and good for you too."

· ·

TOP AND CENTER: *The DeJorias have been working on their weekend summer home for several years—handmade pieces have been commissioned for nearly every room of the house.*

LEFT: *An ornately carved teak tree trunk collected in Thailand: "When we saw its intricacy and all of the animals, we just had to take it home."*

OPPOSITE: *"John Paul is the most romantic man in the world," Eloise vows. After she accepted his formal proposal of marriage, he sent her 1,300 red roses, plus one yellow rose—for Texas.*

MANGO-BANANA SMOOTHIE

Breakfast in a glass—a refreshing "meal," perhaps to follow an early-morning tennis lesson.

For 4

3 ripe mangos, peeled, pitted, and cut into chunks
2 ripe bananas, peeled and cut into chunks
1 cup fresh orange juice
1 cup strawberries, hulled
1 cup blueberries

1. Combine the mangos, bananas, and orange juice in a blender and puree until smooth. Pour the mixture into a small pitcher.

2. Rinse out the blender, add the strawberries and blueberries, and puree until smooth.

3. Layer the two purees in stemmed glasses; layer the remainder of each in a tall glass pitcher and serve at once.

Who won the tennis match or was the final score "love"?

"Everything I've done in my life, all of my experiences—my children, my ten years as an actress, my love for exercise and the outdoors—all of it is part and parcel of what makes my relationship with John Paul so good. It's like, without knowing it at the time, I saved the best for last."—Eloise DeJoria

CITRUS AND FENNEL SALAD

There's not a jot of oil here, and you won't miss it. The secret is in using ingredients that have their own distinctive flavors and textures.

For 4

3 cups mixed salad greens (such as frisée, radicchio, baby lettuces), washed and dried
1 fennel bulb, trimmed and sliced paper-thin
¼ cup walnuts, toasted (optional)
1 cup pomegranate seeds, all traces of white pith removed
¼ cup fresh grapefruit juice
Salt and coarsely milled black pepper
1 large pink or red grapefruit, sectioned and membrane removed

1. Toss together the salad greens, fennel, walnuts, and pomegranate seeds in a large bowl. Sprinkle on the grapefruit juice and season with salt and pepper to taste. Toss to coat the greens.

2. Divide the greens among 4 salad plates and arrange a few grapefruit segments on each plate. Serve at once.

An antique bed and elaborate drapings add to the fairy-tale qualities of the DeJorias' lifestyle.

SWEET CORN AND WILD MUSHROOM RISOTTO WITH TRUFFLES

The sweet corn for this dish is freshly roasted; therefore, it's slightly different in texture and considerably different in flavor from sweet corn cooked any other way. It's worth making a special effort to roast the corn you need, but in a pinch, you can substitute boiled or steamed sweet corn.

For 4

¼ cup peanut oil
1 yellow onion, finely minced
1 large garlic clove, finely minced
2 cups arborio rice
1 cup dry white wine
7 cups vegetable broth, boiling
4 ounces fresh wild mushrooms, cleaned and sliced
3 cups freshly roasted sweet corn kernels
1 teaspoon chopped fresh sage leaves
1 teaspoon chopped fresh thyme leaves
1 teaspoon chopped fresh parsley leaves
Salt and freshly milled black pepper
1 truffle

1. Pour the oil into a nonreactive large sauté pan or saucepan and set over moderately high heat. Add the onion and garlic and sauté until softened but not browned, 3 to 4 minutes.

2. Add the rice and stir until completely coated with the oil and warmed by the heat. Pour in the wine and cook, stirring, until it is absorbed. Add the hot stock, 1 cup at a time, and cook, stirring until it is absorbed.

3. After 3 cups of stock have been added, stir in the mushrooms until coated with the mixture. Continue adding the remaining 4 cups stock, 1 cup at a time, and stirring until absorbed. The entire cooking process will take 20 to 25 minutes.

4. Meanwhile, puree 2 cups of the corn in a blender. Add the pureed corn and the remaining 1 cup whole kernels to the risotto; sprinkle on the chopped fresh herbs. Cook, stirring, until the risotto is creamy—not runny—and the rice is just al dente. Season carefully with salt and pepper to taste.

5. Divide the risotto among 4 heated plates. Shave a generous amount of the truffle over each portion. Serve at once.

His bathtub (hers is different): John Paul DeJoria's tub was hand-carved from a single piece of 2,000-year-old Italian marble. Eloise says, "It's a little too big for one person—just right for two."

BELUGA BATH WITH BUBBLY

If you avoid fats at any cost, you might want to use bath salts or gel in place of the bath oil.

For 2

1 incredible marble bathtub
¼ cup scented bath oil
40 to 100 gallons warm water, depending on the size of the tub
2 people
1 to 2 bottles well-chilled Champagne
7 ounces beluga caviar
4 ounces thinly sliced smoked salmon
4 steamed baby new potatoes, stuffed with caviar
Baby lettuce leaves
Fresh chives, for garnish

1. Combine the tub, oil, and water until the surface is deep in bubbles.

2. Add the people, followed quickly by all of the remaining ingredients. Let the ingredients linger until done. Remove the people from the liquid, wrap in warm towels, and rub gently until dried all over. Send to bed.

....

Thank you for reading and cooking with us.
—Robin Leach

ACKNOWLEDGMENTS

• • • • • • • • • • • •

It's often said that older means wiser—and now that we're well into our second decade with "Lifestyles" and the initial years of the Television Food Network are behind us, there's time to reflect on that saying. Wisdom has been gained and shared with some extraordinary people in the allied businesses of television, hotels, restaurants, food, and wine—and it's safe to say that there's more exercise in our diets and less fat and cholesterol in our system! EVERYBODY SHOULD BE HEALTHY! Exercise shows abound on television, and chefs are preparing more healthful dishes than ever before. With that in mind we set out to create a book that reflects this fervor for good health, but at the same time one that keeps the whole healthy mindset fresh, enjoyable, informative, and *fun*—exactly the way I've approached my "Lifestyles" and "Talking Food" shows.

A lot of people play an important role in life's successes and joys. Many thanks are due to George Carmody, Norman Knittle, Sandy and Pat, Barry Weiner and Jonathan Russo, Cecilia Nord, Rob Hess, and Andrea Ambandos. To my sidekick at TVFN, Kate Connelly; to the unbelievably energetic, enthusiastic staffs of both "Lifestyles" and "Talking Food"; to a new group of friends at the "Modern Cuisine" and "Travel Secrets" TV shows; to the chefs, hotel and restaurant owners and managers whom I'm proud to know as friends all over the world.

When you tackle a project as demanding and as complicated as this—creating a lavish four-color cookbook photgraphed in sixty-five locations across the country and in the Caribbean—it takes an extraordinary team of talented people to bring it all together successfully.

First, our sincere thanks go to the good friends and celebrities who contributed their time, their recipes, and their homes to make the pages herein come fully to vibrant, zestful life!

Then to Liz Baruch and her colleagues, Kristina Scioscio and Jennifer Scher, for the Herculean task of scheduling each and every one of the photo shoots, for obtaining all the necessary legal releases, and the hundreds of other tasks that have made this book possible. Thanks go to Nick LaPenna in the "Lifestyles" office as well, for being a wonderful jack-of-all-trades, and to my executive assistant, Sara Kirkland.

Photographer Lisa Koenig and food stylist and test chef Georgia Downard worked together to make the recipes easy to incorporate into your daily life—you'll find them delicious, healthful, and a breeze to prepare. When she isn't modeling, creating ceramic art, or running her restaurant, Cecilia Nord picks up her camera and takes some extraordinary photographs—just look at the first section of the book!

At Penguin Studio Books, publisher Michael Fragnito, executive editor Christopher Sweet, and editor Martha Schueneman worked tirelessly in our behalf. We'd also like to thank Joseph Rutt and Neil Stuart, who designed the book and its jacket. Last but by no means least, we thank the staff at Duggal color-processing labs in New York, as well as the following individuals, each of whom provided an invaluable contribution:

Liz Applegate, Ken Aretzky, Miguel Bejarano, Ray Bejarano, Tex Bell, Susan Bender, Antoine Bouterin, Chris Brienza, Greg Brittenham, Stacy Burstin, Michael Carlisle, Donna Castellano, Caryl Chinn, John Cirillo, Alan Cohen of Players Steakhouse, Gail Cohen, Jeff Collins, Alexandra Constantinople, Mike Dunmore, Ian Duke, Michael Edmonds, Janie Elder, Stephen Epstein, Rainer Fehringer, Rosana Galvan, Leslie Garson, Andrew Goodenough, Jamie Griffin, Desiree Gruber, Pat Hanlon, Tommy Hayes, David Heil of the David Rickey Company, Ann Heller, Diana Jones, Jumby Bay's William Joseph, Barbara DeYonge, and Ken Dandrade, David Kratz & Co., Martha Land, Jeffrey Lane, Rémi Lauvand, Jennifer Lewis, Kate Lindsay, Michael Lomonaco, Cheryl McClean, Sheila McGrath, Dave Mager, Theresa Manzella, Francine Maroukian, Sari Marvel, Kate Merlino, David Merrill, Roy Mingo, David Morrow, Nancy Mucciardi, Kim Nicely, Tracy Nieporent, Joanne Occhipinti, Carolyn O'Connor, Marvin Paige, Lucky Paulsin, Lyn Paulsin, Kristen Petrocky, William Phillips, Susan Portnoy, Darren Ransdell, Noreen Rasceles, Gary Regan, Jean Renard, Paul Richnow, Rusty Robertson, David Rogers, Randy Rogers, Carl Ruderman, Sager-Bell, Inc., Suzy Salko, Chen Sam, Fernando Saralegui, Catherine Saxton, Alan Schneider of Precison Limousine, Amy Schuler, Benito Sevarin, Barbara Shapiro, Tina Sharpe, Rosana Shiu, Steven Shore, Heidi Skolnik, Elizabeth Sniffen, Bill Squire, Patricia Steele, Craig Sugimoto, Vicki Turner, TVFN's Wayne Fung, Cindy Leiber, Susie Segal, and Joyce Amormino, Tina Ujlaki, Shannon Waggoner, David Wagner, Vida Walter, Walter Weiss, Rosemary Zraly.

PHOTOGRAPHY CREDITS

◆ ◆ ◆ ◆ ◆ ◆ ◆ ◆ ◆ ◆ ◆

Special thanks to the many talented photographers whose work is featured in this book.

Brian Aris—104;

Peter C. Borsari—118;

Fran Brennan—186-91;

Allyn Browne/A & W Photography—84 (bottom);

Patrick DeMarchelier/Almay—52, 53 (bottom);

Maureen Donaldson (photography and food styling)—viii, 38-43, 70-75;

Charles Imstepf—174-79, 240-47;

© George Kalinsky—158, 160;

Lisa Koenig—ii, 36-37, 45-51, 53 (top), 54-61, 64-65, 67-69, 78 (left), 79, 89-93, 96-103, 105-13, 116-17, 119 (top), 132-33, 135, 138-40, 143-45, 146 (left), 147-48, 149 (right), 150-57, 161-73, 180-84, 185 (bottom left and right), 193, 202-27, 230, 232-37;

Fred Lyon—194-201;

Cecilia Nord—front cover photograph, 8-35;

Marc Plantec—239;

Jean Renard—66;

Bonnie Schiffman/Onyx—94, 114-17;

Greg Schneider—120-24, 125 (top left and right);

Tyson Holly Farms® fresh chicken—134;

Antoine Verglas—44;

Joe Viles—81;

© 1995 Courtney Grant Winston—82, 84 (top), 85-87, 126-31.

INDEX

◆ ◆ ◆ ◆ ◆ ◆ ◆ ◆ ◆ ◆ ◆ ◆

Page numbers in *italics* refer to illustrations.